KNOWLEDGE MANAGEMENT

KNOWLEDGE MANAGEMENT

Analysis and Design for Indian Commercial Banking System

O.P. GOYAL

KALPAZ PUBLICATIONS
DELHI-110052

Knowledge Management : Analysis And Design For Indian Commercial Banking System

Rs. 690

ISBN: 81-7835-593-0

Published in 2007 in India by
Kalpaz Publications
C-30, Satyawati Nagar,
Delhi-110052
Phone : 9212729499
E-mail: kalpaz@hotmail.com

Lassertype Setting by: Rudra Computer Graphics
Printed at : Salasar Imaging System, Delhi

In the Memory of My Parents

Late Shri G. S. Gupta
&
Late Shrimati Kiran Devi

CONTENTS

	ACKNOWLEDGEMENTS	**9**
	LIST OF FIGURES, EXHIBITS AND GRAPHS	**11**
	NOMENCLATURE	**13**
1.	INTRODUCTION	**15**
2.	INDIAN COMMERCIAL BANKING SYSTEM	**49**
3.	RESEARCH METHODOLOGY	**83**
4.	PERTINENT ANALYSIS	**91**
5.	SUMMARY OF FINDINGS & RECOMMENDATIONS	**129**

<u>APPENDICES</u>

Appendix – I	Tables : 3.1 through 3.16	**153**
Appendix – II	Schedule –1 & Schedule –2	**179**
Appendix – III	Table : 4.1 through 4.29	**199**
Appendix – IV	Knowledge Management Matrix - Assessment Toolkit	**253**

INDEX **265**

Acknowledgements

The All India Council For Technical Education supported my work on 'Knowledge Management in relation to Indian Commercial Banks', and I thank the esteemed Council for granting necessary financial assistance for the purpose. I am beholden to Professor K.K. Aggarwal, Vice-chancellor, Guru Gobind Singh Indraprastha University, Delhi without whose motivation this work would have not seen its accomplishment. I also thank all the CEOs and other bank executives, academicians and researchers who rendered their full cooperation in making available to me the plethora of meaningful information.

LIST OF FIGURES, EXHIBITS AND GRAPHS

LIST OF FIGURES

1. FIGURE 1.1 : MANAGERS' TOOLS THROUGH THE DECADES : KNOWLEDGE MANAGEMENT HAS BEEN COMING SINCE THE 1950S
2. FIGURE 1.2 : PROCESS OF KNOWLEDGE MANAGEMENT
3. FIGURE 1.3 : THE 10-STEP KNOWLEDGE MANAGEMENT ROADMAP

LIST OF EXHIBITS

1. EXHIBIT 2.1 : STRUCTURE OF INDIAN COMMERCIAL BANKING
2 EXHIBIT 2.2 : COMMERCIAL BANKING SYSTEM IN INDIA
3. EXHIBIT 4.1 : PARAMETER-AND CATEGORY OF BANKS-WISE STATISTICS RELATED TO TECHNICAL EFFICIENCY
4. EXHIBIT 4.2 : PARAMETER-AND INDIVIDUAL BANK-WISE STATISTICS RELATED TO TECHNICAL EFFICIENCY.
5. EXHIBIT 4.3 : ATM BRANCHES OF THE SELECTED BANKS
6. EXHIBIT 4.4 : PERCENTAGE OF THE COMPUTERIZED BRANCHES

7. EXHIBIT 4.5 : GROUP WISE GROWTH IN BUSINESS (ADVANCES + DEPOSITS) ALONGSIDE THE STRENGTH OF THE STAFF (2001-04)
8. EXHIBIT 4.6 : BUSINESS PER EMPLOYEE (2001 : 04)
9. EXHIBIT 4.7 : FORMAL MECHANISM OF STORING/ SHARING THE DATA/ INFORMATION/ KNOWLEDGE
10. EXHIBIT 4.8 : REALIZED BENEFITS FROM THE INVESTMENTS MADE IN EXECUTION OF KNOWLEDGE MANAGEMENT

LIST OF GRAPHS

1. GRAPH 4.1 : OVERALL LEVEL OF TECHNICAL EFFICIENCY
2. GRAPH 4.2 : THE ERROR BARS FOR ALL THE THREE CATEGORIES OF BANKS
3. GRAPH 4.3 : INFORMATION TECHNOLOGY INFRASTRUCTURE
4. GRAPH 4.4 : STRATEGIC ANALYSIS
5. GRAPH 4.5 : ERROR BARS FOR ALL THE THREE CATEGORIES OF BANKS
6. GRAPH 4.6 : HUMAN RESOURCE ANALYSIS
7. GRAPH 4.7 : BUSINESS PROCESS ANALYSIS
8. GRAPH 4.8 : STRUCTURAL ANALYSIS
9. GRAPH 5.1 : KM : IT ARCHITECTURE
10. GRAPH 5.2 : KM SYSTEM

NOMENCLATURE

ALM	Asset Liability Management
ANOVA	Analysis of Variance
ATM	Automated Teller Machine
BPO	Business Process Outsourcing
CEO	Chief Executive Officer
CFMS	Centralized Fund Management System
CIO	Chief Information Officer
CKO	Chief Knowledge Officer
CLO	Chief Learning Officer
CPPD	Computer Planning and Policy Departments
CRM	Customer Relationship Management
CRR	Cash Reserve Ratio
CRS	Constant Return to Scale
DEA	Data Envelopment Analysis
DMU	Decision Making Units
DSA	Direct Selling Agents
DW	Data Warehousing
EIP	Enterprise Information Portal
ERP	Enterprise Resource Planning
FDI	Foreign Direct Investment
HRD	Human Resource Development
HRM	Human Resource Management
INB	Internet Banking
INFINET	Indian Financial Network
IPO	Initial Public Offering
IRS	Increasing Return to Scale
IT	Information Technology
KM	Knowledge Management

M & A	Mergers & Acquisitions
MIS	Management Information System
MOU	Memorandum of Understanding
NDS	Negotiated Dealing System
NPA	Non-Performing Assets
NRI	Non-Resident Indians
OSMOS	Off-site Monitoring Surveillance
PNB	Punjab National Bank
PSB	Public Sector Bank
RDBMS	Relational Data Base Management System
ROA	Return on Assets
ROE	Return on Equity
RBI	Reserve Bank of India
RRB	Regional Rural Banks
RTGS	Real Time Gross Settlement System
SARFAESI	Securitization and Reconstruction of Financial Assets and Enforcement of Securities Interest
SCB	Scheduled Commercial Bank
SHG	Self Help Group
SBI	State Bank of India
SLR	Statutory Liquidity Ratio
SME	Small and Medium Enterprises
VRS	Variable Return to Scale
WWW	World Wide Web

1

INTRODUCTION

The empires of the future are the empires of the mind. **Tom Peterson said "Heavy lifting is out; brains are in."** Every business is a knowledge business; every worker is a knowledge worker. Knowledge is perishable. The shelf life of expertise is limited because new technologies, products, and services continue to pour into the market place. No one can hoard knowledge. People and companies must constantly renew, replenish, expand, and create more knowledge.

WHAT'S KNOWLEDGE?

1.2 "**Knowledge is a fluid mix of framed experience, values, contextual information, expert insight and grounded intuition that provides an environment and framework for evaluating and incorporating new experiences and information. It originates and is applied in the minds of knower. In organizations, it often becomes embedded not only in documents or repositories but also in organizational routines, processes, practices, and norms.**"[1] The idea of different forms of knowledge is given in **Ikujiro Nonaka and Hirotaka Takeuchi's** popular work titled, '**The Knowledge Creating Company**.'[2] According to them Knowledge has two forms: **Explicit** and **Tacit** knowledge, which briefly means as thus:

Tacit (Subjective)	Explicit (Objective)
·Knowledge of Experience (body)	Knowledge of rationality (mind)
·Simultaneous Knowledge (here & now)	Sequential Knowledge (there & then)
·Analog Knowledge (Practice)	Digital Knowledge (theory)

KNOWLEDGE MANAGEMENT

1.3 'Knowledge' is one concept, which is of utmost significance and is full of promises and hard to pin down in this era of information technology. It is mutable and can take on almost all challenges of an organization irrespective of its size, nature, and form of ownership.[3] Its application does not conflict with business strategy, process management, relationship management, adding value to business, and competitive edge differentiating product and service offerings. Rather it aids in doing better and better both the things already being done and the variety of newer things that could be perceived of.[4]

1.4 In this perspective, the phrase 'knowledge management' (KM) could be taken as the process by which the organization generates wealth from its intellectual or knowledge based assets[5]. Alternatively, knowledge management is creating a business value of generating a competitive edge for the organization; it is a powerful means for ensuring the customers delight *via* enabling the organization to go for customization of its products and services in a big way and attaining the enterprise goals from the given financial and intellectual resources.

WHY SO MUCH EMPHASIS ON KNOWLEDGE MANAGEMENT NOW?[6]

1.5 True that centuries back also the organizations were making use of 'knowledge'. But then 'strategy' drives by knowledge help the organization be what **Peter F Drucker** calls "**purposefully opportunistic**." Peter Drucker rightly points out that the most valuable assets of the twenty-first century company are its knowledge and knowledge workers[7]. Drucker like many others saw this coming for over 50 years as is evident from the Figure-1.1. This Figure depicts the vital tools of managers as they evolved from the 1950s to the 2000s. Some of these died much anticipated deaths as fads, and some live till this day. Notably, one consistent and pervasive thread runs through all these – about leveraging knowledge, experience, intellectual assets and their management. And this consistent thread has led businesses to what we now call knowledge management.

1.6 In a global economy, Davenport and Prusak suggest, "Knowledge may be your company's greatest competitive advantage."[8] Having exhausted all other sources of competitive advantage such as technology and market dominance – none of which has sustained their promises – companies are befittingly placing all hopes in knowledge and its effective management. The value proposition of knowledge management is now stronger than ever, as it is no longer a rare competitive differentiator but the only differentiator.

VALUE PROPOSITION OF KNOWLEDGE MANAGEMENT[9]

1.7 A loud talk about knowledge management in this century is primarily for the companies who can reap an immense payoff when a knowledge management solution makes it easier for practitioners to reach out to other practitioners who share common problems or have experience to share. Why all this noise about knowledge management? There are few specific reasons for this:

(i) Companies are becoming Knowledge Intensive, not Capital Intensive

Knowledge is rapidly displacing capital, monetary prowess, natural resources, and labor as the quintessential economic resource.[10] Knowledge is the only input that can help organization cope with radical change and ask the right questions for attempting to find the answers, for without this

FIGURE-1.1:MANAGERS TOOLS THROUGH THE DECADES: KNOWLEDGE MANAGEMENT HAS BEEN COMING SINCE THE 1950S

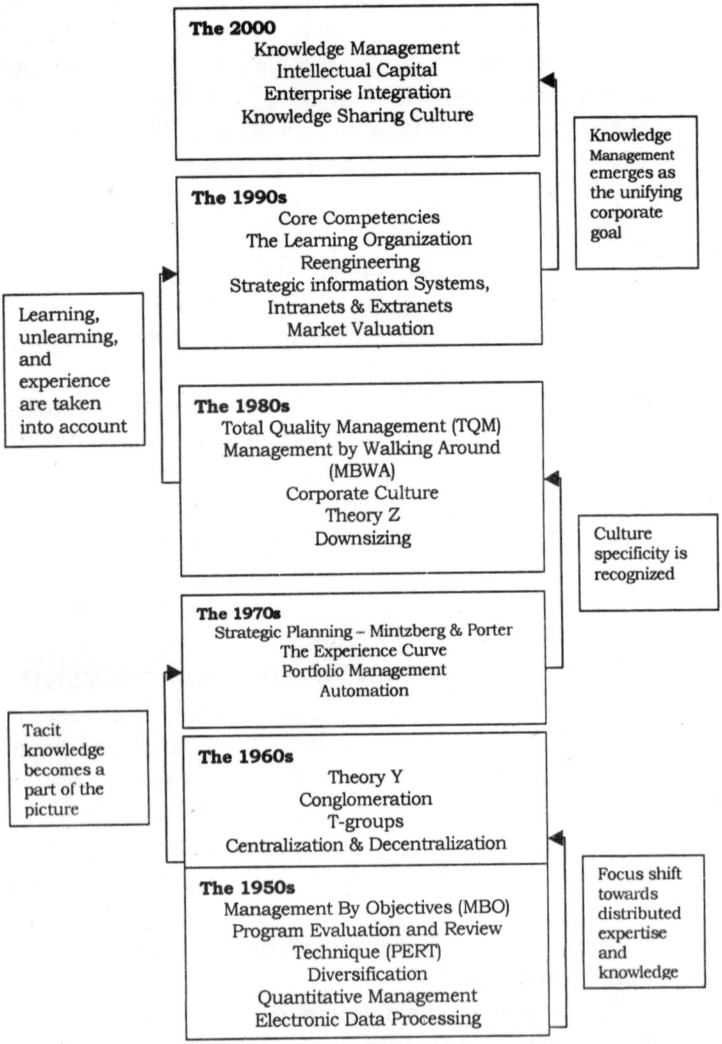

Source: Tiwana Amrit, "The Knowledge Management Toolkit: Practical Techniques for Building a Knowledge Management System", Pearson Education Asia Pvt. Ltd, 2000, p.9.

knowledge we may never even realize how our industry's competitive environment is changing until it's little too late. It is this knowledge that brings quality into any organization's product and service offerings. Further, product life cycles and service time-to-market can be accelerated an unprecedented ways through knowledge. Knowledge management is the only way to reach and apply this knowledge in time.

(ii) Unstable Markets Necessitate "Organized Abandonment"

The markets might undergo radical shifts, leaving the organization in a disastrous position of being with the wrong product, at the wrong time, and in the wrong place. The impact of these forces is witnessed most prominently in high technology environments and financial markets, and increasingly in other markets as well. Knowledge Management enable us to undertake what Drucker calls organized abandonment:[11] reshaping products, getting out of projects and product lines that can pull the business down, and getting into others that maximize growth potential.

(iii) Knowledge Management allows us to lead change

No industry or a firm have a natural advantage or disadvantage; the only advantage it can possess is the ability to exploit universally available knowledge. Thus the knowledge is "the window of opportunity."[12] Since the next critical piece of information could take any form – an evolving social trend affecting preferences, a new management practice, a nascent technology, or a political or economic development in a remote manufacturing location.[13] We cannot manage this change, Drucker reminds. We can only lead change, and stay ahead of it.

(iv) Only the Knowledgeable Survive

"The survival of the fittest firm" is an outmoded thought in the knowledge-based economy. The ability to survive and thrive comes only from a firm's ability to create, acquire, process, maintain, and retain old and new knowledge in the face of complexity, uncertainty and rapid change[14]. It becomes deterministic in the firm's long-term survival. Drucker points out that knowledge is productive only if it is applied to make a difference (rather than simply exist) and suggests that it is this productivity that is going to be the deterministic factor in the competitive position of any company or industry.[15] Knowledge management can make that a reality.

(v) Cross-Industry Amalgamation Is Breeding Complexity

The complexity, uncertainty, and ambiguity are hallmarks of today's production and business systems irrespective of the nature of business or type of industry. And, Knowledge management can allow us to turn this complexity to our advantage.[16]

(vi) Knowledge can provide Effective Decision Support

Providing effective decision support by making knowledge about past projects, initiatives, failures, successes, and efforts readily available and accessible can make a significant contribution toward convalescing this process. There are four diagnostic tools for decision-making that we can focus on: foundation, productivity, competence, and resource allocation. Knowledge management solutions are capable of effectively supporting collaboration and knowledge sharing enable individual workers, teams, and communities to collaboratively make better decisions faster – and act on those decisions to create more economic value for their organization.

(vii) Knowledge Management requires Sharing; information technology (IT) barely supports sharing

Knowledge Management requires a strong culture of sharing that information systems do not inherently support.

Knowledge, as any witness to artificial intelligence research knows, "is not about machines, but about culture."[17] Principles that have traditionally driven information technology design, though with moderate success, no longer apply in designing knowledge management systems.

(viii) Tacit knowledge is mobile

Too often when someone leaves your firm, his or her experience leaves too. This knowledge, skills, competencies, understanding and insight then often go to work for a competitor. Knowledge management can save our organization from losing critical capabilities when that happens.

(ix) Competitors are no longer just on the west coast.

We are becoming increasingly global. Keeping up with developments and ensuring threats or opportunities in other countries is a tedious, time-consuming, and difficult process.

1.8 Knowledge management technology, when given the right source feeds, can deliver relevant and timely knowledge. As companies shift from a product-centric form to a knowledge-centric form, it becomes essential to support various dimensions of this knowledge as a critical asset. Companies – big or small – cannot afford to underinvest in using, reusing, and not losing knowledge that they already have. Knowledge management is therefore imperative for organization, which do not operate in purely cost-driven markets anymore.

1.9 One more aspect is clarified here. Knowledge Management is not solely concerned with technology. Thus it cannot be looked upon as a mere technology problem. It is partly a management problem. Only by aligning the two we can build knowledge management technology that can truly enable effective knowledge management and thus act as a potent competitive tool for an ever more brutally competitive age of shrinking margins, shorter product development times, and fickle customers.

1.10 It may be added that knowledge management is not knowledge engineering too(+). Further, knowledge management is about process, not just digital networks. Management of knowledge has to encompass and improve business processes. Agreed that IT (Information Technology) is the bigger enabler for effective knowledge management if used correctly. However, focusing on the T and not the I in IT will deliver little. Also it should be ample clear that knowledge management system can use the company's intranet as its front end, but intranet is not knowledge management system. The intranet is, however, a part of the equation that provides a stable messaging and collaboration. Knowledge management is not about a one-time investment. Like any other future-oriented investment, it requires consistent attention over a substantial period of time even after it begins to deliver results. KM is also not about enterprise-wise "infobahns". True that enterprise integration helps, the focus of KM is on creating, getting, importing, delivering, and most importantly helping the **right** people apply the **right** knowledge at the **right** time. Lastly, knowledge management is also not about capturing "knowledge." An inevitable loss of context occurs when documents are "sanitized" for use across the company. While a document management system lacks context, experience, and insight, it still has a marginal place in knowledge management technology. What needs to be mentioned is that the knowledge, in its entirety, cannot be captured.

TWO KINDS OF ORGANIZATIONS

1.11 Basically there are two types of organizations that should be pursuing knowledge management irrespective of the their size - small or large. The **first type** is one that has realized the need to keep up with its competitors and remain a legitimate player through the process of maintaining knowledge that is core

---

(+) Knowledge Engineering has been a vital part of computer science but is barely even related to knowledge management. Knowledge management is a business problem and falls in the domain of information systems and management, not in computer science. Knowledge management needs to meld information systems and people in ways that knowledge engineering has never been able to.

to its line of business. Core knowledge is the basic level of knowledge required before you can even "play the game". The **second type** is one step ahead: It already had the core knowledge necessary. This organization realizes that what is innovative knowledge to day will be common place core knowledge tomorrow. Such companies are struggling with their ability to keep ahead, not just viably complete. Of the two kinds, commercial banks in India fall in both the categories. They have been the users of 'knowledge' since the time they came into existence. However, the use of 'knowledge' and the extent of its effective management have increased for them during post-reform period, namely, July 1991 till this date.

KNOWLEDGE MANAGEMNT PROCESS

1.12 Conceptually, the process of knowledge management includes 4 major steps, as depicted in Figure: 1.2.

FIGURE: 1.2 PROCESS OF KNOWLEDGE MANAGEMENT

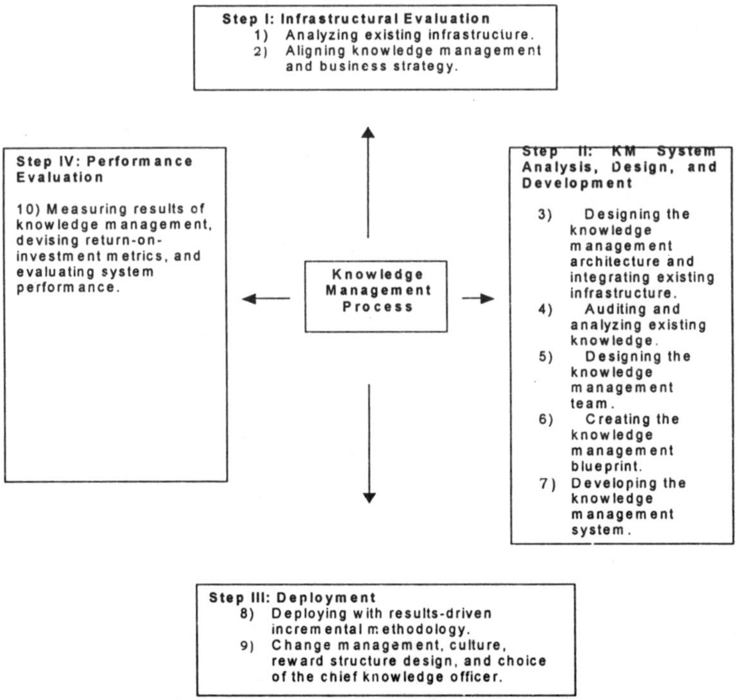

Knowledge Management Roadmap

1.13 The Roadmap of KM, which has four phases, could be divided into 10 Steps as depicted below in Figure 1.3

FIGURE 1.3
THE 10-STEP KNOWLEDGE MANAGEMENT ROADMAP

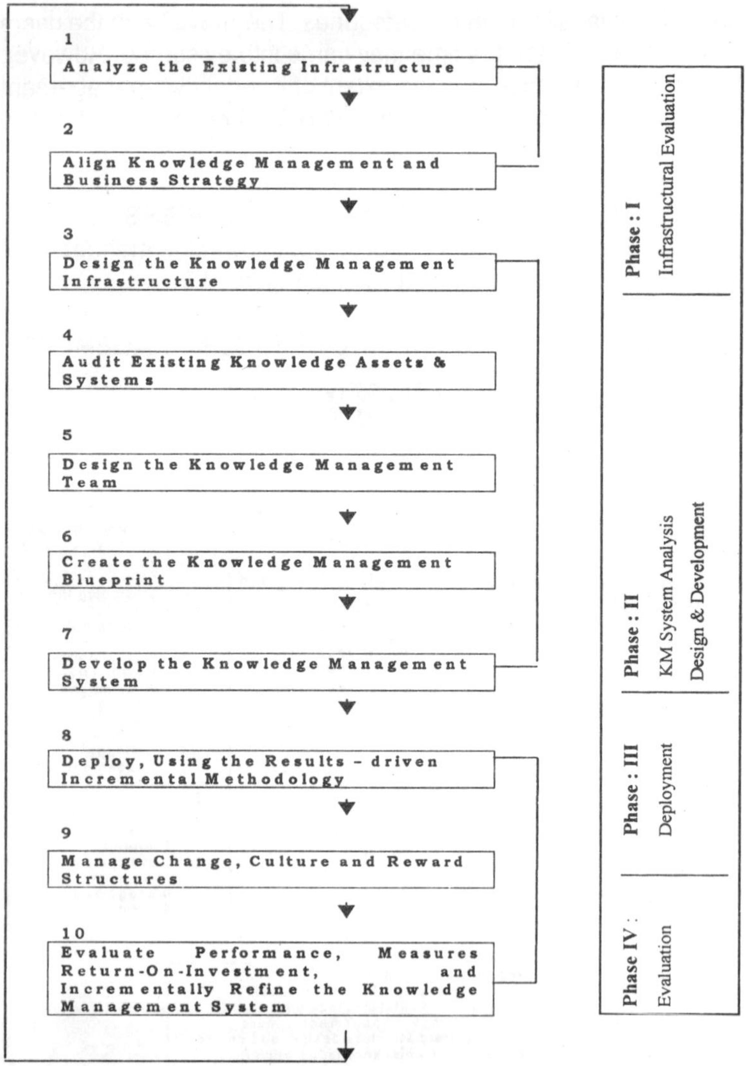

WHOSE RESPONSIBILITY IS FOR KNOWLEDGE MANAGEMENT[18]?

1.14 All the members of the organization are responsible for knowledge management. As a matter of fact the value of any one-person's contribution is determined less by his or her location in the organizational hierarchy than by the importance of the information he or she provides to the entire knowledge-creating system. In fact, creating new knowledge is the product of dynamic interaction among the knowledge practitioners (front-line employees and line managers), knowledge engineers (middle managers) and knowledge officers (top managers). Knowledge practitioners are responsible for accumulating and generating both tacit and explicit knowledge. They consist of "Knowledge Operator," who interface with tacit knowledge from the most part, and "Knowledge Specialists" who interface primarily with explicit knowledge. Knowledge engineers are responsible for converting tacit knowledge into explicit and *vice-versa*. Knowledge officers are responsible for managing the organizational knowledge creation process at the corporate level.

SURVEY OF THE LITERATURE

1.15 The expression 'Knowledge Management' was coined for the first time in 1986 by **Dr. Wiig M. Karl (1993)**[19] who wrote one of the first books with the title, 'Knowledge Management Foundations', published in 1993. A significant contribution was made by **Nonaka I. and Takeuchi H. (1995)**[20] in explaining the type of knowledge and their conversion processes: socialization, externalization, combination, and internalization. Each process involves converting one form of knowledge (tacit or explicit) to another form of knowledge (tacit or explicit). This model focused on the important issue of how knowledge may be created through organizational sharing and is useful for identifying and evaluating certain key activities in the management of knowledge.

1.16 **Wilcox C. Lyle (1997)**[21] defined Knowledge Based Systems as tools of intelligence that assist how organizations are structured, how they respond and react to opportunities, and how vertical and horizontal communication encourage productive competition for resources while creating highly efficient orders of parallel processing (concurrent synchronized management) within the organization.

1.17 **Vander Spek Rob and Spiglrevet Andre (1997)**[22] identified organization into different knowledge areas like promising knowledge areas; key (core) knowledge areas; basic knowledge areas; outdated knowledge areas. They also identified different types of organization, which can be benefited from Knowledge Management[23]: (i) companies which must re-organize due to various circumstance or that have already been reorganized, (ii) companies that have just gone through a major expansion, (iii) industrial companies that want to enter markets where the required knowledge areas are scattered over the whole organization, (iv) companies have completed a re-engineering phase, and (v) networks in which several companies and organizations participate.

1.18 **Beckman T.J. (1999)**[24], presents the organizational perspective and he opined that knowledge could be viewed as processed information embedded in routines, processes, products, rules and culture that enable actions. **Zack H., Michael, Faulkner, and Gray (1999)**[25] observed that Knowledge mapping has become a standard technique in the knowledge management arsenal. By knowing where the knowledge resides, it can be more effectively and efficiently shared and exploited.

1.19 **Skyrme J. David (1999)**[26] argument is that knowledge is an important contributor to the performance, value and future prosperity of the organization. **Stewart A. Thomas (2001)**[27] identified the wealth of knowledge, which presents a practical, prescriptive, four step process for managing knowledge assets. This process is agenda for the companies of twenty first century. It defines the knowledge battleground on which a company competes, shows how to identify the knowledge assets that control an industry, describes how to develop strategies to invest in intellectual capital and compete with it, and offers ways to create millions upon millions of dollars' worth of additional value by managing knowledge more efficiently.

1.20 **The World Development Report[28] (1998)** suggests that growth in developed as well as developing countries is a function of the quality of knowledge in those countries. Knowledge based industries such as information technologies; biotechnology, financial and insurance services, and consultancy have become increasingly more important in terms of their share in gross national product and their growth potential. Knowledge management had its origin in these knowledge-based industries and is claimed to be providing them with competitive advantage.

1.21 **Smith J. Michael (2001)[29]** focusing on the knowledge desired to support and enhance peoples' business functions and aligning Knowledge Management with business objectives and requirements. Collaborative knowledge management is necessary for a company to: (i) Remain Competitive; (ii) Adapt to a rapidly changing environment; (iii) Innovative; (iv) Respond to the demand of e-business; (v) Fully capitalize and develop its people; (vi) Support effective relationships with Suppliers, Partners and Customers.

1.22 **Kucza Timo (2001)[30]** defines Knowledge Management process as one which is divided into co-ordination processes and operational processes. Herein, coordination processes describe what needs to be performed to initiate and control knowledge management activities; operational processes describe what is done when performing knowledge management activities. The co-ordination processes are organized into a cycle of analysis, planning, defining and effecting to support continuous improvement. The operational processes consist of the main processes: identification of need for knowledge, knowledge sharing, knowledge creation, knowledge collection and storage, and knowledge update.

1.23 Technological innovation has been cited as a major reason for the current interest in Knowledge Management **(Covin T.J. and Stivers B., 1997)[31]. Long De David (1997)[32]** suggest that organizational culture is relevant to firm that creates, shares and uses knowledge. He also suggests four ways in which organizational culture influences behaviors central to knowledge creation, sharing, and use. (i) Culture and particularly subcultures shape our assumptions about what knowledge is, and, hence, what knowledge is worth managing. (ii) Culture mediates the relationships between individual and organization-level knowledge. (iii) Culture creates the context for social interaction that ultimately determines the value an organization derives from knowledge. (iv) Culture shapes the processes by which new organizational knowledge – with its accompanying uncertainties – is captured, legitimated, and distributed.

1.24 **Loughridge Brendan (1999)**[33] concluded that the knowledge management practices bear a close resemblance to well established practices in librarianship and information management. However, the emphasis by knowledge management theorists and practitioners is on the importance of knowledge elicitation and knowledge creation, group work and team work, greater involvement in organizational strategy development and support.

1.25 **Zack H. Michael (1999) in his study on 'Managing Codified Knowledge'**[34] shows that to remain competitive, organizations must efficiently and effectively create, locate, capture, and share their organization's knowledge and expertise. This increasingly requires making the organization's knowledge explicit and recording it for easier distribution and reuse. Zack provides a framework for configuring a firm's organizational and technical resources and capabilities to leverage its codified knowledge.

1.26 In another study, **"Developing a Knowledge Strategy"**[35], **Zack H. Michael (1999)** emphasized that most knowledge management initiatives could be viewed primarily as information systems projects. He provides a framework for making that link and for assessing an organization's competitive position regarding its intellectual resources and capabilities. It recommends that organizations perform a knowledge-based SWOT (strengths, weaknesses, opportunities, and threats) analysis, comparing their knowledge to that of their competitors and to the knowledge required to execute their own strategy.

1.27 **Parise S. & Henderson J.C. (2001)**[36] describes a model of the knowledge resource exchange between alliance partners. It focuses on the different dimensions of knowledge resources (tacitness, specificity, and complexity) and their associated value implications, as well as the different roles of the partner bases on its position within an industry network (complementor, competitor, supplier, customer, or other). In order to capture and internalize knowledge obtained through an alliance, a firm must have an alliance learning capability.

1.28 **Dueck G. (2001)**[37] associates the different views of knowledge with personality types. A person's temperament determines that person's view of knowledge—a remarkable coincidence. Therefore, a person's answer to the question "What is knowledge?" is strongly related to the answer to "Who am I?" Hence, an enterprise should be careful when defining knowledge management for its use, lest its definition imply "who the employee should be."

1.29 **Fahey L., Srivastava R., Sharon J. S., Smith D. E. (2001)**[38]: The new business landscape ushered in by e-business has revolutionized business operations but, to date, has not integrated well with internal knowledge management initiatives. The development of e-business focused knowledge, contributes in the enhancement of three core-operating processes: customer relationship management, supply chain management, and product development management.

1.30 **Mack R., Ravin Y., and Byrd R. J. (2001)**[39] identified new tool Knowledge Portals for supporting knowledge work. Knowledge portals are single-point-access software systems intended to provide easy and timely access to information and to support communities of knowledge workers who share common goals. The role of knowledge portals plays in supporting knowledge embedded in portals, such as the gathering of distributed document information, indexing and text search, and categorization.

1.31 **MacMorrow N. (2001)**[40]: The management of information does not really focus on information sharing and is more oriented toward the control, preservation, and retention of information. One could also argue that the usefulness and the meaningfulness of information do not depend as much on its collective consumption or sharing: its individual consumption and use could be very effective from an organizational point of view.

1.32 **Marwick, A.D. (2001)**[41] researches in IBM, emphasize on the technology that should be applied to knowledge management and to assess their actual and potential contribution to the basic process of knowledge creation and sharing within the organization. The knowledge is being applied differently from tacit to tacit; tacit to explicit; explicit to explicit; explicit to tacit.

1.33 **McDonough Brian & Morris Henry (2001)**[42] discovered the important reasons for adopting knowledge management in many organizations. These are as thus : to increase customer retention/satisfaction; improve profits/growth revenue; decrease product development life cycle; provide project workspace.

1.34 **Prusak L. (2001)**[43] argues that consultants developed knowledge management to replace declining revenues from the waning re-engineering movement. Some of them may feel that knowledge management is just a "re-badging" of earlier information and data management methods. In the business community, there is also a strong interest for Knowledge Management.

1.35 **Auditore Peter (2002)**[44] emphasis on the key Knowledge Management Enabling Technologies: B2E Enterprise Information portal, Federated Search, Taxonomy, Classification and Indexing of Information Sources, Document/Information Management System, Collaborative E-commerce Application Environments and/or Workspaces, Simultaneous Collaboration, Business Process Management and Community of Interest Building, Intelligent Agents – web crawlers, Chat-Instant Messaging, Automated-Community Building Software, Visualization Software for Information Systems, and Expert Systems.

1.36 **Douglas Weidner (2002)[45]**: Knowledge Manager connect, collect and integrates for effective knowledge process, i.e. he (i) reinforces natural instincts to build trust and a culture of knowledge sharing; (ii) provide appropriate technology-enhanced collaboration tools; (iii) provide intuitive repositories for accumulating mission critical knowledge ; and (iv) enrich the technology with managerial practice and business process.

1.37 **Soo Christine, Devinney Timothy, Midgley David, and Deering Anne (2002)[46]** covered a range of concepts that were central to organizational knowledge management such as formal and informal network, absorptive capacity, quality of problem solving, and innovation. They come out with the greater formal and informal networking, the greater is information and knowledge acquisition; the more effective decision making that is applied to a large stock of information and knowledge, the more new knowledge is created; the greater is the level of new knowledge creation, the greater is the amount of innovation; the greater the amount of innovation, the greater the market and financial performance.

1.38 **Bontis Nick (2002)[47]** conducted a study at the Institute for Intellectual Capital Research Institute in Dundas, Ontario in 2002 in which a strong evidence was found that knowledge management programmes have resulted in to tremendous amounts of cost savings.

1.39 **Hlupic, V., Pouloudi, A. and Rzevski, G. (2002)[48]**, who identified three main types of activities: knowledge generation involving the creation of new ideas and new patterns; knowledge codification, and knowledge transfer, ensuring exchange of knowledge between individuals and departments.

1.40 **James A. Albers & Steve Brewer (2003)[49]**: Many organizations are turning to the practice of knowledge management for sharing experiences and expertise, integrating knowledge, and generating new knowledge. They examined the relationship between knowledge management and innovation to create a working model that will assist organizations in building innovative qualities and knowledge management practices into their business processes.

1.41 **W. Chan Kim and Mauborngne Renee (2003)**[50]: Knowledge based organizations are totally dependent on the commitment and ideas of their employees. But it is possible for top executives to create processes that help keep managers honest – and that also help build employees' trust. They describe one such process, which grew out of their research into the links between trust, idea sharing, and corporate performance.

1.42 **Kathleen M. Sutchliffe & Klaus Weber (2003)**[51]: The case of competitive advantage, companies are pouring increasingly more money into collecting and organizing information about the world in which they operate. Information improves accuracy, they contended and accuracy helps companies adapt more quickly and effectively to a changing market.

1.43 **Raman, Thothathri A (2003)**[52] realizing that seeking and acquiring knowledge is the way of life of human society stated that knowledge management is what makes the difference between a civilized and modern race and that which is still languishing as underdeveloped. Knowledge management is also the way to keep knowledge growing through sharing and such sharing is best done with no exacting price, either in material or human terms.

1.44 **Malhotra Yogesh (2000)**[53]: The new business environment, characterized by dynamically discontinuous change, requires a re-conceptualization of knowledge management, as it has been understood in information systems practice and research. One such conceptualization is proposed in the form of a sense-making model of knowledge management for new business environments. Application of this framework will facilitate business model innovation necessary for sustainable competitive advantage in the new business environment characterized by dynamic, discontinuous and radical pace of change.

1.45 **Ojha, K. Abhoy (2001)[54]**: Organizational knowledge consists of a combination of the knowledge of all individuals in the organization. It emerges out of a process of conscious and/or unconscious negotiations among all members of the organization. Prior knowledge is necessary for new learning, an organization is constrained by the choices it makes early in its existence. Different organizational forms have differing abilities to support knowledge creation: the functional form is suitable for exploitation, the divisions form suitable to exploitation, the divisions form suitable to exploitation in chosen domains, and matrix domains, and matrix forms suitable for exploration.

1.46 **R. T. Krishnan (2001)[55]**: Creating and using knowledge effectively can be an effective way of cost-based competitive advantage. Knowledge management has become prominent because advances in information technology and connectivity have enabled certain aspects of knowledge management to be performed on a wider scale and at lower cost than before.

1.47 **Hariharan Arun (2002)[56]**: The objective of knowledge management is to support the achievement of business-objectives. Both knowledge-contributions / sharing as well as re-use need to be encouraged and recognized at the individual employee level as well as the company level. This is best done by measuring and rewarding knowledge-performance. Sustained strategic commitment and a corporate culture that is conducive to knowledge-performance are vital for success in knowledge management.

1.48 **Jurgen Kluge, Wolfram Stein, Thomas Licht (2001)[57]** conducted a survey of 40 companies in Europe, Japan, and the United States which showed that many executives think that knowledge management begins and ends with building sophisticated information technology systems. Some companies go much further: they take the trouble to link all their information together and to build models that increase their profitability by improving processes, products, and customer relations.

1.49 **Karl M. Wiig (2000)**[58]: Knowledge Management plays several roles in Public Administration. Each role serves specific constituencies and purposes and is implemented differently. In Public Administration, four knowledge management areas are considered important : (a) Enhance decision making within public services; (b) Aid the public to participate effectively in public decision making; (c) Build competitive societal knowledge and IC capabilities; and (d) Develop knowledge-competitive work force.

1.50 A survey conducted in 1997 of 200 large US firms revealed that 80% of corporations had knowledge initiatives **(KPMG, 2000)**[59]. **Kenan Patrick Jarboe & Athena Alliance (2001)**[60] observed that : economic development organizations can use KM tools to enhance external communications of local companies including marketing and to promote internal communications within local businesses and help companies capture tacit knowledge. Knowledge management tools can be used to enhance external knowledge sharing among the economic development community and to capture and share tacit knowledge within an economic development organization.

1.51 **Hackett Brian (2001)**[61]: A survey was conducted by PriceWaterhouseCoopers and a Working Group of Executives covering 12 companies. This survey described the current status of knowledge management from the perspective of senior line and staff executives where 200 senior executives at 158 global companies responded. It revealed that 80 percent of companies have some KM efforts under way; 6 percent use KM enterprise-wide and 60 percent expect to in five years; 25 percent have a chief knowledge officer or chief learning officer (although half of them not supported with dedicated budget or staff); and 21 per cent have a communicated KM strategy.

1.52 **Antonina Holowetzki (2002)**[62]: Knowledge management (KM) initiatives can not be taken hold unless they are supported by an organization's culture. The study examines cultural factors in the culture knowledge relationship. Applying content analysis methods, theory-based literature and case studies published between 1998 and 2002 are reviewed to examine the relationship between organizational culture and knowledge management. Considered cultural factors being : information systems, organizational structure, reward systems, processes, people, and leadership.

1.53 **Daniele Chauvel and Charles Despres (2002)**[63] report outlines the results of a pilot survey that was sent to selected European firms and published on the Knowledge Board (http.//www.knowledgeboard.com) between October and December 2001. The study was initiated by ECKM: The European Center for Knowledge Management (http://www.eckm.fr) with the objective of establishing a research agenda concerning the way the topic of Knowledge Management (KM) is treated within the Management Development function of European businesses. In addition to being posted on the Knowledge Board, the questionnaire was sent to 93 firms in Europe and 134 companies in France. This databank will serve as the basis for a more robust treatment of KM as a Management Development issue in European business, with a large-scale survey targeted for Q4 2002. Highlights from this study are as follows: 1. Respondents tend to define Knowledge Management as a source of innovation and value creation, with a strong focus on business objectives. 2. Over three-quarters (77.8%) of the companies surveyed have or are establishing a KM program. The majority of existing programs have been in operation between 9 and 24 months. 3. Approximately 45% of the firms have a Knowledge Management officer and half have Management Development programs specifically devoted to KM. 4. The KM-related Management Development programs most frequently cited by respondents include: (a). Team-based topics aimed at synergies and new work designs ; (b). Technologically-based topics aimed at managing information and / or knowledge assets; and, (c). Topics related to the strategic use of information and knowledge assets.

1.54 **Michael Barry & Stephen Clifford (2002)**[64]: Another knowledge management study was conducted in Feb/March 2002 of 740 people interested in KM topics where companies involved in KM initiatives. The survey respondents were highly concentrated in the business and legal service industries. They listed that enhancement of internal collaboration and capturing and sharing best practices were among the top business reasons for undertaking the initiative.

1.55 **Chase Rory (2002)**[65]: Few enterprises also establishes some criteria for knowledge performance like creating a corporate knowledge culture/knowledge leaders; delivering knowledge based products and solutions, maximizing enterprising intellectual capital; creating a learning organization; focusing on customer knowledge.

1.56 **Sviokla J. John (1996)**[66]: Knowledge based expert system, which intended to be the insurance sales process at four insurance companies in USA. Lutheran Brotherhood, National Mutual, Prudential, and Sun Alliance tried to get more than 5000 field salespeople to implement profiling. The study results indicate that in implementing a radically new technology, managers need to assemble "constellation" of actions, consider the political ramifications throughout the organization, manage the momentum of the project, and work to achieve economies of scale.

1.57 In Studies carried at firm level in the U.S. in the manufacturing sector and in the service sector, **Brynjolfsson Erik & Hitt Lorin (1996)**[67], found productivity improvements associated with investment in information technology and the quality of manpower engaged in the task of information technology. However, **Prasad Baba and Harker T. Patrick (1997)**[68] in a study relating to the retail-banking sector in USA, did not find productivity improvements associated with IT investment but observed that productivity improvements are more associated with the manpower engaged in managing information technology.

1.58 **Luen T.W. and Al-Hawamdeh S.(2001)**[69] study shows that private sector organizations are not the only ones embracing knowledge management. The systematic sharing of knowledge is assuming a larger role in all kinds of organizations around the world.

1.59 **Skok W. (2000)**[70]: Some of the recent Knowledge Management initiatives in the United Kingdom include the creation of the post of knowledge officer at the British Council and the appointment of a Chief Knowledge Officer at NatWest Markets.

1.60 **Frada Bursteina, Suzanne Zyngierb, and Zohdy Ratebc (2002)**[71] put their collaborative research in Knowledge Management in the Financial Services Sector in Australia. In this environment, an organizational knowledge management strategy becomes a critical platform for sustaining core business capabilities and harnessing the capacity for innovation. The results of a survey of the top 130 Australian banking and insurance institutions supplemented this data with a series of interviews with business leaders and compared the results with a similar European study. Some of the key findings were: almost all (92%) of surveyed organizations have in place, or are establishing, a plan to manage organizational knowledge ; although most of these are in the initial phases of a knowledge management strategy, they are far ahead of their European counterparts (41% of which have or are establishing a knowledge management plan) ; and, two thirds of banks and one third of insurance companies have developed knowledge management mechanisms for sharing best practice.

1.61 **Daniel Z. Levin, Rob Cross, Lisa C. Abrams and Eric L. Lesser (2002)**[72]: The IBM Institute for Knowledge-Based Organizations (IKO) studied the role of trust in knowledge sharing. Factors such as the strength of the relationship between the knowledge seeker and the knowledge source, the difference between competence-based and benevolence-based trust and the type of knowledge being exchanged were explored. Data from a two-part survey of 138 people in three companies were analyzed to discern how trust affects knowledge sharing and how individuals evaluate the trustworthiness of others when seeking knowledge. By applying this new insight, managers can take explicit actions to help build trust—and, in turn, encourage knowledge sharing.

1.62 On the basis of the study of service companies **Stefan Thomke (2003)**[73] commented that this segment has long suffered from haphazard approaches to innovation. Big Banks like Bank of

America has been running a series of formal experiments aimed at creating a new service concept for retail banking, where they created a new process for service innovation. Bank of America took an unprecedented step in the conservative banking industry: it would create an "innovation market" within the bank's existing branches.

1.63 **Takemura Toshihiko (2003)**[74] In the banking sector we found relevant productivity improvements associated with information system investments, especially software investment.

1.64 **Agrawal M. Narendra (2001)**[75] conducted a study to examine and understand some of the problems being experienced in implementing knowledge management systems in Indian Organizations. It focused on identifying what needs to be done to manage and institutionalize knowledge management processes and to create an organizational culture for managing and motivating knowledge workers. The findings of the study were: a) lack of top management involvement; b) lack of pull for KM system; c) lack of cross-functional ownership; d) obstructive organizational structure; e) dysfunctional reward system.

1.65 **Srinivas Krishna (2001)**[76]: As the demographic pattern of society undergoes change, there is a greater need for products, services and information relevant to ethnic, age and income/ education groups. One size does not fit all in consumer-driven healthcare. A factor that has assumed prominence is privacy of patient information. As the clamor to capture patient information through information technology increased, the fear of the possible misuse of patient data impacted the spread. The most critical challenge faced by the sector is the need for a cultural shift amongst the various members of this sector. The sector needs to develop a mindset that facilitates knowledge sharing.

1.66 **Swami Subramaniam (2001)**[77]: In countries where knowledge management has been a later development, the emphasis has been on the forms of knowledge management, such as IT systems, with none of the experimentation that precedes the implementation of a new management theory. The 'New Biology' has thrown up a multitude of specialized 'insider' disciplines that must be tamed and integrated within the existing discipline of the drug discovery process. Only then can it yield the fabulous potential that is attributed to it. Although new biology is unique for the volume of data needed to be coped with, the basic paradigms of KM still apply. Knowledge sharing through a variety of processes including mentoring, internships, communities of practice and networking, etc. still constitute the key element.

1.67 **Desai Pranay (2002)**[78]: Knowledge Management has taken a top-place on business agenda culminating in a knowledge-based organization. The market runners are well aware about the facts that knowledge management will play a critical role in the near future, enhancing their internal productivity in conjunction with developing them externally, in terms of increased customer satisfaction due to rich knowledge based marketing, developing a competitive advantage. The research findings primarily indicate the importance of knowledge management within an organizational framework and the acceptance of this new management strategy in the Indian context.

1.68 This survey of literature reveals, in nutshell, that broadly there have been two kinds of studies in past. One, those which concerned with the subject of 'Knowledge Management' as such. And, second, those which related to the application of it in variegated segments of the organization. Most of the studies show that Knowledge Management has assumed the top place in the business agenda in the case of knowledge-based organizations.

1.69 The studies concerning with the application of knowledge management have mainly been in areas of Public Administration, Information Technology Companies, Pharmaceutical Sector, Health Sector etc. Only one study also pertained to the Banking and Finance and it had been for the Australian and European Banking and Insurance firms. None of the studies has been for the Indian Commercial Banks. In fact, it is true that the information is the lifeblood for banks and its management is necessary for continuous functioning in the globalized environment. In the near future, banks have to gear up for Basel II compliance. This required lots of information and knowledge management on the part of banks. However, the new technologies can come to the rescue of banks as never before in the banking sector. Our study, which will assess and analyze the current status of knowledge management in the Indian commercial banking sector, will contribute to fill out this strategic gap.

FOCUS OF THE STUDY

1.70 The main objective of this study is **to assess and analyze the present status and future of Knowledge Management for the Indian Commercial Banking Sector** ***via*** **studying their structural, operational, technological, and administrative processes, and gamut of products/services provided by them to their clientele. Designing the necessary framework for an ongoing effective Knowledge Management System for this sector is another objective that study intends to accomplish.**

1.71 In order to achieve these objectives, this study intends to address the following major research issues :-

a) Evaluating the technical efficiency among the selected commercial banks through their growth, productivity and profitability indicators.

b) Role of Information System in Knowledge Management and the current status of the use and impact of information technology on the functioning of and Knowledge Management by Indian Banks.

a) Integration of Knowledge Strategy in the Business Strategy and Knowledge Initiatives in Relation to Banks' Vision, Mission/Goals and Actions.

b) Managing Human Resource for an Effective Knowledge Management.

c) Nature, Source and Purposes for which the Information and Knowledge is utilized.

LIMITATIONS OF THE STUDY:

1.72 It may be mentioned that the utility of financial analysis undertaken in this study is restricted by and such factors as:

- Availability of scarce, unorganized and unstructured literature on the subject.
- Unwillingness of the top management to provide exact information about their strategic policies and plans of actions.
- The dynamic nature of the information available on websites in the form of articles, news, etc.
- Difficulty in proving that an improvements in financial indicators is entirely dependent upon computerization information technology/ knowledge management.
- Accuracy of the analysis being dependent upon the accuracy of the data reported by banks.

PERIOD OF THE STUDY

1.73 For this Study we have chosen the post-economic reforms period broadly commencing from July 1991 and onward; to be more precise it covers the period July 1991 – March 2004. And, our choice has been primarily dominated by the overriding for that it has been the period, which has led to the paradigm shift from conventional growth path to contemporary growth path for the banking industry in India.

1.74 To collaborate it may be mentioned that impacts of economic reforms on the Indian banking sector are more than visible both in width and depth of the financial intermediation process structure of interest rates on deposits and loans and advances, extent of competition, operational transparency, global face in institutional architecture of the system as evidenced in the shape of markets, technology, managerial approach, etc.

NOTES

1. Davenport, Thomas, H., and Laurece Prusak, "Working Knowledge: How Organization Manage What They Know", Harvard Business School Press, Boston, 1998, p.5.
2. Nonaka Ikujiro and Takeuchi Hirotaka, "The Knowledge Creating Company: How Japanese Companies Create the Dynamics of Innovation", Oxford University Press, New York, 1995.

3. Krogh Georg Von, Ichijo Kazuo, and Nonaka Ikujiro, "Enabling Knowledge Creation: How to unlock the Mystery of Tacit Knowledge and Release the Power of Innovation," Oxford University Press, New York, 2000, p.6.
4. Davenport, Thomas, H., and Laurece Prusak, " Working Knowledge: How Organization Manage What They Know," Harvard Business School Press, Boston, 1998, p.163.
5. Bukowitz, Wendi R. and Williams, Ruth L, "The Knowledge Management Field Book," Pearson Education Limited, London, 1999, p.2.
6. Tiwana Amrit, "The Knowledge Management Toolkit: Practical Techniques for Building a Knowledge Management System", Pearson Education Asia Pvt. Ltd, 2000, p.9.
7. Drucker, Peter F., "Management Challenges for the 21st Century", Harper Business, New York, 1999.
8. Davenport, Thomas, H., and Laurece Prusak, op. cit.
9. Tiwana Amrit, op. cit., pp.6-9.
10. Hansen, Nohria M.N., and Tierney T., "What's Your Strategy for Managing Knowledge?" Harvard Business Review, March-April 1999, p.106-116.
11. Drucker, Peter F., op. cit., p.74.
12. Drucker, Peter F., op. cit., p.84.
13. Abramson, Gary, "The Thrill of the Hunt", CIO Enterprise, January 15 1999, pp.35-42.
14. Dhurana, Anil, "Managing Complex Production Process", Sloan Management Review, Winter 1999, pp.85-97.
15. Drucker Peter F., "The Post Capitalist Society", Harper Business Press, New York, 1993.
16. Fabris Peter, "You Think Tomaytoes, I Think Tomahtoes", CIO Enterprise, 1999, pp.46-52.
17. Krochmal, Mo, Tech Guru, "People are Key to Knowledge Management", The New York Times, New York, June 9, 1999.
18. Nonaka Ikujiro and Takeuchi Hirotaka, op. cit.
19. Wiig, M. Karl, "Knowledge Management Foundations: Thinking about Thinking - How People and Organisations Create, Represent and Use Knowledge", Arlington TX: Schema Press, 1993.
20. Nonaka, I. and Takeuchi, H. "The knowledge creating company: how Japanese companies create the dynamics of innovation" New York: Oxford University Press, 1995.

21. Wilcox, C. Lyle, "Knowledge – Based Systems as an Integrating Process", CRC Press LLC, 1997, p.21
22. Vander Spek Rob and Spiglrevet Andre, "KM: Dealing Intelligently With Knowledge", CRC Press LLC, Florida, 1997, pp37-38.
23. Vander Spek Rob and Spiglrevet Andre, op. cit., pp54-55.
24. Beckman, T.J., "The current state of knowledge management" Knowledge management handbook, edited by J. Liebowitz, New York, CRC Press, 1999 pp.1.1-1.22.
25. Zack, H. Michael, Faulkner, and Gray, "Competing on Knowledge: Handbook of Business Strategy", New York, 1999, pp.81-88.
26. Skyrme J. David, "Knowledge Networking: Creating the Collaborative Enterprises", Butterworth Heinemann, 1999, p.5.
27. Stewart, A. Thomas, "The Wealth of Knowledge: Intellectual Capital and the Twenty-First Century Organization" Utopia Limited, 2001, pp.53-55.
28. World Bank, "World Development Report", 1998
29. Smith, J. Michael, "Collaborative Knowledge Management as a Necessary Business Imperative", ICL e-Innovation, February 2001, p4.
30. Kucza Timo, "Knowledge Management Process Model", Technical Research Centre Of Finland, VTT Publications, 2001, p.3
31. Covin, T.J. and Stivers, B, "Knowledge management focus in US and Canadian firms" Creativity and Innovation Management, Vol 6(3), 1997, pp.140-150.
32. Long De David, "Building the Knowledge-Based Organization: How Culture Drives Knowledge Behaviors", Center for Business Innovation, Ernst & Young LLP, May 1997, p26.
33. Loughridge Brendan, "Knowledge Management, Librarians and Information managers: Fad or Future?", New Library World, Volume 100 . Number 1151, 1999, pp.245-253. Also available at http://www.emerald-library.com
34. Zack, H. Michael, "Managing Codified Knowledge", Sloan Management Review, Volume 40, Number 4, summer 1999, pp.45-58.
35. Zack, H. Michael, "Developing a Knowledge Strategy" California Management Review , Vol. 41, No. 3, Spring, 1999, pp.125-145.
36. Parise S. and Henderson J. C., "Knowledge Resource Exchange In Strategic Alliances", IBM Systems Journal, Vol 40, No 4, 2001, pp.908-924.

37. Dueck, G. "Views of knowledge are human views", IBM Systems Journal, Vol 40, No 4, 2001, pp 885-888.
38. Fahey L., Srivastava R., Sharon J. S., Smith D. E., "Linking e-business and operating processes: The role of knowledge management", IBM Systems Journal, Vol 40, No 4, 2001, pp.889-907.
39. Mack R., Ravin Y., and Byrd R. J., "Knowledge portals and the emerging digital knowledge workplace", IBM Systems Journal, Vol 40, No 4, 2001, pp.925-955.
40. MacMorrow, N. "Knowledge management: an introduction", in: Annual Review of Information Science and Technology, edited by M.E. Williams, 2001 pp.381-422.
41. Marwick, A. D. "Knowledge Management Technology", IBM Systems Journal, Vol 40, No. 4, 2001, pp.814-830.
42. McDonough Brian & Morris Henry, "Computer Associate: Building a strong foundation for knowledge management" An IDC white paper IDC & KM Magazine, 2001.
43. Prusak, L "Where did knowledge management come from", IBM Systems Journal, Vol 40, No 4, 2001, pp.1002-1004.
44. Auditore, Peter "Enabling Knowledge Management in Today's Knowledge Economy", KM World, Jan 2002, pp.8-9.
45. Douglas Weidner, "Using Connect and Collect to Achieve the KM Endgame", IT Pro January | February 2002, pp. 18-24.
46. Soo Christine, Devinney Timothy, Midgley David, and Deering Anne, "Knowledge Management: Philosophy, Processes, and Pitfalls", California Management Review (CMR) 44/4 (summer: 2002), pp.129-149.
47. Bontis Nick, "The Rising Star of the CKO", IVEY Business Journal, March/April 2002, pp. 20 – 25.
48. Hlupic, V., Pouloudi, A. and Rzevski, G. "Towards an integrated approach to knowledge management: 'hard', 'soft', and 'abstract' issues" Knowledge and Process Management, Vol 9(2), 2002, pp.90-102.
49. James A. Albers & Steve Brewer, "Knowledge Management And The Innovation Process: The Eco-Innovation Model", Journal of Knowledge Management Practice, June 2003,
50. W. Chan Kim and Mauborngne Renee, "Fair Process: Managing in the Knowledge Economy", Harvard Business Review – Motivating People, Jan 2003, pp. 127-136.

51. Kathleen M. Sutchliffe, Klaus Weber, "The High Cost of Accurate Knowledge", HBR, May 2003, pp.74-82.
52. Raman, Thothathri A., "Knowledge Management: A resource book", Excel Books, 2003, pp. 4-5.
53. Malhotra Yogesh, "Knowledge Management & New Organization Forms: A Framework for Business Model Innovation", Information Resources Management Journal, 13(1), Jan-March 2000, pp. 5-14.
54. Ojha K. Abhoy, "Building a Knowledge Organization: Overcoming Individual and Organizational Barriers", IIMB Management Review, Dec 2001, pp. 64-73.
55. R. T. Krishnan, "Knowledge Management and Competitive Advantage", IIMB Management Review, Dec 2001, pp. 57-63.
56. Hariharan Arun, "Knowledge Management: A Strategic Tool", Journal of Knowledge Management Practice, December 2002, Also Available at www.bharti.com
57. Jurgen Kluge, Wolfram Stein, Thomas Licht, "Knowledge Unplugged: The McKinsey & Company – Global Survey of Knowledge Management", Palgrave, New York, 2001.
58. Karl M. Wiig, "Application of Knowledge Management in Public Administration", Knowledge Research Institute, Inc., Arlington, Texas, USA, May, 2000
59. KPMG Consulting (2000). Knowledge management research report. London: Atos KPMG Consulting. Available at: http://www.kpmgconsulting.co.uk/research/othermedia/wf_8519 kmreport.pdf
60. Kenan Patrick Jarboe & Athena Alliance, "Knowledge Management As an Economic Development Strategy", U.S. Economic Development Administration, Department of Commerce, April 2001, pp.13-14.
61. Hackett Brian, "Beyond Knowledge Management: New Ways to Work and Learn", The Conference Board, Inc. Report 2001 sponsored by Price WaterhouseCoopers.
62. Antonina Holowetzki, "The relationship between knowledge management and organizational culture: An examination of cultural factors that support the flow and management of knowledge within an organization", University of Oregon, Applied Information Management Program, CAPSTONE REPORT, Dec 2002, p. 51.

63. Daniele Chauvel, Charles Despres, "Knowledge Management and the Management Development Function in European Business", The European Center for Knowledge Management, April 2002 pp.1-17.
64. Michael Barry & Stephen Clifford, "eINFORM" Volume 3, Issue 8, 2002, www.idc.com
65. Chase Rory "2002 North American Most Admired Knowledge Enterprises", TELECOS Inc., Feb/March 2002
66. Sviokla J. John, "Knowledge Workers and Radically New Technology", Sloan Management Review, summer 1996, pp. 24-40.
67. Brynjolfsson Erik & Hitt Lorin, "Productivity, Profit and Consumer Welfare: Three Different Measures of Information Technology's Value", MIS Quarterly, June, 1996. Also available at http://ccs.mit.edu/papers/CCSWP190.html
68. Prasad Baba and Harker T. Patrick, "Examining the Contribution of Information Technology Toward Productivity and Profitability in U.S. Retail Banking", Financial Institutions Center of The Wharton School, University of Pennsylvania, Philadelphia, 1997
69. Luen, T.W. and Al-Hawamdeh, S. "Knowledge management in the public sector: principles and practices in police work" Journal of Information Science, Vol 27, 2001, pp.311-318.
70. Skok, W. "Managing knowledge within the London taxi cab service" Knowledge and Process Management, Vol 7(4), 2001, pp. 224-232.
71. Frada Bursteina, Suzanne Zyngierb, and Zohdy Ratebc, "Knowledge Management in the Financial Services Sector: understandings and trends in Australia", Proceedings of the 3rd European Conference on Knowledge Management (ECKM2002), 24-25 September 2002, Trinity College Dublin, Ireland, MCIL, pp.113-125.
72. Daniel Z. Levin, Rob Cross, Lisa C. Abrams and Eric L. Lesser, "Trust and knowledge sharing: A critical combination", IBM Institute for Knowledge-Based Organizations, 2002, pp.1-8. ibm.com/services/strategy.
73. Thomke Stefan "R & D comes to service: Bank of America's Path breaking experiments", Harvard Business Review, April 2003, pp.71-79.

74. Takemura Toshihiko, "Information System Investment, Productivity Information System Investment, Productivity and Efficiency in Japanese Banking and Efficiency in Japanese Banking Industry" Graduate School of Economics, Osaka University, Research Center of Socio-network Strategies, Kansai University, 2003.
75. Narendra M Agrawal, "Creating an Organizational Culture for Knowledge Management", IIMB Management Review, Dec 2001, pp.74-82.
76. Srinivas Krishna, "Knowledge Management in the Healthcare Sector", IIMB Management Review, Dec 2001, pp.83-90.
77. Swami Subramaniam, "Knowledge Management in the Pharmaceutical Industry", IIMB Management Review, Dec 2001, pp.91-97.
78. Desai Pranay, "Knowledge Management" Research Report, India, Griffith University - School of Management & BML Consulting, Brisbane, Australia, 2002.

2

INDIAN COMMERCIAL BANKING SYSTEM

Commercial Banks be it a case of developed nation or a developing one, could be treated as service-rendering organization. As have already been said in the preceding chapter, they have been the users of knowledge since their existence. However, the pace of developments in technology in general and in the sphere of information technology in particular has relatively been high. Also the post-reform period in India has not only accompanied with opening of the economy and its integration with global markets but also with series of reforms in the financial sector which included the banking system – the core of the financial sector of an economy. In order to appreciate in the right perspective the relationship between Commercial Banks and the Knowledge Management it would be appropriate to understand the nature and functions of these banks in India with reference to Banking Regulation Act, 1949, structure of commercial banking system in India, changes that have taken place in the operational focus of these banks during the post-nationalization era *vis-à-vis* the pre-nationalization period. The review of the banking policy in early 1990 by the Committee on Banking Sector Reforms and its major recommendations and the subsequent impacts on the functioning of the banks shall further of interest in this context.

COMMERCIAL BANKS

2.2 Commercial Banks are one kind of financial institutions. Each one of them represents a 'Company' as defined in Section 3 of the Companies Act, 1956; and includes a foreign company within the meaning of Section 591 of that Act. Further this company is a "banking company" in terms of Section 5 (c) of the Banking Regulation Act, 1949. As per this clause the **"banking company" means any company which transacts the business of banking in India"** and **"banking" means the accepting, for the purpose of lending or investment, of deposits of money from the public, repayable on demand or otherwise, and withdrawal by cheque, draft, order or otherwise "Section 5(b) of the Banking Regulation Act, 1949"**. In addition to the business of "banking", as defined above, a banking company may engage in any one or more of the following forms of business, namely:

(i) the borrowing, raising, or taking up of money; the lending or advancing of money either upon or without security; the drawing, making, accepting, discounting, buying, selling, collecting and dealing in bills of exchange, hoondees, promissory notes, coupons, drafts, bill of lending, railway receipts, warrants, debentures, certificates, scrips and other instruments and securities whether transferable or negotiable or not; the granting or issuing of letters of credit, traveler's cheques and circular notes; the buying, selling and dealing in bullion and specie; the buying and selling of foreign exchange including foreign bank notes; the acquiring, holding, issuing on commission, underwriting and dealing in stock, funds, shares, debentures, debenture stock, bonds, obligations, securities and investments of all kinds; the purchasing and selling of bonds, scrips or other forms of securities on behalf of constituents or others, the negotiating of loans and advances; the receiving of all kinds of bonds, scrips or valuables on deposit or for safe custody or otherwise; the providing of safe deposit vaults; the collecting and transmitting of money and securities;

(ii) acting as agents for any Government or local authority or any other person or persons; the carrying on of agency business of any description including the clearing and forwarding of goods, giving of receipts and discharges and otherwise acting as an attorney on behalf of customers, but excluding the business of a managing agent[18] or secretary and treasurer of a company;

(iii) contracting for public and private loans and negotiating and issuing the same;

(iv) the effecting, insuring, guaranteeing, underwriting, participating in managing and carrying out of any issue, public or private, of State, municipal or other loans or of shares, stock, debenture, or debenture stock of any company, corporation or association and the lending of money for the purpose of any such issue;

(v) carrying on and transacting every kind of guarantee and indemnity business;

(vi) managing, selling, and realizing any property which may come into the possession of the company in satisfaction or part satisfaction of any of its claims;

(vii) acquiring and holding and generally dealing with any property or any right, title or interest in any such property which may form the security or part of the security for any loans or advances or which may be connected with any such security.

(viii) undertaking and executing trusts;

(ix) undertaking and administration of estates as executor, trustee or otherwise;

(x) establishing and supporting or aiding in the establishment and support of associations, institutions, funds, trusts and conveniences calculated to benefit employees or ex-employees of the company or the dependents or connections of such persons; granting pensions and allowances and making payments towards insurance; subscribing to or guaranteeing moneys for charitable or benevolent objects or for any exhibition or for any public, general or useful object;

(xi) the acquisition, construction, maintenance and alteration of any building or works necessary or convenient for the purposes of the company;

(xii) selling, improving, managing, developing, exchanging, leasing, mortgaging, disposing of or turning into account or otherwise dealing with all or any part of the property and rights of the company;

(xiii) acquiring and undertaking the whole or any part of the business of any person or company, when such business is of a nature enumerated or described in this sub-section;

(xiv) doing all such other things as are incidental or conducive to the promotion or advancement of the business of the company; and

(xv) any other form of business which the central government may, by notification in the Official Gazette, specify as a form of business in which it is lawful for a banking company to engage.

2.3 If the legal framework as provided by the Banking Regulation Act – 1949 in respect to functioning of commercial bank is analyzed then, it's obvious that prime function of these banks can broadly be classified into four categories, namely, mobilization of savings, promotion of productive investments and regulation of their direction, raising the levels of savings and investments and other growth-oriented functions. It needs no emphasis that the main function of commercial banks remains as that of acting as "go-betweens" in the saving and investment mechanisms.[1]

(i) Mobilization of Savings

2.4 Commercial banks, as compared to the ultimate deficit spending units, are better placed in mobilizing the surplus funds of the savers because they offer savers financial claims that have features not possessed by the usual primary securities – stocks and bonds of investors. A prime consideration for the saver is liquidity; the ability to obtain his funds quickly, if need be with little risk of loss. With commercial banks how funds are most liquid need not be explained. Another reason, because of which savers prefer commercial banks is the fact that the later issue a wide variety of claims – indirect securities – which apart from their suitability to a wide group of savers also possess the advantage of constant or determinable redemption value, low investment costs and the divisibility claims into convenient units of low or higher denominations.

2.5 Savings cannot be directed into most profitable use if the decision –makers do have or use the needed information concerning the alternative forms of securities. A variety of information would be required in this context, such as, information concerning past performance of the firm in so far as it bears on the future; the honesty, ability and enterprise of its management and the nature of its plans for the future; future demand for the output of the firm and of the industry of which it is a part; and so on. Commercial banks help the saver in this expensive and irksome task by doing the job of collecting the necessary information and conducting research and analysis at no extra cost. Thus, the indirect claims issued by the commercial banks are more profitable to the saver in this sense. Further, in the absence of commercial banks, each owner of investible funds would have to perform for himself the routine and technical job of seeking out securities, ensuring their validity, purchasing them, providing safe custody, protecting his interests against the issuer, collecting income and principal accruals and selling the securities. Commercial banks perform all these functions for savers at much low cost. Also, these banks with their diversified advance portfolio, are able to reduce to the minimum the risk associated with investments.

2.6 Another aspect of the mobilization of savings in a developing country like ours is that savings are widely scattered.

Commercial banks, with their wide branch network help pool these small and scattered savings and use them for the purposes of productive investments. A further inter-related aspect is that in underdeveloped countries savings are institution-elastic, being responsive to the stimulus of new saving facilities provided by financial intermediaries like commercial banks. This will no doubt affect the volume of saving as well as its direction.

(ii) Facilitating Investments and their Direction

2.7 By pooling the scattered savings commercial banks make it possible to finance a large number of investors at reasonable cost and in appropriate quantum. In case the investment demand for a single project is of a heavy magnitude, the commercial banks can collectively meet the capital needs of such a venture. Again, the commercial banks are better disposed than the individual to channel the funds into investments, which are more profitable for the economic growth of a developing economy.

2.8 In developing economics where private sector is still dominant the objectives of balanced growth, regional and sectoral, are often not taken care of by private investors. Commercial banks, under the impetus of monetary and fiscal controls, can become the instruments for according preferential treatment in matter of loans and credits to industrial ventures or development projects claiming high priority in the development programmes of the country. Commercial banks may be responsible to some extent – for sponsoring, encouraging and discriminating between various industries, so that sectoral balances is promoted. Also, these banks can afford to offer liberal and concessional terms in the form of lower rates of interest, and other fees/charges and other conditions relating to margin requirements, securities, etc. for socially desirable productive projects. Thus these institutions can channel investible funds to the most productive and desirable ventures with a view to promoting a balanced growth region-wise and sector-wise of the economy.

(iii) Raising the Level of Savings and Investments

2.9 Commercial banks in developing countries also assist in raising the level of saving and investment and thus allow the rate of growth to rise at a faster rate than what it would have been otherwise. In such countries savings are said to be interest-elastic. They respond easily to the stimuli of new saving facilities provided by banks. When the aggregate output is rising, commercial banks can raise the rate of saving by raising rates of interest offered on deposits. In turn, this would further raise the incomes of savers, and at least, a part of it can be expected to flow back to the banks as deposits. When the level of saving rises, the level of investment would normally go up. In addition to this automatic increase, commercial banks can also raise their level of investment by creating liabilities to the extent of some multiple of their currency / deposit balances.

(iv) Other Functions

2.10 Some of the commercial banks also take up certain other essential promotional jobs as well. A couple of them extend technical assistance to the borrowers in planning and implementation of their projects. They impose, through adherence to certain criteria of appraisal, minimum financial discipline on the borrowing units and control the efficiency of the borrowing enterprises through tools based on the financial data obtained from them. A few of them also undertake marketing and investment research surveys, techno-economic feasibility and profitability cost-benefit studies of a specific growth sector or a region, particularly the backward regions, so as so to identify the potential for growth, thus helping in identifying new entrepreneurship. Furthermore, they can plan, promote and develop industries to fill the growth gaps, which exist in such economies. Above all, banks may also provide assistance in organizing and imparting training to the talented managerial personnel / prospective entrepreneurs.

COMMERCIAL BANKS IN INDIA

2.11 Prior to July, 1969, all the commercial banks (99) in India were in private sector excepting, of course, the State Bank of India and its Subsidiaries ; of the 99, 73 were scheduled and 26 were non-scheduled. On July 19, 1969, however, 14 major commercial banks were nationalized. Further, in April, 1980, another six commercial banks were taken over by the Government.

Features of Commercial Banking System In India

2.12 Commercial banks in India may broadly be classified on the basis of two criteria: (i) statutory, and (ii) ownership. On the statutory basis, the banks are of two types; (i) Scheduled banks; and (ii) Non-scheduled banks. On the ownership basis, the banks may be classified into two groups: (i) Public sector commercial banks, and (ii) Private sector commercial banks. In the category of scheduled banks, there are private sector banks and public sector banks[2].

Scheduled and Non-Scheduled Banks

2.13 In India the commercial banking system is comprised of scheduled and non-scheduled commercial banks. Scheduled banks are those commercial banks, which are included in the Second Schedule of the Reserve Bank of India Act, 1934*; it's only after the fulfillment of the pre-laid down conditions that the name of any bank becomes eligible for inclusion in this Schedule – however, the same needs no reiteration.

2.14 While these banks have certain obligations to RBI such as maintaining a part of their cash reserves with it, they also enjoy certain facilities like borrowings from RBI etc. the banks which do not qualify for inclusion in the second schedule of the RBI, they are clubbed in the category of Non-scheduled Banks. Incidentally it may be added that such banks are gradually disappearing from the Indian banking scene. These scheduled banks comprise commercial banks, regional rural banks, urban co-operative banks and state co-operative banks.

---

* As per the Reserve Bank of India Act, 1934, a commercial bank to qualify for inclusion in the Second Schedule, must satisfy the following conditions:

(i) It must have a minimum paid-up capital and total reserves of Rs. 5 lakhs.

(ii) It must be either a company as defined in Sec. 3 of the Indian Companies Act, 1956, or a corporation, or a company incorporated by or under any law in force in any place outside India, or an institution notified by the Central Government in this behalf, or a state co-operative bank.

(iii) It must also satisfy the Reserve Bank of India that is affair are not being conducted in a way detrimental to the interest of its depositors.

Exhibit 2.1

STRUCTURE OF INDIAN COMMERCIAL BANKING

(*As on March 31, 2004*)

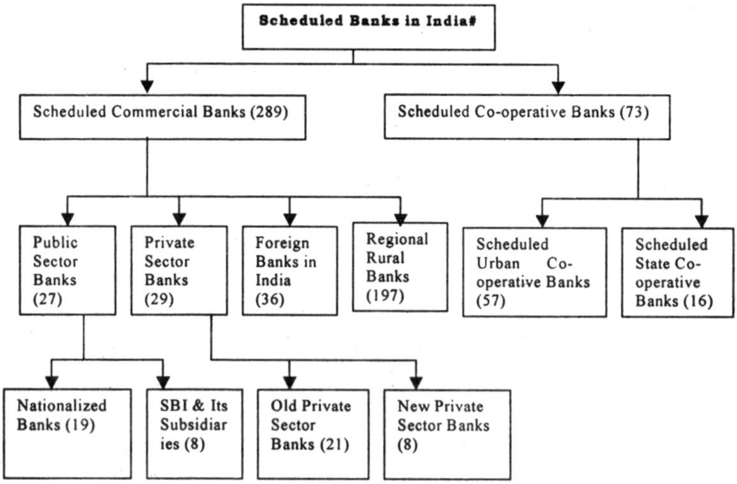

As indicated in the Second Schedule of the RBI Act, 1934.
Note: Figures in brackets indicate number of banks in each group.
Source: Reserve Bank of India Annual Report for the year 2004.

2.15 As may be seen in Exhibit 2.1, the number of scheduled and non-scheduled banks stood at 289 and 4 respectively as on March 31, 2004. Among scheduled banks the majority of them have been incorporated in India and their head offices are located in our country, while some are incorporated in foreign countries with their Head Offices outside India. The banks falling in the former category are popularly known as Indian Commercial Banks and those in the later are treated as Foreign Banks. Pertinent also it would be to mention in the context, that the foreign banks are also scheduled banks and generally specialize in transaction involving foreign exchange and/or innovative services like internet banking, credit/debit cards, consumer credits meeting human motives. Among the total scheduled banks, 253 are Indian and the remaining 36 are foreign banks. From out of the 253 Indian Commercial Banks, as many as 197 are Regional Rural Banks which came into existence in 1975 and onward to cater to the need of the residual economy of India, such as the credit requirements of small farmers, artisans, and agriculture workers. They in fact operate mainly at the district level. The rest of the commercial banks, namely, 56 can further be divided into two categories on the basis of the patter of their ownership i.e. public sector commercial banks and private sector commercial banks.

2.16 The Central Government entered the banking business into the nationalization of the Imperial Bank of India (now the State Bank of India and its Associates) in 1955. In 1969, Fourteen (14) large banks were nationalized and again in 1980, six more banks were taken over by the Government. These nationalized banks, which are 27 in all, are popularly called Public Sector Banks. The remaining 29 are private sector banks. It would of further interest to note that of the 29, majority (22 in number) are old private sector banks i.e. found in existence in the pre-reform era and rest of have come into existence in the post-reform era consequent of upon one of the recommendation made by the Narasimhan Committee on Banking System (Referred to in details in the subsequent paras).

2.17 Scheduled Commercial Banks (SCBs) collectively serve Rs 15,750 billion in deposit accounts as on March 31, 2004. SCBs have a presence throughout India; with approximately 70% of bank branches belonging to the public sector banks are located in rural or semi-urban areas of the country.

Public Sector Banks

2.18 Public sector banks constitute the largest category in the Indian banking system. They include the State Bank of India and its 7 associate banks, 19 nationalized banks and 196 regional rural banks. As of March 31, 2004, apart from the regional rural banks, the other public sector banks have over 46,500 branches. Public sector banks collectively account for approximately 73.2% of the outstanding gross credit and 77.9% of the aggregate deposits of the scheduled commercial banks. The large network of public sector banks enable them to fund themselves out of low cost deposits. The State Bank of India is the largest public sector bank in India. As of March 31, 2004, the State Bank of India and its 7 associate banks had 13,505 branches, accounting for 27.5% of the aggregate deposits and 25.5% of the outstanding gross bank credit of all scheduled commercial banks.

Private Sector Banks

2.19 After the first phase of bank nationalization was completed in 1969, public sector banks made up the largest portion of Indian banking. In July 1993, as part of the banking reform process and as a measure to induce competition in the banking sector. RBI permitted entry of the private sector into the banking system. This resulted in the emergence of nine private sector banks. These banks are collectively known as "new" private sector banks. There are ten "new" private sector banks at present. In addition, 20 private sector banks existing prior to July 1993 are further found in operation as on March 31st, 2004.

Foreign Banks

2.20 As of June 30, 2004, there were 32 foreign banks with 215 branches operating in India. As on end-March 2004, foreign banks account for 5.1% of aggregate deposits and 7% of outstanding gross bank credit of scheduled commercial banks. As part of the liberalization process, RBI has permitted foreign banks to operate more freely, subject to requirements largely similar to those imposed on domestic banks. Foreign banks operate in India through branches of their parent banks. In fiscal 2003, the government announced that foreign banks would be permitted to incorporate subsidiaries in India. Subsidiaries of foreign banks will have to adhere to all banking regulations, including priority sector landing norms, applicable to domestic norms. The primary activity of most foreign banks in India has been in the corporate segment. However, in recent years, some of the larger foreign banks have started to make consumer financing a larger pat of their portfolios based on the growth opportunities in this area in India.

2.21 With the growth of public sector banks in the Indian economy, the structure of commercial banking has completely changed in the post-nationalization years. The structure and operations of banks have undergone a rapid transformation in recent years. Consequent upon the revolution in information technology and the associated increase in competition, both at national and international levels, financial intermediaries have become increasingly global in geographical coverage and universal in their financial operations, encompassing a wide range of activities including banking, securities markets activities and insurance.

2.22 The relative importance of the different constituents of the Commercial Banking System of India is reflected in Exhibit 2.2

OPERATIONAL FOCUS : PRE Vs POST – NATIONALIZATION PERIOD

2.23 Broadly speaking pre-nationalization period of the commercial banking in India was characterized by three major operational features. One, the industrial sector claimed the lion's share in bank credit; and, within the industry, the large sized industrial units cornered the bank credit. Second, the banks were neither keen nor geared to meet the credit requirements of farmers and other non-industrial sectors of the economy. Lastly, banks at times used to finance socially undesirable activities like hoarding of external commodities.

2.24 In pre-reforms period the commercial banks in India functioned in a highly regulated environment such as administered interest rate structure, quantitative restrictions on credit flows, high levels of Cash Reserve Ratio, pre-emption of significant proportion of lendable resources for the priority sectors and the government under Statutory Liquidity Ratio. It was with reference to this situation that in 1969 the Government nationalized 14 commercial banks of the private sector. Keeping in view four primary objectives: (a) to break the ownership and control of banks by a few business families; (b) to prevent concentration of wealth and economic power; (c) to mobilize savings of the masses from every nook and corner of the country; and (d) to pay greater attention to the credit needs of the priority sectors like agriculture, small industries, professionals and education etc. In response to these objectives, we witnessed reallocation of sectoral credit in favour of agriculture,

Exhibit 2.2 : COMMERCIAL BANKING SYSTEM IN INDIA
(Between Pre-Reform Year 1990-91 and Post-Reform Year 2003-2004)
(Contd....62)

(Amount in Rupees Crores)

Serial Number	Constituents	Number		Number of Branches		Total Number of Employees	
		1990-91	2003-04	1990-91	2003-04	1995-96	2003-04
(1)	(2)	(3)	(4)	(5)	(6)	(7)	(8)
I	**Scheduled Banks**						
	(i) Public Sector Banks	28	27	42,938	48,150	880,423	752,627
	(ii) Private Sector Banks	24	30	3,939	5,903	57,967	64,461
	(iii) Foreign Banks	23	36	150	222	12,870	11,804
	(iv) Regional Rural Banks	196	196	14,697	14,772	67,765	65,433
	All Scheduled Banks	**271**	**289**	**61,724**	**69,047**	**1,019,025**	**894,325**

Exhibit 2.2 : COMMERCIAL BANKING SYSTEM IN INDIA
(Between Pre-Reform Year 1990-91 and Post-Reform Year 2003-2004) *(Contd...63)*

Constituents	Deposits (Amount)		Advances (Amount)		Investments (Amount)	
	1990-91	2003-04	1990-91	2003-04	1990-91	2003-04
	(9)	**(10)**	**(11)**	**(12)**	**(13)**	**(14)**
(i) Public Sector Banks	210,811	1,226,838	131,622	632,741	71,476	625,678
(ii) Private Sector Banks	9,432	268,550	4,949	170,894	3,139	134,802
(iii) Foreign Banks	11,733	79,757	7,119	60,508	4,222	41,586
(iv) Regional Rural Banks	5,028	57,010	3,511	25,481	227	17,444
All Scheduled Banks	**237,004**	**1,632,155**	**147,201**	**889,624**	**79,064**	**819,510**

Exhibit 2.2 : COMMERCIAL BANKING SYSTEM IN INDIA
(Between Pre-Reform Year 1990-91 and Post-Reform Year 2003-2004)

	Constituents	Total Income (Amount)		Total Expenses (Amount)		Profit (Amount)	
		1990-91	2003-04	1990-91	2003-04	1990-91	2003-04
		(15)	(16)	(17)	(18)	(19)	(20)
	(i) Public Sector Banks	24,317	137,603	23,852	98,127	465	16,547
	(ii) Private Sector Banks	1,035	33,154	996	24,943	38	3,484
	(iii) Foreign Banks	2,186	13,010	1,968	8,024	217	2,242
	(iv) Regional Rural Banks	737	6,244	717	5,475	19	769
	All Scheduled Banks	**28,275**	**190,011**	**27,533**	**136,569**	**739**	**23,042**
II	**Non-Scheduled Banks**	Not Available					

Sources: (i) Annual Accounts Data of Scheduled Commercial Banks (1990-91)
(ii) Statistical Tables Relating to Banks in India for the year ended on March 31, 1996 and March 31, 2004.
(iii) Report on Trend and Progress of Banking in India for 2003-04

including of procurement of food grains, poultry farming, dairy and piggeries, small industries, exports, professionals, and self-employed persons, artisans and other weaker sections of the society. Also rapid branch expansion took place in the country[3].

Impact of liberalization on the Indian Financial Sector

2.25 Until 1991, the financial sector in India was heavily controlled and commercial banks and long-term lending institutions, the two dominant financial intermediaries, had mutually exclusive roles and objectives and operated in a largely stable environment, with little or no competition. Long-term lending institutions were focused on the achievement of the Government's various socio-economic objectives, including balanced industrial growth and employment creation, especially in areas requiring development. Long-term lending institutions were extended access to long-term funds at subsidized rates through loans and equity from the Government and from funds guaranteed by the Government originating from commercial banks in India and foreign currency resources originating from multilateral and bilateral agencies.

2.26 The focus of the commercial banks was primarily to mobilize household savings through demand and time deposits and to use these deposits to meet the short-term financial needs of borrowers in industry, trade and agriculture. In addition, the commercial banks provided a range of banking services to individuals and business entities.

2.27 Since 1991, various financial sector reforms have transformed the operating environment of the banks and long term lending institutions. In particular, the deregulation of interest rates, emergence of a liberalized domestic capital market, and entry of new private sector banks, along with the broadening of long-term lending institutions. RBI has permitted the transformations of long-term lending institutions into banks subject to compliance with the prudential norms applicable to banks.

REVIEW OF BANKING REFORMS

2.28 Most large banks in India were nationalized in 1969 and thereafter were subject to high degree of control until reforms began in 1991. In addition to controlling interest rates and entry into the banking sector, these regulations also channeled lending into priority sectors. Banks were required to fund the public sector through the mandatory acquisition of low interest bearing government securities or statutory liquidity ratio bonds to fulfill statutory liquidity requirements. As a result, bank profitability was low, non-performing assets were comparatively high, capital adequacy was diminished, and operational flexibility was hindered.

Committee on the Financial System (Narsimham Committee I)

2.29 The Committee on the Financial System (The Narsimham Committee I) was set up in August 1991 to recommend measures for reforming the financial sector. The government implemented many of the recommendations made by the committee, which addressed organizational issues, accounting practices and operating procedures. The major recommendation that were implemented included the following:

(i) With fiscal stabilization and the government increasingly resorting to market borrowing to raise resources, the statutory liquidity ratio or the proportion of a bank's net demand and time liabilities that were required to be invested in Government securities was reduced from 38.5% in the pre-reform period to 25.0% in October 1997. This meant that the significance of the statutory liquidity ratio shifted from being a major instrument for financing the public sector in the pre-reform era to becoming a prudential requirement;

(ii) Similarly, the cash reserve ratio or the proportion of a bank's net demand and time liabilities that were required to be deposited with RBI was reduced from 15.0% in the pre-reform period to the current level of 4.5% ;

(iii) Special tribunals were created to resolve bad debt problems;

(iv) Most of the restrictions on interest rates for deposits were removed. Commercial banks were allowed to set their own level of interest rates for all deposits except savings bank deposits ;

(v) Substantial capital infusion to several state-owned banks was approved in order to bring their capital adequacy closer to internationally accepted standards. By the end of fiscal 2002, aggregate recapitalization amounted to Rs 217.5 crores. The stronger public sector banks were given permission to issue equity to further increase capital ; and,

(vi) Banks were granted the freedom to open or close branches.

Committee on Banking Sector Reforms the Financial System (Narsimham Committee II)

2.30 The Second Committee on Banking Sector Reform (Narsimham CommitteeII) submitted its report in April 1998. The major recommendations of the committee were in respect to capital adequacy requirements, asset classification and provisioning, risk management and merger policies. RBI accepted and began implementing many of these recommendations in October 1998.

Effects of the Reforms

2.31 The recommendations of the Narasimham Committee in 1991 provided the blueprint for the first generation reform of the financial system. While these reforms were being implemented, the world economy also witnessed significant changes, coinciding with the movement towards global integration of financial services (Narasimham Committee, 1998). Against such backdrop, the Report of the Narasimham Committee II (NCR-II) on Banking Sector Reforms provided the framework for the current reform process[4].

2.32 The visible impact of reforms is evident in both a widening (as reflected in the financial interrelations ratio) as well as the deepening (as evidenced by the intermediation ratio) of the intermediation process and its positive influence on growth. In addition to banks, various other intermediaries, including financial institutions, mutual funds and non-banking financial companies, are also engaged in the process of intermediation. Steps have been initiated to strengthen public sector banks and infuse competition into the banking system. To increase competition, new banks in the private sector have been allowed to enter the industry and foreign banks have been given more liberal entry[5].

2.33 A set of micro-prudential measures have been stipulated, aimed at imparting strength to the banking system as well as ensuring safety and soundness on a prospective basis in order to fix the true position of bank's balance sheet. The banking system has attained greater transparency. This applies both with regard to prudential norms (disclosure of capital adequacy ratios-tier I and tier II separately, net non performing assets (NPAs) ratios, provisions and more recently, the maturity profile of loans and advances, investments, movements in NPAs and lending to sensitive sectors, such as capital market, real estate and commodities) as well as securities portfolio (greater 'marking-to-market').

2.34 A positive externality of the reform measures have been the building up of the institutional architecture in terms of markets, technological and legal infrastructure and improving the managerial competence and the quality of human resources, which are pre-requisites for the efficient functioning of markets. Several new initiatives on the technological front, including among others, the setting up of the Indian Financial Network (INFINET), a Wide Area Satellite based Network using VSAT technology, Shared Payment Network System, initiatives for Electronic Fund Transfer have already been undertaken. A Real Time Gross Settlement (RTGS) system, with system requirement specifications to take into account international best practices and the specific requirements of Indian banking is being developed[6].

Summary of Reforms in the Banking Sector[7]

2.35 On the above basis we may summarize the major reforms that took place in the banking sector of India as under:

A. Prudential Measures

- Introduction and phased implementation of international best practices and norms on risk-weighted capital adequacy requirement, accounting, income recognition, provisioning and exposure.
- Measures to strengthen risk management through recognition of different components of risk, assignment of risk-weights to various asset classes, norms on

connected lending, risk concentration, application of marked-to-market principle for investment portfolio and limits on deployment of fund in sensitive activities.

B. Competition Enhancing Measures

- Granting of operational autonomy to public sector banks, reduction of public ownership in public sector banks by allowing them to raise capital from equity market up to 49 per cent of paid-up capital.
- Transparent norms for entry of Indian private sector, foreign and joint-venture banks and insurance companies, permission for foreign investment in the financial sector in the form of Foreign Direct Investment (FDI) as well as portfolio investment, permission to banks to diversify product portfolio and business activities.

C. Increasing Role of Market Forces

- Sharp reduction in pre-emption through reserve requirement, market determined pricing for government securities, disbanding of administered interest rates with a few exceptions and enhanced transparency and disclosure norms to facilitate market discipline.
- Introduction of pure inter-bank call money market, auction-based repos-reverse repos for short-term liquidity management, facilitation of improved payments and settlement mechanism.

D. Institutional and Legal Measures

- Settling up of *Lok Adalats* (people's courts), debt recovery tribunals, asset reconstruction companies, settlement advisory committees, corporate debt restructuring mechanism, *etc.* for quicker recovery/ restructuring. Promulgation of Securitisation and Reconstruction of Financial Assets and Enforcement of Securities Interest (SARFAESI), Act and its subsequent amendment to ensure creditor rights.
- Setting up of Credit Information Bureau for information sharing on defaulters as also other borrowers.

- Setting up of Clearing Corporation of India Limited (CCIL) to act as central counter party for facilitating payments and settlement system relating to fixed income securities and money market instruments.

E. Supervisory Measures

- Establishment of the Board for Financial Supervision as the apex supervisory authority for commercial banks, financial institutions and non-banking financial companies.
- Introduction of supervisory rating system, move towards risk-based supervision, consolidated supervision of financial conglomerates, strengthening of off-site surveillance through control returns.
- Recasting of the role of statutory auditors, increased internal control through strengthening of internal audit.
- Strengthening corporate governance, enhanced due diligence on important shareholders, fit and proper tests for directors.

F. Technology Related Measures

- Setting up of INFINET as the communication backbone for the financial sector, introduction of Negotiated Dealing System (NDS) for screen-based trading in government securities and Real Time Gross Settlement (RTGS) System.

2.36 Banking sector reforms in India were introduced in order to improve efficiency in the process of financial intermediation. It was expected that banks would take advantage of the changing operational environment and improve their performance. Towards this end, the Reserve Bank initiated a host of measures for the creation of a competitive environment. Deregulation of interest rates on both the deposit and lending sides imparted freedom to banks to appropriately price their products and services. To compete effectively with non-banking entities, banks were permitted to undertake newer activities like investment banking, securities trading and insurance business. This was facilitated through amendments in the relevant Acts, which permitted PSBs to raise equity from the market up to a threshold limit (49 per cent) and also by enabling the entry of new private and foreign banks. This changing face of banking led to an erosion of margins on traditional banking business, promoting banks to search for newer activities to augment their fee incomes. At the same time, banks also needed to devote focused attention to operational efficiency in order to contain their transactions costs. Simultaneously with the deregulation measures, prudential norms were instituted to strengthen the safety and soundness of the banking system.

RELATIONSHIP OF KNOWLEDGE MANAGEMENT WITH THE COMMERCIAL BANKS

2.37 In a pre-liberalization period, the computer hasn't produced the spurt of productivity that we all expected is that we are still with bits and bytes of information. We still haven't learned how to learn into certifiable knowledge. That's because most of us are still building traditional systems, that is, system that provide merely tactical information, rather than smart systems that provide competitive advantage – systems that provide knowledge. Financial services has always look beyond the ordinary toolset is an attempt to develop system that would not only process data but turn the data into this elusive thing called knowledge.

2.38 Indian banking overhangs from the past, the low level of computerization, excess manpower with lack of skill set compatibility, higher NPA's, lack of innovation in product and services, and unresponsive to customer needs. Banking has emerged as on the riskiest business. Information is the lifeblood for banks in mitigating and managing risks. In the near future, banks have to gear up for Basel II compliance. This required lots of information and knowledge management on the part of banks. However, the new technologies can come to the rescue of banks as never before in knowledge management. Collection, compilation, analysis and retrieval of massive data have never been so easy. With the explosive spread of the Internet and web technologies, it is much easier to provide access to information users 'anywhere, anytime'.[8]

2.39 Things have been changed over the number of years; now banks are focusing on their customers and increasing the value of their interactions by providing consistent, seamless access to relevant information at every stage point. The difference at every stage point is the value of information and knowledge, which is increasing day by day. A successful bank is built on sound business decisions and the key to good decision-making to accurate knowledge – about its business, the market, its competitors, and its customers. Without it, a bank is at a serious disadvantage. But how can a bank gain this knowledge and mission critical intelligence, in a way that makes sense to its bottom line?

2.40 For a successful banking business, management and analysis of large data and information play key roles in devising new strategies, products and services. With the cost of technology falling and their capacities increasing day by day, data warehousing has become affordable. Banks should set up their own intranets and extranets, spread over wide geographic locations[9].

2.41 Knowledge can be effectively utilized in Risk Management because information is to the very basis of risk management. This is critical in today's age of information overload. However, before it can be processed, analyzed or acted upon, the right information must first be made available at the right time to the systems and individuals who need it.

2.42 Knowledge management system is the tool that would give banks an edge is respect of service providing to their constituents, better housekeeping, optimizing the use of funds – and building up of MIS for empirical decision making which has a relationship with the critical aspect of asset-liability management which in turn has a direct impact on the balance sheet of banks as a whole. In order for computerization to take care of the emerging needs, the recommendations of the Committee on Technology Upgradation in the Banking Sector (1999)[10], have a direct bearing. These are:

- Need for standardization of hardware, operating systems, system software, application software to facilitate interconnectivity of systems across branches.
- Need for high levels of security.

- Communication and networking – use of networks which would facilitate centralized databases and distributed processing.
- Need for a technology plan with periodical upgradation.
- Need for business process re-engineering.
- Need to address the issue of human relations in a computerized environment.
- Sharing of technology experiences.
- Innovative customer-oriented delivery mechanisms.
- Improvement in decision-making process.
- Extended banking business reach and hours as well as increased business volume and better fund utilization, thereby facilitating reduced operational cost.

Impact of Information Technology

2.43 A study of the technological progress in the banking sector is important because banks play an important role in providing financing and mobilizing savings, especially in emerging markets as compared to mature markets, where the well-developed capital markets perform such functions. Technological efficiency can result in lower transaction costs and increased revenues for banks. For instance, technology can allow banks to cross-market new and existing products to customers. Technology can also generate a high rate of innovation in new financial products. Further, information technology can make it easier for banks 'to screen out good from bad credit risks or to monitor corporations, thus reducing the adverse selection and moral hazard problems,' that would otherwise impede the efficiency of financial markets[11]. From an accounting standpoint, technology can speed up the financial reporting process and the timeliness with which banks make public disclosures via regulatory reports. Better quality public disclosures can translate into an overall improvement of financial market transparency. Such disclosures can also provide useful and accurate data to bank supervisors, which in turn could enhance the oversight of banks. Finally, the use of technology can improve/enhance systems for administrative control such as enabling better management of risk, which if disclosed in regulatory reports to supervisors and in annual reports to investors, can improve bank transparency and enable the banks to reduce their cost of capital[12].

2.44 One of the benefits that technology has ushered in is the capacity for centralized data storage with decentralized processing, resulting in initiatives such as 'Anywhere Banking', 'Anytime Banking', 'Shared Networks' etc., which need to be popularized by more banks. For banks, one of the prime thrust areas is the reduction of the non-performing assets (NPAs); and for quick information flow on assets and for timely action for the reduction of NPAs, technology could provide a pivotal role, by means of sound management information systems based on data warehousing which helps in data mining for obtaining results in any manner so as to facilitate better decision making using empirical data.

2.45 Internet banking is emerging as a buzzword – but then it requires a great deal of security when online banking and funds related activities based on Internet are implemented. Suitable firewalls, proxy servers, authentication of messages, and other security features would have to be developed.

2.46 Yet another development gaining importance is the *usage of cards* – especially smart cards which can be used for access, security purposes by staff / authorized people and as multi-purpose cards by constituents of banks for operating on their accounts and for facilitating movements of funds in a secure and electronic manner.

2.47 Banks have been also accorded *greater operational flexibility* in conducting their business. As part of the process, commercial banks have adopted several initiatives to strengthen their business practices, including, among others, greater product sophistication, increased customer orientation, improved risk-management, particularly credit risk management techniques, updated management information systems, greater focus on electronic banking channels, sharing and exchange of credit information, and diversification into newer business areas.

2.48 The widespread adoption of technology by the banking industry has also opened lot of scope for its use by RBI for an effective performance of its core central banking functions such as banking supervision, currency management, credit and monetary policies, etc.

Regulation and Supervision

2.49 The technology has enabled the emergence of non intrusive focused supervision with a view to prevent frauds and disturbance to financial stability. Given the geographical size of the country, the volume and value of notes and coins in circulation, the market preference for cash, currency, handling practices, etc., Currency Management is a formidable task in India ; however, the technology offers immense opportunities to improve performance on this score.

2.50 The management of the monetary policy poses a challenge in the current day scenario. The proliferation of IT has redefined the toolkit of economic indicators normally practiced for execution of monetary policy. The task of compiling statistical information has been made easier. Not only that it has become simpler to assess the impact of variegated variables on price levels with the help of IT tools. The issue of digital money has assumed due importance. The technology has transformed the conduct of the payment and settlement system, aside setting the stage for unprecedented growth in financial activity across the globe. However, the domestic payment system and financial stability has become more vulnerable to international shocks. This has made the task of formulation and implementation of monetary policy more complex and full of operational risks.

2.51 The proliferation of IT has also set the stage for improving and managing risks in payment systems

- Electronic Trading Systems
- Real Time Gross Settlement System (RTGS)
- Reduction of systemic risk in inter bank payment systems
- The Centralised Funds Settlement System
- Facilitating effective liquidity management
- The Negotiated Dealing System
- A modern electronic dealing platform for gilts

- Enabling Straight Through Processing
- The Securities Settlement System
- Providing centralized depository and settlement services
- Seamlessly integrated with the NDS and RTGS Systems
- The Clearing Corporation of India
- Secured netting services with central counterparty arrangements
- G-Sec and Forex segments
- Elimination of settlement risks with liquidity saving elements

EMERGING CHALLENGES IN INDIAN BANKING

2.52 The challenges in the current millennium for the banking industry are enormous and can be dealt with effectively only when the banking institutions also make knowledge as engine for growth. Connecting different knowledge sources can create innovative products. It is, therefore, that the World Development Report for the year 1998-99 was exclusively devoted on this aspect.

2.53 In the near future, banks will be characterized by how they deal with interest rate risks? How they adhere to Basel-II adequacy norms? How to attain profitability and cope with the real time gross settlement system? In the next millennium, banks should strive to achieve significant increase in their productivity, efficiency and profitability.

(i) Competition and Consolidation[14]

2.54 The deregulation in interest rates, grant of functional autonomy to banks in the area of credit, entry of foreign banks and emergence of new private banks has made the banking environment more competitive. While the total share in bank credit continues to be dominated by public sector banks, the share of foreign banks is showing an increasing trend. In the changed scenario, it has now become extremely important for Indian banks to remain competitive for survival. Universally there is a move towards consolidation and convergence. It has been our contention that the Government and supervisory authorities should only provide a conducive environment for consolidation and convergence through appropriate fiscal and monetary policies supported by a sound regulatory and supervisory framework.

(ii) Management of Non Performing Assets (NPAs)[15]

2.55 Management of NPAs continue to be the foremost challenge of the Indian banking system. In the recent past there has been a conscious and persistent effort through the prescription of strict objective norms for the identification and classification of NPAs. This was also supplemented by the sustained efforts both by the Government and the RBI for setting up the requisite infrastructure as also systems/ procedures for effecting recoveries/ reduction of NPAs. In addition, banks have been advised to strengthen their credit administration machinery and put in place effective credit risk management systems to reduce the fresh incidence of NPAs.

(iii) Risk Management Systems[16]

2.56 In view of the diverse financial and non financial risks confronted by banks in the wake of the financial sector deregulation, the risk management practices of banks have to be upgraded by adopting sophisticated techniques like VaR, Duration and Simulation and adopting internal model-based approaches as also credit risk modelling techniques, at least by top banks. Banks need to evolve an integrated risk management system depending on their size, complexity and the risk appetite. As a step towards enhancing and fine-tuning the existing risk management practices in banks RBI has recently issued the draft guidance notes on credit and market risks.

(iv) Corporate Governance[17]

2.57 An adequate institutional and legal framework is in place in India for effectively implementing a code of sound corporate governance in banks. The statutes have built-in legal provisions that prohibit or strongly limit activities and relationships that diminish the quality of corporate governance in banks. As a major step towards strengthening corporate governance in banks, they have been advised to place before their Board of Directors the Report of the Consultative Group of Directors of banks and FIs set up to review the supervisory role of Boards of banks. The recommendations include the responsibility of the Board of Directors, role and responsibility of independent and non-executive directors, fit and proper norms for nomination of directors in private sector banks, etc. The banks were advised to adopt and implement the recommendations on the basis of the decision taken by their Board.

(v) Technology Issues[18]

2.58 The delivery of products and services need extensive use of information technology necessitating high magnitude of investment. However, with a view to enhance the quality of customer service as also to enhance the quality of control, one of the prime thrust areas for the future would be completion of branch computerisation and networking of banks. This would also necessitate putting in place of appropriate legal and security systems.

(vi) Customer service[19]

2.59 The objective was to evolve a level of banking services which is efficient, effective and customer-oriented and which should seek to emulate the "best practices" in the industry the world over. Indian banking, realizing the challenges thrown by global competition is undergoing significant developments and improvements in the field of customer service. This has by and large been possible due to increased use of technology in banking resulting in branch computerization, growth of retail banking and automation of banking processes. Extension of reach of customer service and rationalisation of costs of operations were the by-products of this process. Modern clearing operations, electronic funds transfer system and centralized funds management system are some projects receiving priority of RBI to enhance customer service in the banking sector.

(vii) Treatment of Weak Banks[20]

2.60 A sound banking system by definition presupposes that all the banks, or at least a majority of them within the system are strong and good as viable concerns. However, every system has its own instances of weak links and the banking system is no exception. It is, therefore, desirable to discuss the options available to the weak banks for ensuring resilience of the system. While the root cause of a bank becoming weak can be traced to managerial inadequacies, existence of high NPAs is one of the prominent manifestations. It is often argued that the problem of weakness in the banking sector has had its roots in directed lending on behest of the Government, and that the latter has the responsibility to bail out the weak institutions.

(viii) Transparency and Disclosure[21]

2.61 In the Indian context, the transparency and disclosure standards have been enhanced to meet international standards. The range and extent of disclosures has been gradually increasing over the last couple of years in order to provide a clearer picture of balance sheets to the financial community. Since March 31, 2000, banks operating in India have been disclosing in their published accounts information relating to maturity pattern of loans and advances, investment securities, deposits and borrowings, foreign currency assets and liabilities, movements in NPAs and provisions and lending to sensitive sectors (capital market sector, real estate sector and commodities sector). The Memorandum of Understanding (MOU) signed with the Reserve Bank each year has compelled bank management to adhere to certain minimum performance standards. More so, when banks are raising capital from the market, they are accountable to the public/shareholders. Such transparency of operations is essential to minimize informational asymmetry between the regulator and regulated and facilitate effective monitoring of banks.

2.7 FUTURE OF INDIAN BANKING[22]

2.62 What will happen to the commercial banking industry in the coming decades? That depends on how successfully banks can provide value to their customers. The fiscal year 2002-03 was the most happening year for the Indian banking industry. The industry was able to post extraordinary results on multiple fronts – higher incomes and lower expenditure, profitability growth, declining Non-Performing Assets (NPA) levels, improved Return on Assets

(ROA), successful Initial Public Offerings (IPO's) of Public Sector Banks and high valuation to banking stocks. Much of the profits of the Indian banking sector are on account of retail banking and treasury operations. Inspite of economic slowdown and industrial sickness, banks have been able to record profits on account of shift in focus. There has been a clear shift in focus of the Indian banks as they focused more on retail banking in contrast to their primary focus of working capital financing and term loans.

2.63 Consumer banks are discovering that customer acquisition and retention depend on the ability to provide the highest level of customer experience management at any time, from any location from any device. Bank customer will need to collect and disclose new information. Customer will face new structure as a result of increased transparency.

1.Capturing the promise of the customer: Banks are changing their focus from gaining new customers to holding on to their current ones and generating more value from them. Leading banks turning to a back to basics approach that emphasize excellent services, process improvements, and more targeted technology investments.

2.Leveraging Human Capital: Every bank around the world is facing increasing pressure to improve performance. After several years of deep cost cutting, CEOs are turning their attention to their largest asset – human capital. Executives are a l s o questioning established assumptions when it comes to employee hiring, compensation and jobs responsibility. In addition new analytical tools are being used to quantify the role of human factors in generating financial results and identify them to boost business outcomes

3.Offshoring: London, Frankfurt, New York, Tokyo and now Banglore, in emerging markets world wide, a new generation of financial centers are becoming familiar location for bankers looking to increase their profit margins. Offshoring relocating business functions are processes to lower cost locations – is becoming an imperative for banks struggling to cut cost and increase shareholder value.

4. Basel II (Seize the opportunity): Additional discussions over the new Basel Capital Accord, or Basel II, will continue into 2004 as members of the Basel Committee try to hammer out a final version by a promised mid year deadline. Although the new rules are not due to be implemented until 2006, banks should already have started making the fundamental changes in risk management and information system that will be required for compliance.

***5. Corporate Governance* (A global movement to raise standards):** Across the globe, the movement toward improved corporate governance is firmly taking hold, with an unprecedented number of initiatives.

6. Investing in New Technology: The last several years of focusing on cost reduction, along the failure to achieve the benefits expected from major IT projects, have led banks to rein in their investment in new technology. To remain competitive, however banks will need to renew their commitment to upgrading their technological capabilities, ensuring that their new investments are practical, client focused, and clearly generate value.

7. Maintaining a Strategic Focus: In a world, where short term results dominate the headlines and financials institutions must respond quickly to the growing demands of regulators and investors, its easy to understand why long term planning is well down on an organization priority list.

8. Globalization: It would provide opportunities for Indian corporate entities to expand their business in other countries. Banks in India wanting to increase their international presence could naturally be expected to follow these corporate and other trade flows in and out of India. In the years to come, the Indian banking system will be experiencing the following changes.

a. The power of financial muscle.
b. Competition among equals.
c. M & A route, which provides a quick step forward for increasing the operational efficiency and functioning.
a. Competition from new banks.

9. Mergers and acquisitions: It would gather momentum, as managements will strive to meet the expectations of stakeholders. This could see the emergence of 4-5 world class Indian Banks. As Banks seek niche areas, we could see emergence of some national banks of global scale and a number of regional players.

10. Diversification: With excess capital would help banks to diversify their Intellectual and Cash Capital into other profit venturing business like insurance, brokerage, home loan, consumer durables loan, personal loan and other financials services to every form of customer.

NOTES

1. Goyal O.P., "Financial Institutions and Economic Growth of India", 1979, p.4.
2. Mithani, D.M., "Money, Banking, International Trade and Public Finance", Himalaya Publishing House, 2002, pp.309-310.
3. Banerjee Amalesh, Singh K. Shrawan, "Banking and Financial Sector Reforms in India" Deep & Deep Publications New Delhi, Indian Economic Association, 2000, pp.64-65.
4. Jalan, B, "Finance and Development-Which Way Now?", RBI Bulletin, January 2000, pp.29-45.
5. Reddy, Y.V., "Financial Sector Reform: Review and Prospects", RBI Bulletin, January 1999, pp.33-93.
6. Bhide, M. G., A. Prasad and Saibal Ghosh, "Emerging Challenges in Indian Banking", Center For Research On Economic Development And Policy Reform, Working Paper No. 103, Paper presented at the Conference on Indian Economic Policy: Trade, Finance and Public Finance at Stanford University, July 2001, pp.10-20.

7. Rangarajan, C, "Banking Sector Reforms: Rationale and Relevance", SICOM Silver Jubilee Memorial Lecture, Mumbai, 1998.
8. Shekhar & Shekhar, "Banking Theory & Practice", USB Publishers Distributors, New Delhi, 1999, pp.335-356.
9. Kamth K. V., "Impact of Technology & Globalization – An Indian Perspective", ICICI – London Biennial meeting Dec 12,2001.
10. RBI Report "Committee on Technology Upgradation in the Banking Sector" at www.rbi.org.in, July 17, 1999, Chapter 1, pp.3-4.
11. Mishkin, F. and Strahan, P., "What will technology do to financial structure?", Brookings-Wharton Papers on Financial Services, 1999, pp. 249–277.
12. Basel Committee, "Report on enhancing bank transparency", Paper No. 41, 1998, http://www.bis.org/publ/bcbs41.pdf,
13. World Development Report "Knowledge for Development", Published for the World Bank, Oxford University Press 1998/99
14. Kamesam Vepa, "Challenges Before The Indian Banking Industry", Reserve Bank of India on August 31, 2002 at the Annual General Meeting of the Indian Banks' Association at Mumbai.
15. Ibid.
16. Ibid.
17. Ibid.
18. Ibid.
19. Muniappan G. P., "Management Challenges in Banking", Reserve Bank of India at the NIBM Annual Day Celebrations January 6, 2003.
20. Bhide, M. G., A. Prasad and Saibal Ghosh, op. cit., pp.16-35.
21. Ibid.
22. Deloitte, Financial Service Industry "Global Banking Industry Outlook" 2004 Top Ten Issues.

3

RESEARCH METHODOLOGY

UNIVERSE OF THE STUDY

The universe of this Study covers all the scheduled commercial banks found operating in India in public and private sectors and as foreign, cooperative, and regional rural banks.

SURVEY POPULATION

3.2 Of the kinds of the banks referred to above, only those banks, which are in the public sector, private sector and are operating as Foreign Banks have been included in the Survey Population of this Study. Thus, we have excluded from the ambit of the survey population of this Study the entire family of the Cooperative Banks and the Regional Rural Banks on account of two basic reasons. First, these banks are grossly found wanting in terms of the availability of technological structure, aside having inadequately trained base of human resources. Second, chunk portion of both of them indicates an erratic trend on the score of profitability and thereby making it difficult to take up the warrantedkind of analysis for their programmes. Thus, the Survey Population of this Study is comprised of 84 banks in all; of these, 27 are public sector banks, 23 belongs to private sector and 34 are in the category of foreign banks*. The full details of

* This statistics relates to the period ended as on March 31, 2003; Source : RBI, Annual Report for the period ended March 31, 2003; and, RBI, Trend & Progress Report for the period ended March 31, 2003.

this survey population may be seen in Table 3.1 of Appendix I

SAMPLING FRAMEWORK AND SELECTION CRITERIA

3.3 After identifying certain criteria such as size as indicated by total assets, total income, net profit as on March 31, 2003 and making use of MS-excel and SPSS V.12, ranking has been computed for all the banks using the methodology elaborated step by step in subsequent para 3.4. The author has selected two banks having Rank 1 and Rank 2 each from the categories of public, private and foreign sector banks. It may be pertinent to mention here that the composite rank of each bank has been arrived at by combining the proportionate weights assigned for each of the above referred parameter. The complete data of all the banks included in the Survey Population may be seen in Table 3.1 through 3.16 presented as part of Appendix I.

3.4 Step by Step methodology adopted for the purpose has been as described here under:-

1. **First Step:** All the 84 banks (Public-27/ Private-23/ Foreign-34) were first of all arranged in an ascending order (from best to worst) according to the values obtained by concerned banks in respect to each of the identified indicators. Table 3.3, 3.8 and 3.13 of Appendix I highlights the results obtained in respect to this step.

2. **Second Step:** The number of times a bank maintained an identical rank in identified parameters of Net Profit, Total Income and Total Assets, the same has been depicted in the form of frequency distribution in Table 3.4, 3.9 and 3.14 of Appendix I.

3. **Third Step:** Weights are assigned to each rank in descending order. Since there are 27 public sector banks, the weightage pattern in respect to these banks is 1st to 27th ; likewise it is 1st to 23rd in case of private sector banks and 1st to 34th in case of Foreign Banks. Weights were then normalized. These weights are presented in Table 3.5, 3.10 and 3.15 of Appendix-I.

4. **Fourth Step:** The sum of the number of times a bank appeared in the respective ranks as weighed by the weights assigned as per Step Third, the obtained values of weights for the respective banks are also presented in Column 6 of Table 3.5, 3.10 and 3.15 of Appendix-I for Public, Private and Foreign Banks, respectively.

5. **Fifth Step :** On the basis of the values referred to in Step Four, the overall ranking has been depicted in Table 3.6, 3.11 and 3.16 of Appendix I.

3.5 A few observations in respect to the banks included in the sample are as thus:

- Among public sector banks, the State Bank of India (SBI) is found at the top followed by Punjab National Bank and Canara Bank, respectively. SBI is the market leader with maximum number of branches, highest profit, total income and total assets.
- In Private Sector, the outstanding performers have been ICICI Bank and HDFC Bank. UTI Bank and J&K Bank followed them on the above-mentioned criteria but with a big margin.
- In the category of Foreign Banks the Standard Chartered Bank and Citi Bank have been found leading followed by HSBC Bank.

3.6 Rank could be assigned to 84 banks only as the same was not possible in case of a few private and foreign sector banks either on account of non-publication of annual report and/or incurring net loss in the 2002-2003. This, however, does not mean that the operations of excluded banks have been inferior but it only means operations of these banks have not been profitable. Hence these banks were not considered. The prerequisites for analyzing the efficiency in the banks has been based on some key parameters i.e. year of establishment, number of people employed, profitability, number of ATMs, retail branches etc. The drop in the total income of foreign banks as a sector was partly on account of the decision of a few banks to shut down their branch /es in India. Many banks also reduced their funded exposure in the country and focused instead on fee-based income. During 2001-2002 CommerzBank, Dresdner Bank and KBC Bank closed down their Indian operations, while in 2002-2003 Siam Commercial Bank and Tornto Domination Bank decided to leave the country. The oversea-Chinese Banking Corporation is in the process of winding up of its operations in India and will make a complete exit from the country by the end of the year. A few banks like Deutsche Bank and Barclays produced extremely strong results while some others actually witnessed a dip in net profit.

METHODS EMPLOYED FOR DATA COLLECTION / INFORMATION GATHERING

3.8 This study has been completed with the help of both the secondary and primary data. The main sources of secondary data have been Reports on Currency and Finance, Trend and Progress, Annual Report, Banking and Technology and all other publications of the Reserve Bank of India. The different reports for the period: 1991, 2004 were accessed through website: www.rbi,org.in ; however, the author also collected a couple of hard copies of these publications as could be available from the market.

3.9 Further, the Websites of different commercial banks were also accessed for gathering necessary data about the banks included in the sample. This apart, various published and unpublished reports of the concerned banks and different organizations to whom the banks have outsourced the function of KM were also referred to.

3.10 Thousands of articles have been written on knowledge management, and an Internet search using the keyword, Knowledge Management and Knowledge Management in Banking Sector at *www.Google.com*, *www.MSN.com*, *www.Altavista.com*, *www.Yahoo.com*, *www.theeconomictimes.com*, *www.financialexpress.com* reveals tens of thousands of hits. Various published and unpublished reports of technological (software development, maintenance, outsourcing, etc.) and management consulting firms were also used for updating our records. On line service and internet gateway has further come to the rescue of the author in supplementing the secondary data information at the time of analysis and presentation.

3.11 The main source of primary data have been Schedule 1 and 2 designed by the author for gathering needed information from the chosen respondents from the selected commercial banks and other concerned entities and categories of persons. Schedule 1 has been addressed to the Top Management of the commercial banks included in this study and Schedule 2 to the respondents of middle management and other respondents selected from software and management consultancy firms, researchers and academicians including information technology firms. While the Officers of the level of Vice President, Director (Executive and Non-Executive), Chief Manager and Sr. Chief Manager have been included in the category of top management, the Branch Manager, Operations Managers, IT Managers, Marketing Executives and Other Sr. Assistant Executives have been included in the category of middle management.

3.12 Schedule 1 includes a set of structured and non structured (open-ended) questions covering various aspects of operations of banks such as awareness about the knowledge management, status of information and its sharing, HRD practices and technological support to decision making for securing information from the respondents of top management. Face to face personal interviews and in couple of cases telephonic interviews were also conducted. The same procedure was adopted for gathering information from the respondents falling in the category of middle management and software and management consultancy firms including information technology firms and researchers and academicians.

3.13 It may also be mentioned here that the Schedule 2 included only structured questions pertaining to HR issues, strategic issues, operational issues, technological issues and structural issues. It this case, the respondents were required to indicate their appropriate response (in numbers) from among the five responses designed on a five-point Likert Scale : (A) Not at all true =1, (B) Rarely true =2, (C) Sometimes true =3, (D) Mostly true =4, and, (E) Almost always true =5. It may be of interest to make a mention of one more aspect. The respondents from the chosen banks like State Bank of India, HDFC, ICICI and Standard Chartered were conducted at their registered and head office situated in Mumbai. In the case of Punjab National Bank and Citi Bank, the concerned respondents were contacted at New Delhi. Furthermore, the respondents falling in the category of middle management and others were contacted only at New Delhi branches/other concerned offices. The full contents of Schedule 1 and 2 may be perused in Appendix II. The primary information so collected has been supplemented on the basis of personal interaction from the officers having expertise in the field *via* tapping their memories and experience[1].

SAMPLING

3.14 On the basis of stratified random sampling, we selected 60 and 200 respondents from the Officials falling in the category of Top Management and Middle Management of the banks selected for this Study, respectively. This apart 90 respondents were also identified from software and management consultancy firms, information technology firms, researchers and academicians. Thus in all, the total number of chosen respondents added to 350. Of these, actual responses could be gathered only from 206 respondents comprising of 39 from the category of top management, 150 from middle management and 17 from the other category, namely, management software and consultancy firms including IT companies and researchers and academicians.

PATTERN OF ANALYSIS AND STATISTICAL TOOLS EMPLOYED

3.15 After due editing and coding of raw data (of course employing statistical softwares like, SPSS and Microsoft Excel) necessary classification was done and appropriate codes, both numeric and alphanumeric were assigned for undertaking conclusive analysis. In doing so, we also fallowed the rules of missing values and don't know rules. Emphasis in analysis has been on visual presentation also using graphs over and above the presentation of relevant statistics in the tabular shapes. Classical statistical tools of adjudging significance and confidence level have been used wherever required. In order to analyze the profitability, growth and productivity of banks, we have used Data Envelopment Analysis (DEA)[2]. Descriptive statistics like, mean, median, mode and Standard Deviation and F-Test have further been widely used for undertaking warranted analysis as per the determined objectives and focus of this study.

NOTES

1. Cooper, Donald R., Schindler Pamela S., "Business Research Methods", Tata McGraw Hill, India, 2003, p.154.
2. Anderson R. David, Sweeney J. Dennis, Williams A. Thomas, "An Introduction to Management Science: Quantitative Approaches for Decision Making", South Western College Publishing, 2000, USA, pp.182-183.

4

PERTINENT ANALYSIS

I. EVALUATING THE TECHNICAL EFFICIENCY AMONG SELECTED BANKS THRUOGH THEIR GROWTH, PRODUCTIVITY AND PROFITABILITY INDICATORS.

The performance of the banks included in the sample for this Study have been adjudged on the basis of growth, productivity and profitability for the purposes of evaluating their technical efficiency. For the purpose we employed the technique of Data Envelopment Analysis (DEA), which is a widely accepted theoretical framework for analyzing the performance. Basically it is a Study of non-parametric linear technique used to construct empirical production frontiers and evaluate the relative efficiency of production units[1]. DEA evaluates the relative efficiency of identical units, referred to as decision making units (DMUs). While in traditional approaches, all measures of efficiency focus on average and estimation of parameters and utilize only a single optimized regression equation presumed to be appropriate for every DMU; in DEA the performance measure of each DMU is optimized. In DEA, we calculate the best possible performance for each DMU *vis-à-vis* all other observed measures.

4.2 **Farrell** (1957)[2] attempted to measure the efficiency of production in single input and output case. Farrell's study involved the measurement of price and technical efficiencies and the derivation of the efficient production function. Farrell applied his model to estimate the efficiency of US agricultural output in relation to other countries. However, he failed in providing a way to summarize all the various inputs and outputs into a single virtual input and single virtual output.

4.3 **Charnes, Cooper and Rhodes** (1978)[3] extended Farrell's idea and proposed a model which generalizes the single-input, single-output measure of efficiency of Decision-Making Unit (DMU) in a multiple-input, multiple-output setting. A DMU is an entity that uses inputs to produce outputs. This approach to performance measurement is called Data Envelopment Analysis (DEA). The technique of DEA involves the use of Linear Programming (L P) to solve a set of inter - related problem to determine the relative efficiency of DMUs. In banking, a bank constitutes a DMU. We can also consider a branch to be a DMU when we are considering the performance of various branches. The efficiency of a DMU (using the engineering-like efficiency measure, i.e. efficiency as a ratio of virtual output produced to virtual input consumed) is computed as:

$$\text{Efficiency} = \frac{\sum \text{ Weighted Outputs}}{\sum \text{ Weighted Inputs}}$$

4.4 Data Envelopment Analysis is an approach which compares the efficiency of organizational unit such as local authority departments, schools, hospitals, shops, bank branches and similar entities which constitute relatively a homogeneous set of units. The analysis will measure output(s) achieved from the input(s) provided and will compare the group of DMUs by their strength in turning input into output. At the end of the analysis DEA will be able to evince which units are (relatively) efficient and which are (relatively) inefficient.

4.5 In DEA mathematical programming is applied to assess the 'relative' efficiency of variety of institutions using a variety of input and output data. The term 'relative' is rather important here since an institution identified by DEA as an efficient unit in a given set of data may be deemed inefficient when compared, using another set of data. One starts using DEA by building a relative ratio consisting of total weighted outputs to total weighted inputs for each institution. The relatively 'most efficient' units become the efficient frontier and the relative efficiency of other units are compared with the efficient frontier and are then determined using a mathematical method (simplex method of linear programming). The term efficiency used in DEA is the relative efficiency and not the absolute efficiency. Accordingly, summary analysis cannot be done by using different DEA runs.

4.6 It is a deterministic non-parametric approach to measure bank performance. It is a very promising tool for monitoring efficiency in banking industry (Berger and Humphrey, 1997)[4]. In banking industry, the DEA model is preferable to econometric approach of efficiency measurement because it has a number of advantages:

- It can simultaneously analyze several inputs and outputs, which is an attractive characteristic because production in the banking industry often involves multiple inputs and multiple outputs ;
- It does not require any assumptions about the functional form of the technology; and,
- It calculates a maximal performance measure for each production unit relative to all other production units in the observed population with the sole condition that each production unit lies on or below the extreme frontier.

4.7 In the case of a bank, which has a number of branches, the goal of management is to ensure that each one of these branches achieve the best possible performance; the problem, therefore, is deciding what this means and how best to go about measuring it. The inputs of the branches such as staff, office space, material costs, etc., can be measured. Managers can develop performance ratios such as the business per member of staff or profit per unit of office space utilized. All these attempts to measure performance may not produce a clear picture as branches may exhibit considerable variation depending on the performance indicator chosen. Further, in most cases attempts are made to find a comprehensive performance measure by giving a priori weight to a variety of performance ratios.

DEFINING INPUT AND OUTPUT FACTOR

4.8 Although the DEA model avoids the problem of agreeing on a common set of weights for the inputs and outputs, it cannot, of course, avoid the problem of selecting which inputs and outputs should be included in the comparisons. Clearly, any resources used by a unit should be included as input. A unit will convert resources to produce outputs so that the outputs should be treated as the amount of products or services produced by the unit and these products or services may be produced at different levels of quality. Hence, the outputs may include, a range of performance and activity measures. In addition, environmental factors, which may affect the production of these outputs, must be identified and included in the assessment model.

4.9 The total number of inputs and outputs relative to number of DMUs can affect the discriminating power of DEA. The number of factors selected (inputs and outputs) need to be small compared to total number of DMUs to strengthen discrimination power or DEA. This arises due to the flexibility in the choice of weights in determining the efficiency of each individual unit. In seeking to be seen efficient a unit can allocate almost all its weight to a single input/output. The unit for which one particular ratio of output to input is highest can allocate all its weight to that ratio and appear efficient. The total number of such ratios will be the product of the number of inputs and outputs and this product is a reasonable indicator of the minimum number of efficient units. Hence, with four inputs and three outputs at least 12 or so units will appear efficient, so that the total number of units in the set need to be much greater than 12 for the method to be of any discriminatory value. Usually, the total number of DMUs should be at least twice the number of inputs plus output factors. The higher the number of DMUs, the better is the discrimination power.

4.10 Each input/output weight assigned in a DEA model depends on the value and mix of the inputs and outputs because in solving the DEA algorithm weights are assigned independently so as to optimize the solution and to maximize each unit's efficiency score – so changing the value of an input or output changes the weight. The efficiency score of a unit is equal to the sum of its virtual outputs. The sum of the virtual inputs is always equal to one.

ORIENTATIONS IN DEA

4.11 One of the basic choices in selecting a DEA model is whether to use an input-orientation or an output-orientation. The difference is subtle but important and can typically be best understood by considering whether a DMU emphasized on reducing input while achieving the same level of output or emphasizes on producing more output given the same level of input.

4.12 DEA offers three possible orientations in efficiency analysis (Charnes 1994)[5]:

(a) Input-oriented models are models where DMUs are deemed to produce a given amount of output with the smallest possible amount of input.

(b) Output-oriented models are models where DMUs are deemed to produce the highest possible amount of output with the given amount of input.

(c) Base-oriented models are models where DMUs are deemed to produce the optimal mix of input and output.

RETURN TO SCALE

4.13 Return to scale refers to increasing or decreasing efficiency based on size. For example, a manufacturer can achieve certain economies of scale by producing thousand circuit boards at a time rather than one at a time – it might be only 100 times as hard as producing one at a time. This is an example of Increasing Returns to Scale (IRS).

4.14 On the other hand, the manufacturer might find it more than trillion times difficult to produce a trillion circuit boards at a time because of storage problems and limitations on the worldwide copper supply. This range of production illustrates Decreasing Returns to Scale (DRS). Combining the extreme two ranges would necessitate Variable Returns to Scale (VRS). Constant Return to Scale (CRS) means that the producers are able to linearly scale the inputs and outputs without increasing or decreasing efficiency. This is a significant assumption. The assumption of CRS may be valid over limited ranges but its use must be justified. This aside, CRS efficiency score will never be higher than VRS efficiency scores.

4.15 Few of the recent studies, which have used DEA to measure efficiency in the banking sector in different countries of the world are detailed in Table 4.1 of the Appendix- III.

MODEL OF DEA

4.16 As indicated earlier, **Charnes, Cooper and Rhodes** were the initial proponents of DEA and the first one to cast the concept in the form of a fractional linear programming problem and denoted it as the 'DEA Ratio Model' , which is as detailed under:

$$\text{Maximize } E_m = \frac{\Sigma U_{jm} Y_{jm}}{\Sigma V_{im} X_{im}}$$

$$\text{Subject to} = \frac{\Sigma U_{jm} Y_{jn}}{\Sigma V_{im} X_{in}} <= 1 \qquad n = 1,2,\ldots,N$$

$$U_{jm}, V_{im} >= 0 \qquad I = 1,2,\ldots I; \qquad j = 1,2,\ldots J$$

Where

E_m = the efficiency of the m th DMU,
Y_{jm} = j^{th} output of the mth DMU,
U_{jm} = the weight of that output,
X_{im} = i^{th} input of the mth DMU,
V_{im} = the weight of that input,

Y_{jm} and X_{in} are j^{th} output and i^{th} input, respectively of the nth DMU, n= 1,2,...,N. Note that here n includes m.

4.17 In the solution to this model the efficiency of mth unit is maximized subject to efficiencies of all units in the set having an upper bound of 1. The key feature of above model is that the weights U_{jm} and V_{im} are treated as unknown. They will be chosen so as to maximize the efficiency of mth target unit. The efficiency of mth target unit will either equal to 1 in which case the unit is inefficient. In order to convert inefficient unit into an efficient unit, the solution would lie in comparing the peer group members of inefficient units alongwith the peer group members of efficient units.

$$\text{Maximize } E_m = \sum U_{jm} Y_{jm}$$
$$\text{Subject to: } \sum U_{im} Y_{im} = 1$$
$$\sum U_{jm} Y_{jn} - \sum U_{im} Y_{in} <= 0 \qquad n= 1,2,\ldots,N$$
$$U_{jm} <=0 \quad V_{im} <= 0 \qquad I=1,2,\ldots I; \quad J=1,2,\ldots J$$

4.18 The DEA model is a fractional linear programme but may be converted into linear form in a straightforward manner so that the methods of linear programming can be applied. The simplest way to convert these fractional programmes to linear programmes is to normalize either the numerator or the denominator of the fractional programming objective function. The weighted sum of the inputs **is constrained to be unity** in this linear programme. As the objective function is the weighted sum of outputs that has to be maximized, this formulation is referred to as the output maximization DEA programme.

DATA SOURCE

4.19. The data revealing the growth, productivity, and profitability as published by the RBI in its publications titled 'Trend and Progress Report of India - 2003-2004', 'Statistical Tables Relating to Banks in India - 2003-2004' for 26 public sector banks, 24 private sector banks, and 21 foreign sector banks have been used for analysis. These indicators have been depicted in Table 4.2 in Appendix III.

EMPLOYING THE OUTPUT ORIENTED MODEL

4.20 The CCR output oriented model (output maximization) has been employed to evaluate the data. And, for each indicator data has been evaluated separately. The method adopted to determine the relative performance efficiency of public, private and foreign sector units involved multiple computations using each units as the target DMU in the objective function of the model at a time. With the help of DEA, we have attempted to find out which of the decision-making units (DMUs) determines an envelopment surface while considering related inputs and outputs. Units that determine the envelopment surface are deemed to be efficient, and units that do not lie on the surface are categorized as inefficient.

4.21 **Berger and Humphery (1997)** suggested that the intermediation approach is more suited for analyzing bank level efficiency vis-à-vis the production approach which is well suited for measuring branch level efficiency for the simple reason that at the bank level management aims at reducing the total costs and not just non-interest expenses, while at the branch level a large number of customer service processing takes place and bank funding and investment decisions are mostly not under the control of branches. Therefore, we utilized this most commonly used "intermediation approach" for measuring input and output variables of banks.

4.22 Data envelopment is obtained by solving a linear programming model for each DMU. The DMUs included in the model comprise the reference set. DMUs in the reference set appear in the constraints of the linear programming model; the model is only solved for each of the units in the analysis set. A DEA computer program was used to solve linear programming model. Inputs and outputs for each indicator are shown in the Tables 4.3 through 4.11 included in Appendix III.

4.23. The results obtained by employing DEA technique are also summarized in the Tables 4.3 through 4.11 of Appendix III for Growth, Productivity and Profitability indicators. The results indicate the presence of a marked deviation in the efficiency scores on the frontier of best practice. The mean of technical efficiency turned out to be 0.962 for public sector banks, 0.838 for private sector banks, and 0.868 for foreign sector banks in respect to profitability indicator. Similarly the mean of technical efficiency of growth indicator turned out to be 0.743 for public sector, 0.567 for private sector, 0.571 for foreign sector, and the identical mean for productivity indicator for public sector has been 0.549 ; these have been 0.276 and 0.540 for private and foreign sector banks, respectively. The average of technical efficiency among all the banks is displayed in Exhibit : 4.1

4.24 This implies that the overall level of technical efficiency in Indian Public, Private and Foreign sector banks is to the tune of 8%, 14%, and 6 % in terms of profitability, 15%, 17%, and 10% in relation to growth, and 25%, 22% and 18% in terms of productivity parameters. This suggests that by adopting best practices, banks can reduce their inputs on an average by at least upto the average level of inefficiency as depicted vide item No. 4 in Exhibit 4.1 for different performance indicators for the three categories of banks. However, the potential reduction in inputs from adopting best practices would vary from one bank to another.

4.25 The efficiency score of SBI in terms of profitability indicator is 0.886; it can be interpreted that this bank has attained 88% level of operating efficiency which alternatively means that the SBI has so far been able to attain the 88 per cent of efficiency as evaluated *via* its outputs generated with the given level of inputs. The identical results for the rest of the banks are summarized in Exhibit 4.2.

4.26 The results obtained on the score of profitability are almost 100 per cent in case of all the selected banks, excepting SBI and Standard Chartered which attained the levels of 88 per cent and 98 per cent, respectively. Category-wise, the

Exhibit : 4.1

PARAMETER-AND CATEGORY OF BANKS-WISE STATISTICS RELATED TO TECHNICAL EFFICIENCY

Item No	Particulars	Growth			Productivity			Profitability		
		Public	Private	Foreign	Public	Private	Foreign	Public	Private	Foreign
(1)	(2)	(3)	(4)	(5)	(6)	(7)	(8)	(9)	(10)	(11)
1.	No. of DMUs	26	24	21	26	24	21	26	24	21
2.	No. of Efficient DMSu	8	7	8	1	2	2	15	8	11
3.	Avg. Efficiency (Mean)	0.743	0.567	0.571	0.549	0.276	0.54	0.962	0.838	0.868
4.	Avg. Inefficiency	0.345	0.763	0.751	0.821	2.62	0.85	0.039	0.193	0.152
5.	Overall Level of Effi. (In Percentages)	15	17	10	25	22	18	8	14	6

Exhibit : 4.2

PARAMETER-AND INDIVIDUAL BANK-WISE STATISTICS RELATED TO TECHNICAL EFFICIENCY.

Item No.	*Parameters*	*Name of the Selected Public Sector Bank*			*Name of the Selected Private Sector Bank*			*Name of the Selected Foreign Bank*		
		SBI	PNB	Avg	ICICI	HDFC	Avg	CITI	STAN	Avg.
(1)	(2)	(3)	(4)	(5)	(6)	(7)	(8)	(9)	(10)	(11)
1	Growth	1.000	0.554	0.743	1.000	1.000	0.567	0.662	1.000	0.571
2	Productivity	0.771	0.446	0.549	1.000	0.723	0.276	1.000	0.413	0.540
3	Profitability	0.886	1.000	0.962	1.000	1.000	0.838	1.000	0.988	0.868

accomplishments on this score have been 96 per cent, 83 per cent and 86 per cent for the public, private and foreign sector banks, respectively.

4.27 The picture emerging in relation to growth parameter has, however, been as thus : PNB indicates the bare 55 per cent level of operational efficiency as against 100 per cent level for SBI, ICICI, HDFC and Standard Chartered and 66 per cent for CitiBank. The average level of efficiency has been highest (74 per cent) for Public Sector Banks followed by almost 57 per cent in case of Private and Foreign Sector Banks.

4.28 Against productivity indicator, the most efficient ones have been ICICI (100 per cent) and CitiBank (100 per cent) followed by SBI (over 77 per cent), HDFC (over 72 per cent), PNB (nearly 45 per cent) and Standard Chartered (41 per cent). Category-wise Public Sector and Foreign Banks with an average efficiency level of 54 per cent stand a top. Private Sector Banks have only been able to indicate an efficiency level of slightly higher than 27 per cent.

4.29 The analysis presented above further confirms that Pubic, Private and Foreign Banks are not equally efficient technically. To substantiate, the sum of the scores secured out of 300 (100 for growth, 100 for productivity and 100 for profitability), the level of technical efficiency have been as thus : ICICI (300), HDFC (272), CitiBank (266), SBI (265), Standard Chartered (239), and PNB (199).

RATIO ANALYSIS

4.30 The level of technical efficiency as observed among the banks chosen for this study has further been refined with the help of data published by the RBI in its Trend and Progress Report and Statistical Tables Relating to Banks in India for the year ended March 31, 2004 in respect to major financial ratios and matching these for preparation of a check list of Very Strong (VS), Strong(S), Not So Strong (NSS), Weak (W) and Very Weak (VW) using Likert Scale of 5 to 1 and consequential ranking obtained for the chosen banks. This analysis has been assigned the additional weightage of 100 and therefore, the final ranking obtained is based on the average weight of 400 (300 for growth, productivity and profitability and 100 for 20 financial ratios). These ratios broadly relates to capital adequacies, earning, liquidity and liability. These ratios are displayed for the public sector banks, private sector banks and foreign banks in Table 4.12, 4.13, 4.14 respectively of the Appendix-III. The combined results obtained through DEA and overall ranking may be seen in Graph 4.1.

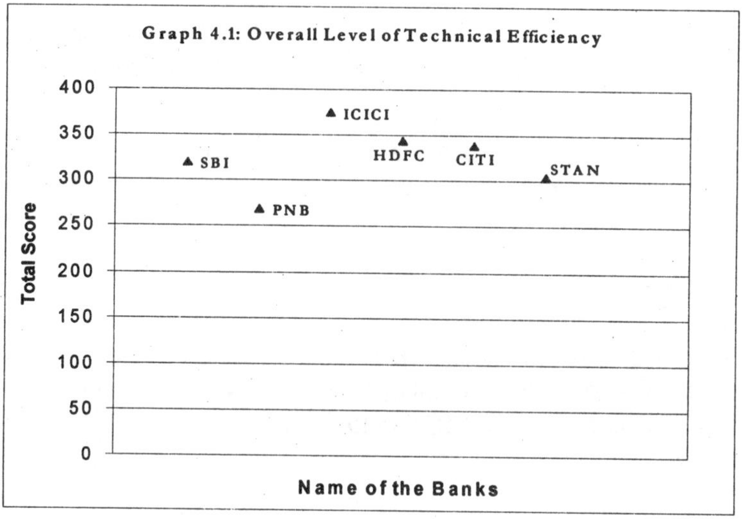

II. ROLE OF INFORMATION SYSTEM IN KNOWLEDGE MANAGEMENT AND THE CURRENT STATUS OF THE USE AND IMPACT OF INFORMATION TECHNOLOGY ON THE FUNCTIONING AND KNOWLEDGE MANAGEMENT BY INDIAN BANKS

4.31 Information Technology not only opened vast range of gainful business opportunities to banks, but also enabled them to perform their existing businesses more efficiently and effectively. RBI in its Trend & Progress Report for the year 2002-03, therefore, referred that different banks are proposing to make big investments in the information technology infrastructure. To quote:

- State Bank of India (SBI) information technology programme aims at achieving efficiency in operations, meeting customer and market expectations and facing competition ;
- The Punjab National Bank (PNB) considers technology as a key driver in business development and continued its efforts in upgradation of technology;
- At ICICI, technology is the key driver of its growth strategy and continues to leverage information technology as a strategic tool for its business operations to gain competitive advantage by offering customer convenience and improved service as well as improving productivity and efficiency ; and,
- At HDFC, technology enables the bank in offering innovative products and services with greater convenience and at an affordable price.

Customer Status

4.32 With a view to adjudge the use and impact of information systems (inclusive of technology) on the functioning and knowledge management by Indian banks we may peruse the facts/details gathered pertaining to following aspects.

ATM Branches

4.33 The availability of ATM equipped branches help banks to service high net worth customers and increase their profit margins. Recognizing this opportunity different banks, of course, at varying pace, installed many ATMs. The SBI Group (SBI and its Associated Banks) installed 2,247 ATMs during the financial year 2003-04, taking the aggregate number to 3814 ATMs covering 1,152 centres spread across the length and breadth of the country, thereby creating a truly national network of ATMs with an unparalleled reach. Further, the SBI has entered into bilateral tie-ups with other banks like, HDFC Bank and UTI Bank for sharing of ATM networks. Out of 404 ATMs in PNB (with a card base of 5.60 lakh), 351 are networked providing online withdrawal facility. An ATM sharing arrangement of PNB also exists with four (now three) other Banks, namely, Oriental Bank of Commerce, Global Trust Bank (merged with Oriental Bank of Commerce w.e.f. August 14, 2004) Indian Bank and UTI. In the case of private sector banks every branch is being linked with ATM. Not only that, ATMs are also being installed by these banks at corporate houses, shopping centres, and other prominent market places. They are also tying up with other public and foreign sector banks and non-bank financial companies for displaying their networks. The status of ATM branches during the four-year period 2000-04 of the chosen banks, is as depicted in Exhibit : 4.3. From the figures included in this Exhibit, it is evident that it reflects from zero to two thousand seven hundred sixty times increase in ATMs ; of course, this increase has been of varied magnitude in case of different banks.

Exhibit 4.3

ATM BRANCHES OF THE SELECTED BANKS

Sr. No.	*Name of the Bank*	*2000-2001*	*2001-2002*	*2002-2003*	*2003-2004*
(1)	(2)	(4)	(5)	(6)	(7)
1	SBI	0	1017	2065	2760
2	PNB	0	100	252	404
3	ICICI	510	720	1675	1700
4	HDFC	207	479	732	910
5	CITI	15	18	18	245
6	STAN	19	19	100	107

Source : Statistical Tables Related to Banks in India for the respective years.

Internet Banking

4.34 This channel is an extremely comprehensive product for both retail and corporate use. At SBI, 1994 branches, covering 555 centers, are extending internet banking (INB) service to their customers. All functionalities other than Cash and Clearing have been extended to individual retail customers. A separate Internet Banking Module for Corporate customers has been launched and available at 1305 branches. Bulk upload of data for Corporate, Inter-branch funds transfer for Retail customers, Online payment of Customs duty and Govt. tax, Electronic Bill Payment, SMS Alerts, E-Poll, IIT GATE Fee Collection, Off-line Customer Registration Process and Railway Ticket Booking are some of the new features of this mode of banking. The PNB also introduced Internet Banking, which has 8300 users as of now. At ICICI and HDFC in private banks and CITI and STAN in foreign banks are providing Internet services at their every branch for individuals and corporate clients.

Computerization

4.35 In SBI, all the branches of the Bank are now fully computerized; this strategy has contributed to improvement in customer service. The PNB bank achieved 100 per cent branch computerization and 97 per cent of Bank's business is captured through computers. Exhibit 4.4 displays the percentage of computerized branches of the banks included in this study by the close of 2003-2004.

Exhibit : 4.4
PERCENTAGE OF THE COMPUTERIZED BRANCHES
(As at the end of 2003-04)

Sr. No.	*Name of the Bank*	*Percentage of the Computerized Branches*
(1)	(2)	(3)
1	SBI	100
2	PNB	100
3	ICICI	100
4	HDFC	100
5	CITI	100
6	STAN	100

Source : RBI : Statistical Tables Relating to Banks in India for the 2003-04

4.36 Since the computerization has been done by banks at its different levels, namely, branch-level, service-branch-level, regional/zonal offices-level, head-office-level, etc. therefore, the impact of computerization must be viewed accordingly. For example, computerization of service operations has certainly contributed to the reduction in the reconciliation problems in the clearing operations. Similarly, the use of information technology at regional office and head office levels has sharpened, *inter alia*, the MIS capability of banks thus contributing to overall efficiency in decision-making mechanism. Computerization of branches, which directly interact with customers, has contributed to higher customer satisfaction besides handling higher volume of businesses and reduced transaction costs. The impact of such benefits in boosting financial performance of banks is, however, difficult to quantify in precise terms. Thus, while it is very difficult to pinpoint as to how much of the improvement in financials is directly attributable to computerization, it is possible to derive indirect linkages by assuming computerization as one of the factors for improvement in efficiency.

Business vis-à-vis Staff Strength

4.37 One of the core benefits of computerization is the ability of the banks to generate high volume of business with low number of people. The Exhibit 4.5 shows bank group wise growth in business (advances + deposits) alongside the strength of the staff over the four-year period 2001-04 :

Exhibit : 4.5

GROUP WISE GROWTH IN BUSINESS (ADVANCES + DEPOSITS) ALONGSIDE THE STRENGTH OF THE STAFF (2001-04) (Contd...108)

Sr. No.	*Name of the Bank*	*Year Ended*			
		2001	*2002*	*2003*	*2004*
(1)	(2)	(3)	(4)	(5)	(6)
1	SBI	15.93 (-7.96)	6.45 (-2.50)	13.93 (-0.22)	14.49 (-0.93)
2	PNB	20.13 (-9.92)	17.03 (-0.77)	17.81 (1.93)	16.45 (0.24)
3	ICICI	73.10 (234.15)	237.97 (71.45)	28.22 (37.66)	28.34 (43.19)

Exhibit : 4.5

GROUP WISE GROWTH IN BUSINESS (ADVANCES + DEPOSITS) ALONGSIDE THE STRENGTH OF THE STAFF (2001-04)

Sr. No.	*Name of the Bank*	*Year Ended*			
		2001	*2002*	*2003*	*2004*
(1)	(2)	(3)	(4)	(5)	(6)
4	HDFC	38.20 (40.56)	50.15 (33.64)	39.49 (28.03)	41.08 (18.40)
5	CITI	38.64 (12.84)	14.16 (-0.40)	14.05 (0)	17.62 (46.25)
6	STAN	10.19 (0)	58.40 (0)	90.72 (0)	16.28 (42.88)

Note : Figures in parentheses indicate percentage change in staff strength.

Source : RBI : Statistical Tables Relating to Banks in India for the year 2001 through 2004.

4.38 As may be perused in Exhibit : 4.5, while there has been a continual growth in the 'banking business' year after year, the corresponding increase in staff since 2001 has been on the negative side. It is thus clear that computerization enabled banks to generate and handle higher volume of business with lesser number of people

Business Per Employee

4.39 Since computerization has enabled banks to handle higher business by employing reduced number of employees, the business per employee has gone up across all bank groups in recent years, which is evidenced by the amounts of the business accomplished in different banks per employee as indicated in Exhibit 4.6.

Technological Solutions

4.40 The Exim Bills Software, which has been customized for the SBI's operations, has enabled it to transact its foreign as well as inland trade finance and bills business also on the same central database. This new software has not only resulted in the quantum jump in process efficiency but it also reduced operating costs aside ensuring accurate and timely MIS support. Introduction of single window services at more than 10,000 branches across the SBI Group has enabled customers to conduct their transactions efficiently. The Bank is aiming at introducing single window at all of its branches.

Exhibit 4.6 : BUSINESS PER EMPLOYEE (2001 : 04)

(Amount in Rupees Lakhs)

Sr. No.	*Name of the Bank*	*Year Ended*			
		2001 (Amount)	*2002 (Amount)*	*2003 (Amount)*	*2004 (Amount)*
(1)	(2)	(3)	(4)	(5)	(6)
1	SBI	136.58	173.01	190.77	210.56
2	PNB	141.95	167.76	195.64	228.22
3	ICICI	815.22	466.49	1120.00	1010.00
4	HDFC	643.00	778.00	865.00	866.00
5	CITI	1336.24	1566.82	1660.19	1666.92
6	STAN	617.78	800.82	840.54	780.11

Source : RBI : Statistical Tables Relating to Banks in India for the year 2001 through 2004.

4.41 Many things have already been undertaken by public/private/foreign sector banks, using technology in a big way such as :

- Regulatory requirements indicated by the RBI for preparation of Off-Site Monitoring Surveillance (OSMOS) Reports on a regular basis in electronic format.
- Regulatory requirement of filing of statutory returns such as the one under Section 42 of the Reserve Bank of India Act, 1934 for working out Cash Reserve Ratio (CRR) and Statutory Liquidity Ratio (SLR) obligations in electronic format.
- Carrying out the entire Asset Liability Management (ALM) through computers.

- Submission of Balance Sheets and Profit & Loss Accounts through shared networks.
- Inter-Branch Reconciliation of Accounts.

4.42 The Exhibit 4.7 brings out that storing/sharing of data/ information / knowledge is being managed in the banks selected for this Study mostly *via* their respective MIS Divisions, Organizing of Conferences/ Workshops/ Training programmes and with the help of appointment of Full Time/Part Time Consultants. It would be pertinent here to mention that in the case of SBI, the KPMG and Mckinsey & Co. were appointed as Consultants for designing its perspective plans relating to use of information technology. And, these firms assisted SBI in preparing plans for :

(a) Migration from distributed to centralized computing ;
(b) Implementation of an integrated core banking system with capability for online real-time transaction processing ;
(c) Multiple delivery Channels such as ATM and internet banking;
(d) Automated Treasuring and Risk Management System integrated into the core banking system ;
(e) Data warehousing, Data Mining, and Workflow capabilities; and
(f) Integrated into an Inter-Bank Payment Gateway.

EXHIBIT 4.7
FORMAL MECHANISM OF STORING/ SHARING THE DATA / INFORMATION / KNOWLEDGE

Sr.	*Source*	*Number of Responses*	*Percentage to total number of responses*
(1)	(2)	(3)	(4)
1.	MIS Division	18	25.4
2.	Constitution of Standing/Adhoc Committee/s	2	2.8
3.	Re-designing of Job-Profile/s	8	11.3
4.	Organizing of Conferences/Workshops/Training	31	43.7
5	Appointment of Full Time/Part-Time	8	11.3
6.	Consultant/s	4	5.6
	Holding of Brainstorming Session/s		
	Total Responses	**71**	**100.00**

4.43 Similarly, PNB took assistance from some technology companies for its different operations. It partnered with Infosys

(FINACLE) for core services, standardization of systems and strengthening electronic delivery channels. The HDFC bank outsourced the technology part to IBM for a period of five years ; this outsourced arrangement included : application management, customer relationship management and data centers. As a matter of fact, there has been a quantum jump in the nature and level of technology applied in the banking sector. This has had a perceptible impact on 'banking from a distance'. Fund transfers and management services and concepts such as online/e-banking are all getting established strongly. A beginning has also been made in innovations on deposit side such as introduction of deposit products linked with insurance and many other conceivable benefits to suit to the varied motives of the savers.

4.44 The Error Bars – the standard errors of means-are plotted in Graph 4.2 , which clearly defines the role of technology among different groups of banks, namely, public, private and foreign. The equality of variance assumption among

Graph 4.2 THE ERROR BARS FOR ALL THE THREE CATEGORIES OF BANKS

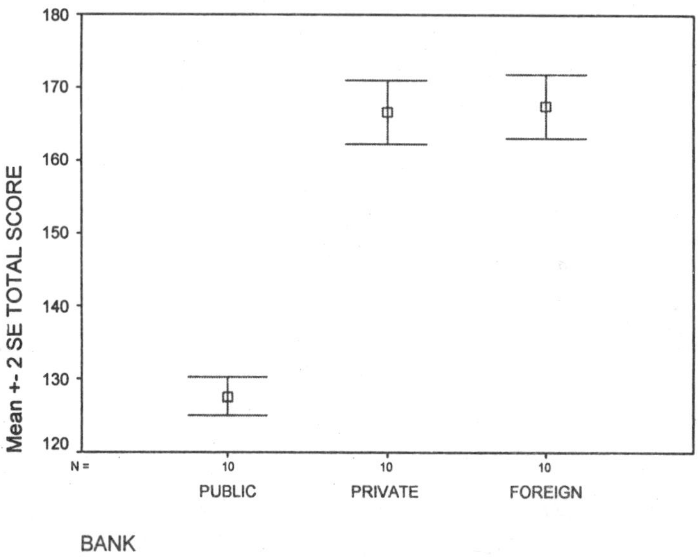

the public, private and foreign sector banks has been verified by employing one way ANOVA (F) Test. The descriptives and scores so obtained are displayed in Table 4.15, 4.16 and 4.17 of Appendix III.

4.45 As may be seen in the Graph at pre page, increase in Error Bar is discernible in the case of private and foreign sector banks. However, at the same time we also notice decrease in the equality of variance across the different groups of banks. The values of standard deviation and standard error further confirm that the role of technologies have varied from one group of banks to another. Accordingly, it is on a much higher side in case of private and foreign sector banks *vis-à-vis* the public sector banks.

4.46 The scores obtained in respect to different banks as they relate to overall 'information technology infrastructure' are summarized in the Table 4.18 of Appendix III ; however, when plotted on the Graph 4.3, the emerging picture is obvious at glance.

Graph 4.3 Information Technology Infrastructure

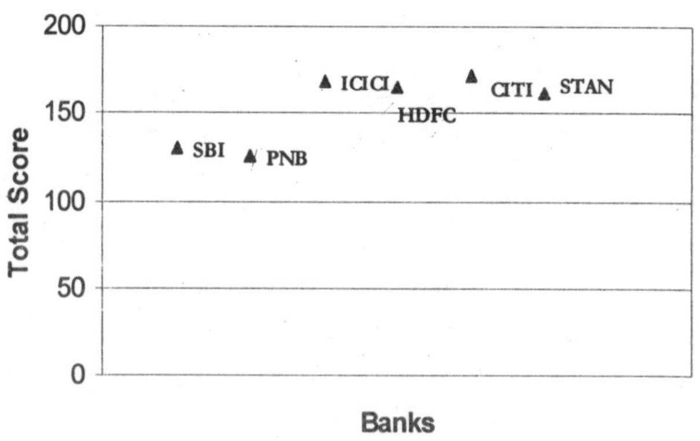

4.47 In the context, we may highlight the following aspects of technology, as it pertains to the banks covered *via* this study, in order to draw attention to higher variance zones among the group of banks :

1. Banks does not have range of well-organized and integrated techniques for transferring knowledge, meetings, e-mail, bulletin boards, online-forums and databases.
2. Information is not ready and accessible at one place in the public sector banks.
3. The physical environment does not encourage and facilitate learning and knowledge sharing.
4. Few technological tools are being used such as : Messaging and e-Mail Systems, Data-Warehousing/Data Marts, Search Engines – Intelligent Agents – Information Retrieval Systems, Business Process Management, and Workflow Management System.
5. The electronic and physical spaces where the knowledge is stored are not updated among public sector banks.

III INTEGRATION OF KNOWLEDGE STRATEGY IN THE BUSINESS STRATEGY AND KNOWLEDGE INITIATIVES IN RELATION TO BANKS VISION, MISSION/GOALS AND ACTIONS.

4.48 The **SBI's vision** statement read as thus :

- To be a Premier Indian Financial Services Group with global perspectives, world-class standards of efficiency and professionalism with core institutional values.
- To retain its position in the country as a pioneer in Development Banking.
- To maximize shareholder value through high-sustained earnings per share
- To be an institution with a culture of mutual care and commitment, a satisfying and exciting work environment and continuous learning opportunities.

In consonance with the above vision, the **SBI's mission** statement is as thus : **To retain the Bank's position as the premier Indian Financial Services group, with the world class standards and significant global business, committed to excellence in**

customer, shareholder and employee satisfaction, and to play a leading role in the expanding and diversifying financial services sector, while continuing emphasis on its development banking role.

State Bank Group, being the largest, is offering the full range of financial services comparable to that offered by the best banks in the world. SBI thrust is on increasing its already high share of Government business, which it perceives as a profit center. However, the SBI continues to emphasize upon lending to the retail, agricultural, SME and infrastructure sectors. The seven associate banks of State Bank of India (SBI) have proposed a branch-swap strategy in an effort to reduce their cost of operations and to enable the banks to focus on their individual regional strengths.

4.49 **PNB's mission and objectives** are as thus :

- to provide excellent professional services and improve its position as leader in the field of financial and related services;
- build and maintain a team of motivated and committed workforce with high work ethos; and,
- use latest technology aimed at customer satisfaction and act as an effective catalyst for socio-economic development.

4.50 The HDFC Bank, which represents the category of private sector banks, intends to be a World Class Indian Bank ; the objective is to build sound customer franchises across distinct businesses so as to be a preferred provider of banking services for target retail and wholesale customer segments and to achieve a healthy growth in profitability, of course, consistent with risk absorption capability. HDFC Bank's business philosophy is to attain Operational Excellence, Customer Focus, Product Leadership, and People orientation.

4.51 The Mission and Objectives of ICICI Bank, another bank representing private sector in this study, provides singular focus on its customers. Strategies are therefore built around this focus to seek new ways to make banking safer, simpler and smarter. Constant efforts are put in to anticipate customer needs and offer value added propositions to fulfill them. The multi-channel, technology driven distribution system enables customers 24*7, countrywide access. The Banks committed team of employees, equipped with world-class technology and financial skills, works to devise new solutions, enhance responsiveness to customer needs and improve services. With focus on technology and customer convenience, it is also able to fulfill the aspirations of NRIs and Indian companies operating abroad.

4.52 Our investigations revealed that in all categories of banks, there is a common practice of creating some Research and Market Intelligence Cell with a view to remain innovative, ensure customer satisfaction and keep abreast of market developments. These banks have further been found to have been constantly interacting with industry bodies, trade associations, farming community, academic /research institutions, aside initiating studies, pilot projects in areas of perspective interest for evolving better financial models.

4.53 On the whole there is no common understanding among public sector banks in respect to where and how the 'knowledge management' has to be practiced. As a matter of fact, they are not only not aware about the precise meaning of the term 'knowledge management' but are also confused as to how it could be applied successfully in the banking sector. In sharp contrast to this, the ICICI Bank is practicing knowledge management through its Innovation and Creativity Department at its Registered Office ; right now this Department is involved in streamlining the routine business processes. Likewise, HDFC is being assisted by its IT Department in transiting the tool of knowledge management for the Bank's benefit.

4.54 While foreign banks, follows their parental proceedings, they put technology at the top and its being a responsibility of each and every individual which has to be linked with the vision and mission of the organization. But no such program is being followed carrying the title of KM Program. But they are following some knowledge-based tools for sharing and disseminating the data and knowledge from vertical to horizontal levels.

4.55 Banks are also building up a proper risk management structure that is crucial for the banks in the future. Banks find the need to develop technology based risk management tools. The complex mathematical models programmed into risk engines providing the foundation of limit management, risk analysis, computation of risk-adjusted return on capital and active management of banks' risk portfolio.

REALIZED BENEFITS

4.56 The investments made for execution of the knowledge management *via* IT have broadly led to reduced time frame in MIS, better risk management, efficient tracking of Non-Performing Assets (NPAs), creation of new business, better regulatory compliance, swifter re-adjustment to market changes, immediate and creative response to customer needs, reduction in transaction costs and finally in improved productivity and enhanced profits. Initiatives in these directions have made banks more customer-centric and have equipped them with the ability to extend their services like ;

- **"any where, any time and any channel banking"** ;
- **"single view across channels"** ;
- **"customer relationship management"** ; **and,**
- **"flexibility and swiftness in product design and delivery".**

4.57 It would be interesting here to mention that 38 respondents selected from among the top managements of the banks included in this study formally acknowledged that investments made in the execution of knowledge management *via* information technology did help them in 'improving the level of efficiency', and 'identification of new markets' followed by 'growth' in revenue generations/ developing new products/

services, improving market share and 'gaining competitive advantage' ; see, please, Exhibit 4.8 given hereunder also.

EXHIBIT 4.8 : REALIZED BENEFITS FROM THE INVESTMENTS MADE IN EXECUTION OF KNOWLEDGE MANAGEMENT

Sr. No.	*Nature of Benefit*	*N*	*Sum of Ranks of the Responses*	*Mean*
(1)	(2)	(3)	(4)	(5)
1	Developing New Products / Services	38	161.00	4.2368
2	Identify New Markets	38	170.00	4.4737
3	Improving Efficiency	38	178.00	4.6842
4	Improving Market Share	38	134.00	3.5263
5	Growth in Revenue Generation	38	164.00	4.3158
6	Gaining Competitive Advantage	38	159.00	4.1842

4.58 To find out the current status of all the banks on the strategic front, we formulated 20 questions and the responses to the same were gathered from the executives belonging to middle level managements of the banks ; these responses were obtained on a 5-point scale wherein these ranged from "Very Much Agree" to "Very Much Disagree". While the total scores secured by different banks in regard to the status of integration

Graph 4.4: Strategic Analysis

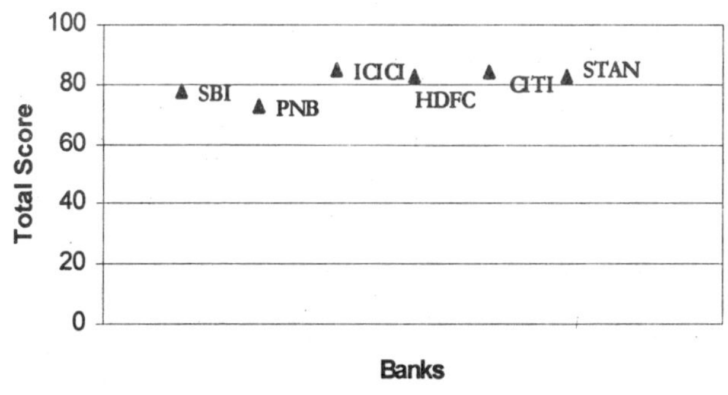

of Knowledge Management while formulating business strategies are depicted in Table 4.19 of Appendix III, the same are plotted in Graph 4.4 on the preceding page 117 for immediate inferences.

4.59 The results obtained by using one way Anova Test are summarized in Table 4.20, 4.21 and 4.22 of Appendix III. The obtained statistics relating to standard deviation and standard error, etc. confirms that strategies have varied from one bank to another bank and a significant favourable variance is noticed in case of private and foreign sector banks as compared to each group of public sector banks. On this basis, we may even infer that the vision and mission statements of public sector banks does not reflect the aspiration of business leadership when compared to the banks falling in the private and foreign sector groups. To make it more elucidate, the banks of private and foreign sector are more customer centric, they intend to leverage their competitive edge and they have been found to incorporate these aspects in the statement of their vision, mission and objectives.

IV MANAGING HUMAN RESOURCE FOR AN EFFECTIVE KNOWLEDGE MANAGEMENT

4.60 The key to the success of any organization lies in how efficiently the organization manages its' human resources. The principle applies equally and perhaps more aptly to service institutions like banks. The issue is all the more relevant to the public sector banks who are striving hard to keep pace with the technological changes and also meet simultaneously the challenges of globalization. In the banks belonging to private and foreign sectors, the quality of 'human resource' is really superb ; there exists an environment that values people and the work that they do. The value to the people signifies that they are committed to hiring, developing, motivating and retaining the best people with them.

4.61 In banks we have a very young and dynamic workforce and most of the banks have the firm belief that its employees are the most valuable corporate asset. It's with this backdrop that we may review the wide ranging initiatives that have been taken by the selected banks in past couple of years.

4.62 The SBI reviewed its Human Resource Management Policies and Practices and as part of this review (a) appointed an internationally reputed consultant for overviewing and revamping of its recruitment policy ; (b) constituted a task force to conduct a thorough and indepth examination of its promotion policy for officers and career path for 'award staff' ; (c) establishing an Advisory Council, comprising of outside experts and inside executives, for enhancing the efficiency of the Bank's training programmes ; (d) implementing of e-learning solution at State Bank Academy, Gurgaon, to facilitate online training and assessment ; and (e) revamping of the performance management system with a focus on competency based assessments and career progression implications. It would be of interest to mention here that the State Bank's Corporate Learning Centre has latest software packages, a Library with more than 8,000 books on variety of subjects and national and international 120 periodicals and 100 video cassettes. Not only that it has in it the facility for indoor/ outdoor games ; gymnasium ; jogging track ; video – conference enabled two conference halls with a seating capacity of 40 and 80 persons, respectively and an auditorium with a seating capacity of more than 300 persons.

4.63 The Bank (SBI) further affected important organizational changes. These changes include :

- Streaming of staffing pattern at administrative offices in circles for a leaner and agile structure ;
- Creation of new official positions to give structural support in different new areas, as emerged consequential to the adoption of BPR initiatives undertaken by the Bank ;
- Empowerment of the functionaries at different levels in respect to their financial authority ; and,
- Further rolling out of six sigma in order to boost up the benefits accruing through process improvements.

4.64 Another public sector bank, namely, PNB, two private sector banks, ICICI and HDFC and foreign sector banks, CITY and STAN too took lot of initiatives for leveraging their human capital for developing and maintaining their positions of competitive advantage. To substantiate, all banks continued to focus on training for its employees both on the job and through training programmes conducted by external agencies. Some of them have also opted for stock options so as to motivate their employees. In order to meet global standards and remain competitive, they are also recruiting specialists in various fields such as Treasury Management, Credit & Risk Management and Information Technology. Linkage has also been forged between reward and compensation packages with the skills and performance of the employees.

4.65 In the context, it would be interesting to note that application of knowledge management *via* Information Technology has resulted in tremendous savings to banks on the score of human resources, as they have not been required to increase the staff in the proportion their businesses have gone up. Not only that, the quality of staff recruited by them have gone up and the banks have been enabled to provide steadily enhanced value-added, innovative and customer-centric services.

4.66 The analysis of the responses gathered from the respondents belonging to middle level managements further indicates that banks have taken several steps for cultivating a knowledge-sharing environment. Among these, the most important ones are : (a) evaluation of operative staff for their contribution to learning and knowledge sharing ; and (b) evaluation of managerial staff for their success in creating an environment conducive to learning and knowledge sharing.

4.67 The Error Bar – the standard errors of means – as plotted in the Graph 4.5 given below for all the three categories of banks depicts that banks belonging to foreign sector have been out performers in so far as handling of issues related to human resources is concerned, followed by private sector and public sector banks. The equality of variance, when tested *via* use of one way ANNOA Test, reveals that it decreases across the bank groups ; for details see, the full results in Table 4.23 and 4.24 of Appendix III.

GRAPH 4.5 ERROR BARS FOR ALL THE THREE CATEGORIES OF BANKS

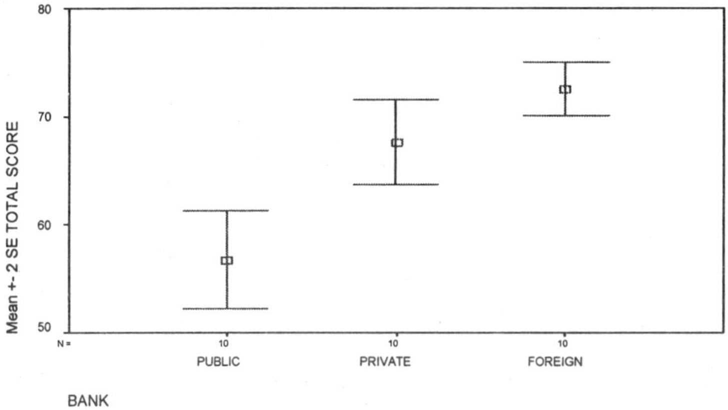

4.68 As is evident from the total scores of different banks (see, Table 4.25 of Appendix III) and their graphical representation in Graph 4.6 the variance among banks is high on account of three major reasons :

1. No system for rewarding employees exists in banks for sharing knowledge.
2. Public sector banks do not have any mechanism for measuring intellectual capital.
3. No emphasis is given on knowledge management in the training and development programmes of the banks.

Graph 4.6: Human Resource Analysis

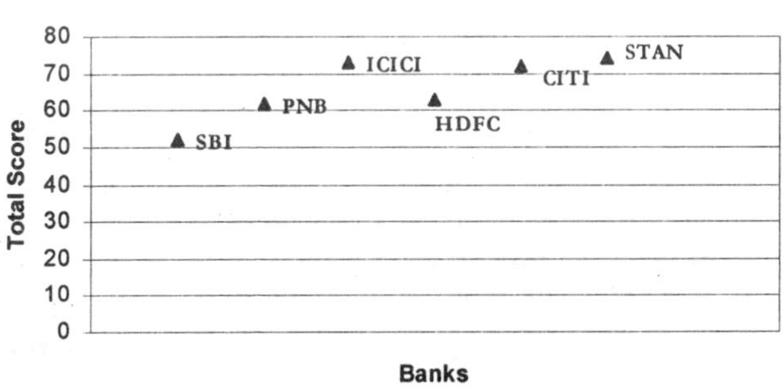

V. NATURE, SOURCE AND PURPOSES FOR WHICH THE INFORMATION AND KNOWLEDGE IS UTILIZED

4.69 As summarized by the respondents, they use wide variety of information as published in the Annual Reports of the RBI, World Development Reports, Specific Reports and their Analysis, Policy Briefs and Discussions, Specific Bank Reports and Publications, Information and Analysis available exclusively through Bank Websites. Naturally, therefore, important sources of access of this information are 'Direct Reading of these Publications', 'Searching Bank Websites', 'Interacting with the Operative and Managerial Staff working in Banks', 'Attending Bank Training Events', (work-shops, seminars, conferences, study tours), 'Consulting Books and Journals available in Libraries/Information Resource Centres'. In the context, it may, however, be mentioned that the chunk portion of respondents feel that Internet and Intranet are assuming potential source of providing comprehensive body of pertinent information. But then, they apprehend certain negative impacts also such as : decline in the availability and responsiveness of bank employees ; decline in one to one interaction ; and, neglect of that segment of population by banks who are not internet-savvy.

4.70 When enquired as to how often and extensively report/information is sought by respondents in their respective banks, the overwhelming majority of them reported that it's quite frequently that they ask for multi-facet kind of information/ reports, etc. and in fact pleasantly they also divulged that whatever information/ reports they ask for is made available to them promptly. This, of course, is but a very healthy sign !

4.71 Set of questions were put to respondents for adjudging the impact of availability of information / knowledge on their work. Interestingly quite a good number of respondents struggled out for identification of the specific area/s where availability of information has critically affected their functioning. In doing so, most of them admitted that information/knowledge made available by banks have not only enhanced their confidence and analytical skills and competence but have had a positive impact in streamlining the operational procedures and specific 'know-how', better understanding the intricacies of project financing, enhancement of institutional competence in systematization of information systems, computerization of libraries/information resource centres, developing websites, and in strengthening of their knowledge sharing initiatives that are called for particularly in the context of providing of global products/services.

4.72 In matters of dissemination of information by banks to their various stakeholders in general, and clients in particular, virtually all the respondents were of view that the performance of banks on this score has rather been poor on account of several factors such as excessive reliance on internet (in real life majority of people still lack easy access to internet), inadequate mailing and distribution list and proactive educational initiatives such as organizing of workshops, services and public forums for the benefit of general public, absence of transparency and open discussions with stakeholders and collaboration with national and local media, and meager number of publications at individual bank level that results into poor dissemination of information pertaining to banks in universities and other libraries.

4.73 The views of the respondents differ in respect to how the policy decisions are actually taken among different sets of bank-groups. In respect to public sector banks, they opined that it is on the basis of the experiences of the members of the board (of managements) and the expert knowledge that most of the decisions are taken. And, as against this, the decisions in case of private and foreign banks are taken primarily after considering the strategies of competitive banks and demands and expectations of the customers.

4.74 With a view to adjudge the equality of variance among pubic, private and foreign sector banks one way Anova Test has been applied. The obtained results are summarized in Table 4.26 and 4.27 of Appendix III. While the overall position as determined by the scores obtained for different banks, as indicated in Table

4.28, is obvious from the Graph 4.7, identified items wherein variances among groups of banks have been are detailed hereunder :

1. Banks are using standard templates for opening an account, internet banking, ATM, credit card etc.
2. Routine knowledge is well documented.
3. Measurement systems do not encourage individual and organizational creativity.
4. People have complete explanations when they make information requests.
5. Information is shared across all levels of the organization.
6. Banks are scanning the external environment for new ideas, information etc.

Graph 4.7: Business Process Analysis

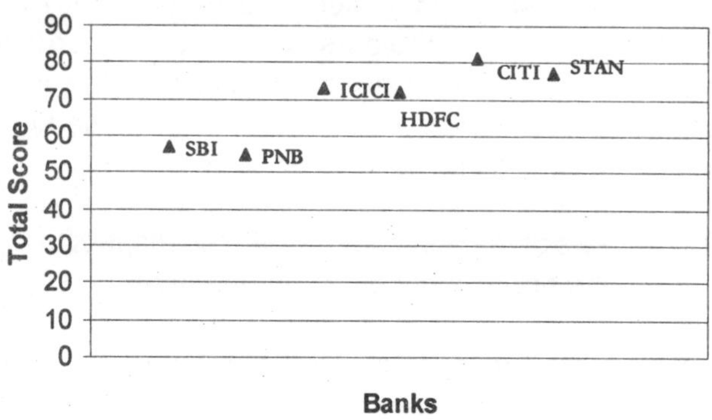

VI THE STRUCTURE OF BANKS

4.75 In regard to structure, the bank-wise scores obtained are summarized in the Table 4.29 of Appendix III ; however, the bank-wise obtained scores have been plotted in Graph 4.8 for an instant analysis on this score. Thus from the Graph under reference it is apparent that the most conducive structure for practicing the knowledge management is found in case of ICICI and CITI (score : 77 each) followed by STAN, HDFC (score : 76 and 75, respectively) and SBI and PNB (score : 52 each).

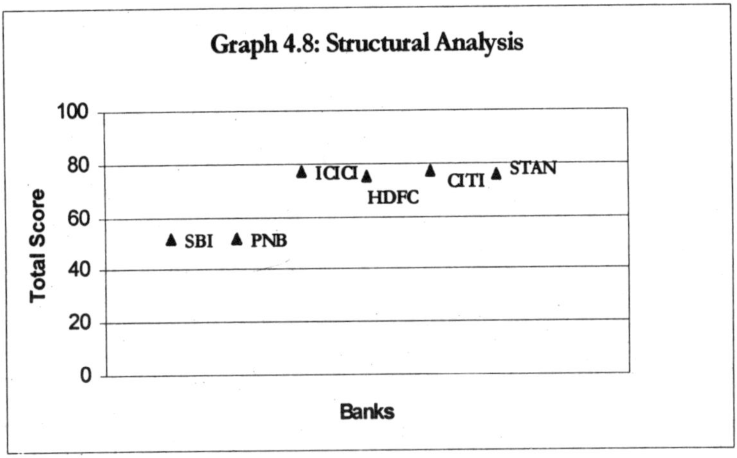

4.76 The other findings in respect to the structure of banks are as thus :

- In the organizational structure of none of the bank included in this study carries the distinct position of 'Knowledge Managers'/ 'Chief Knowledge Officer'(CKO)/ 'Chief Learning Officers' (CLO)/ 'Chief Information Officer' for shouldering the responsibilities of task specifically concerning with knowledge management.
- Likewise, top management of none of these banks has formally designed and implemented the 'Knowledge Management Programme'. However, evidences are found which, in an intriguing manner, suggest that there has been emphasis in the functioning of these banks on 'Learning' and 'Innovativeness'. As a matter of fact, a new division under the name, 'Product and Service Innovation' has been created in ICICI Bank. And, use of technologies, like, Customer Relationship Management (CRM), Project Management, Enterprise Resource Planning (ERP) and Data Warehousing (DW) is in extensive use.
- The last but not least feature that requires its mention relates to 'outsourcing'. Most of these banks have

started resorting to outsourcing of their marketing and other delivery functions. They have started appointing direct selling agents (DSAs) for selling their products like, credit and debit cards, smart-cards and other innovative services/ products. It indicate to the selling of bank products outside the four walls of a bank branch and thereby generating of earnings which are fee-based.

4.77 The overall status of Knowledge Management can be visualized from the Graph 4.29 which highlights the sum total of scores secured by each one of the selected bank on the broad yardsticks employed in analysis. Accordingly, the ICICI Bank of the private sector occupies the first place followed by Citi Bank, HDFC, Standard Chartered, SBI and PNB.

Graph 4.9: Status of Knolwedge Management

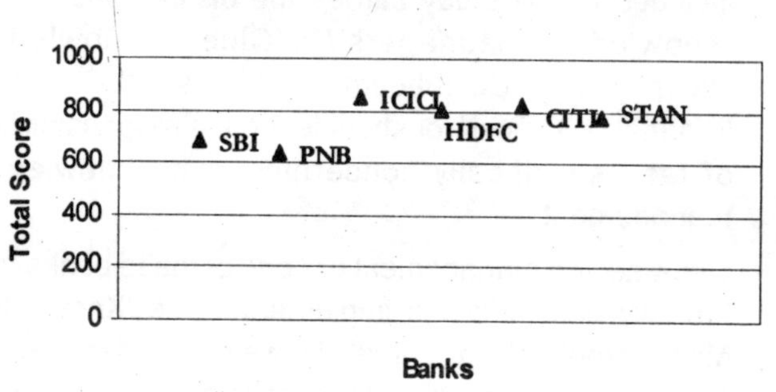

NOTES

1. Anderson R. David, Sweeney J. Dennis, Williams A. Thomas, "An Introduction to Management Science: Quantitative Approaches for Decision Making", South Western College Publishing, 2000, USA, pp.182-183.
2. Farrell, M.J., "The measurement of productive efficiency", Journal of Royal Statistical Society Series A (General), Vol.120, No.2, 1957, pp.253-281.

3. Charnes, A., Cooper, W.W., and Rhodes, E., "Measuring the Efficiency of Decision Making Units", European Journal of Operational Research, Vol.6, 1978, pp.429-444.
4. Berger A. N. and D.B. Humphrey, "Efficiency of Financial Institutions: International Survey and Directions for Future Research", European Journal of Operational Research, Vol. 98, 1997, pp.175-212.
5. Charnes, A; W Cooper; A Y Lewin and L M Seiford, "Data Envelopment Analysis: Theory, Methodology and Application", Kluwer Academic Publisheres, Boston, 1994.
6. Choutdhari Sanjay, Tipathy Arabinda, "Measuring Bank Performance: An Application of DEA", Prajnan, Vol. XXXII, No.4, 2003-2004, pp.287-304.

5

SUMMARY OF FINDINGS AND RECOMMENDATIONS

This Chapter has been divided broadly into two sections. While Section :1 covers the major findings of the study, the Section :2 deals with the recommendations that may be considered not only by the banks included in this Study but also by other Indian commercial banks keen for consciously implementing knowledge management in their functioning.

SECTION : 1

SUMMARY OF FINDINGS

5.2 True that different authors have defined the phrase knowledge management differently but for the purposes of this study, it has been construed to refer **the process by which the organization generates wealth from its intellectual or knowledge based assets.** Thus knowledge management aids in creating a business value of generating a competitive edge for the organization ; it acts as a powerful instrument for ensuring customers delight and in accomplishing the organizational goals from the given financial and intellectual resources.

5.3 The most valuable assets of the 21st century companies are its 'knowledge' and 'knowledge workers' ; although, the vital tools of managers evolved over a period from 1950s to 2000s.

Management by Objectives (MBO), Programme Evaluation and Review Technique (PERT), Diversification, Quantitative Management and Electronic Data Processing constituted the vital tools in 1950s. In 1960s, the complexion of these tools changed to cover Theory 'Y' and Conglomeration and T-groups. Further, it turned out to include Strategic Planning, Experience Curve, Portfolio Management and Automation in 1970s. In 1980s, Total Quality Management (TQM), Management by Walking Around (MBWA), Corporate Culture, Theory 'Z' and Downsizing assumed the place of significant managerial tools. Core Competencies, Learning Organization, Reengineering, Strategic Information Systems, Intranets & Extranets and Market Valuation substituted these techniques in 1990s which were followed by Knowledge Management, Intellectual Capital, Enterprise Integration and Knowledge Sharing Culture in 2000s.

5.4 Commercial banks in India have been the users of knowledge since the time they came into existence. However, the extent of the use of knowledge swelled significantly during the Post-Reform period, i.e. since July, 1991 till this date.

5.5 Conceptually, the process of knowledge management has four major steps, namely, **Step 1– Infrastructural Evaluation :** (i) Analyzing existing infrastructure ; and (ii) Aligning knowledge management and business strategy ; **Step 2 – KM System Analysis, Design, and Development :** (i) Designing the knowledge management architecture and integrating existing infrastructure, (ii) Auditing and analyzing existing knowledge, (iii) Designing the knowledge management team, (iv) Creating the knowledge management blueprint, and (vii) Developing the knowledge management system ; **Step 3 – Deployment :** (i) Deploying with results-driven incremental methodology, and (ii) Change management, culture, reward structure design, and choice of the chief knowledge officer ; and **Step 4 – Performance Evaluation :** (i) Measuring results of knowledge management, devising return-on-investment metrics, and evaluating system performance. Accordingly, the road map of knowledge management could be divided into 10 steps as thus : (i) Analyzing the Existing

Infrastructure ; (ii) Alignment of Knowledge Management with Business Strategy ; (iii) Designing the Knowledge Management Infrastructure ; (iv) Auditing Existing Knowledge Assets & Systems; (v) Designing the Knowledge Management Team ; (vi) Creating the Knowledge Management Blueprint ; (vii) Developing the Knowledge Management System ; (viii) Deployment and Using the Results – driven Incremental Methodology ; (ix) Managing Change, Culture and Reward Structures ; and, (x) Evaluating Performance, Measuring Returns-On-Investments, and Incrementally Refining the Knowledge Management System. To this it may be added that in so far as the responsibility for knowledge management is concerned, all the members of the organization are, in fact, responsible for its execution be they may fall in the category of front line employees and line managers, middle level managers or are from the top management category. It would be pertinent to mention here that knowledge management practioners are responsible for accumulating and generating of both tactic and explicit knowledge. And, Knowledge Officers are responsible for managing organizational knowledge creation process at the corporate level.

5.6 Quite a sizeable contribution to the subject of knowledge management has been from the authors and scholars belonging to the western part of the world ; some of the studies have, however, been accomplished by the scholars of our nation too. Further, the bulk of studies have been conceptual. Studies concerning with the application of knowledge management have rather been a few. Also, the same have been found relating to areas of public administration, information technology, pharmaceutical health centres, etc. Only one study has been found related to banking and finance and this too covered Australian and European Banking and Insurance Firms. In so far as the Indian Commercial Banks are concerned the author has not come across with any study as such. Hence, this modest endeavour.

5.7 Primarily this study has been undertaken with a view to assess and analyze the present status and future of Knowledge Management for the Indian Commercial Banking Sector *via* studying their structural, operational, technological, and administrative processes, and gamut of products/services provided by them to their clientele. Designing the necessary framework for an ongoing effective Knowledge Management System for this sector is another objective that study intends to accomplish. The major research issues focused in this study being as thus : Evaluating the technical efficiency among the selected commercial banks through their growth, productivity and profitability indicators; Role of Information System in Knowledge Management and the current status of the use and impact of information technology on the functioning of and Knowledge Management by Indian Banks ; Integration of Knowledge Strategy in the Business Strategy and Knowledge Initiatives in Relation to Banks' Vision, Mission / Goals and Actions ; Managing Human Resource for an Effective Knowledge Management ; and Nature, Source and Purposes for which the Information and Knowledge is utilized. The period covered by the author has been : July , 1991 to March, 2004.

5.8 Within the regulatory framework as determined by the Banking Regulation Act, 1949, the main functioning of commercial banks in India has been as that of acting as "go-betweens" in the saving and investment mechanisms. Thus they are found involved in mobilization of savings ; facilitating investments and their direction ; raising the level of savings and investments ; and, undertaking couple of promotional jobs. As on March 31, 2004, Indian commercial banking system included 289 scheduled commercial banks and 73 scheduled cooperative banks. Of the 289 scheduled commercial banks, 27 were in public sector, 29 in private sector and 36 were having their origin in countries other than India ; the rest 197 were Regional Rural Banks. From among the various constituents of the Indian Commercial Banking System, public sector banks, although relatively less in number, occupy the most dominant place, be they are adjudged from the angle of number of branches, total number of employees, amounts of deposits, advances, investments, total income-expenses and net profits.

5.9 Marked shift in the functioning of Indian Commercial Banks have been witnessed during the post-reform period commencing from July, 1991 onwards. Thus, until 1991 the financial sector in India was heavily guarded and accordingly the focus of the commercial bank was primarily on mobilization of household savings through demand and time deposits and on the use of these deposits to meet the short term financial needs of borrowers in industry, trade and agriculture in addition to providing of a range of banking services to individuals and business entities. However, the operating environment of banks has changed significantly since 1991 on account of varied financial sector reforms like, deregulation of interest rates, emergence of globalized capital markets, entry of new private sector banks, redefining of capital adequacy requirement, asset classification and provisioning, risk management and merger policies, reduction of public ownership in public sector banks, granting of permission for foreign investment in financial sector in the form of foreign direct investment as well as portfolio investment, granting of permission to banks for diversifying their product portfolio and business activities, setting up of Lok Adalats, Debt Recovery Tribunals, asset reconstruction companies, corporate debt restructuring mechanism, promulgation of Securitisation and Reconstruction of Financial Assets and Enforcement of Securities Interest Act, setting up of Credit Information Bureau for information sharing on defaulters as also other borrowers and setting up of Clearing Corporation of India Limited, establishment of Board for Financial Supervision, introduction of supervisory rating system, recasting of role of statutory auditors, strengthening of corporate governance and setting up of INFINET as the communication backbone for the financial sector, introduction of Negotiated Dealing System (NDS) for screen-based trading in government securities and Real Time Gross Settlement (RTGS) System.

5.10 Cause and effect relationship is perceived between Knowledge Management and effective functioning of the commercial banks. True that Indian Banking System inherited from its past a low level of computerization, excess manpower with absence of skill set compatibility, higher level of non performing assets, lack of innovations in products and services and lackadaisical attitude towards the customers need, yet with the advent of all the age of information technology, commercial banks in India have realized that they must focus on their customer and on the increasing value of their communications by providing consistent, seamless access to relevant information at every stage. These banks are now fully convinced that information plays key roles in devising new strategies and products and services. It is felt that Knowledge Management will enable them in providing better services to their constituents aside better housekeeping, optimizing the use of funds and building up of MIS for empirical decision making which has a relationship with the critical aspect of asset-liability management which in-turn has a direct impact on the balance sheet of the banks as a whole. As a matter of fact, it is for these reasons that a Committee was constituted on Technology Upgradation in Banking Sector which submitted its wide ranging recommendations in 1999 and the same came to be implemented in a gradual manner.

5.11 Some of the issues which are assuming the shape of challenges for the current millennium include : Competition and Consolidation; Management of Non Performing Assets (NPAs) ; Risk Management Systems; Corporate Governance ; Technology Issues ; Customer Service ; Treatment of Weak Banks ; and, Transparency & Disclosure.

5.12 While the banks are busy in developing appropriate technological based solutions to meet these challenges, the future of Indian Commercial Banking System shall by and large be determined by its success in winning the confidence of its customers, leveraging human capital, off-shoring, affecting fundamental changes in risk management and information system in order to comply with new Basel Capital Accord, improving corporate governance, optimizing the investments in new technology, maintaining a strategic focus, managing globalization, merger and acquisitions and warranted diversification.

5.13 The universe of this study covers all the scheduled commercial banks found operating in India in public and private sectors and as foreign, cooperative and regional rural banks.

However, in the survey population of this study only those banks which are in the public sector, private sector and are operating as foreign banks stands included. Obviously, therefore, we have excluded the entire set of cooperative banks and regional rural banks from the ambit of this research endeavour. Further, two banks each having Rank 1 and 2 from the categories of public, private and foreign sector banks were selected by the author for an in-depth study after having ranked them *via* adoption of a well defined scientific method. The names of these banks being : SBI and PNB from the public sector ; ICICI and HDFC from private sector ; and, Standard Chartered and Citi Bank from foreign sector.

5.14 The information / data has been collected for this study both through the secondary and the primary source. Two Schedules were prepared for collecting primary data. Schedule :1 was addressed to top managements and Schedule :2 was employed for gathering information from middle level managerial respondents including software and management consultancy firms and researchers and academicians. In all, 350 respondents were approached which included 60 from top managements, 200 from middle level managements and 90 from software and management consultancy firms and researchers and academia. The author has designed and followed a pattern of analysis, as warranted by the objectives of this study and has employed the Data Envelopment Analysis, Non Parametric Leaner programming, descriptive statistics – mean, median, mode, standard deviation, F-Test, Anova Test, etc. for reaching to the meaningful conclusions.

5.15 On the yardstick of technical efficiency, as measured *via* growth, productivity and profitability and identified financial ratios, ICICI bank stands first followed by HDFC, Citi Bank, SBI, Standard Chartered and PNB which occupies the second, third, fourth, fifth and sixth places, respectively.

5.16 The Information Technology opened numerous gainful business opportunities for banks and also enabled them to perform their existing businesses more efficiently and effectively. The impact of information system, inclusive of technology on the functioning of banks is quite discernible when we look at the growth of ATM branches, internet banking, percentage of computerized branches, ability of the banks to generate high volume of businesses with low number of people and statistics pertaining to business per employee. Not only this, the impact of IT is also visible from the variety of technology solutions developed by banks for use to handle their traditional business as also for handling their innovative products and services. However, it is confirmed by this study that the role of technology have varied from one group of banks to another.

5.17 The banks covered by this study makes us further believe that these banks have taken large number of initiatives for practicing knowledge management. There have been investments on the part of almost all the banks for the execution of knowledge management *via* IT and there are clear evidences which reflect reduction in time frame in MIS systems of banks, better risk management, efficient tracking of non performing assets, creation of new business, better regulatory compliance, swifter adjustment to market changes, reduction in transaction costs and finally in improving productivity and enhanced profits. These initiatives have made banks more customer centric like : **"any where, any time and any channel banking" ; "single view across channels"; "customer relationship management" ; and, "flexibility and swiftness in product design and delivery".** There has been a formal acknowledgement on the part of respondents surveyed that investments made in the execution of knowledge management did help these banks in improving their level of efficiency, identification of new markets, growth in revenue generations and gaining competitive advantage, etc.

5.18 The study further reveals that there have been serious efforts also in the direction of managing human resources for an effective knowledge management. While the description of these efforts differ from one bank to another but on the whole it could be said that in so far as private and foreign sector banks are concerned there exists an environment that values people and the work that they do. They are taking initiatives for leveraging human capital for developing and maintaining their positions of competitive advantage. Further, it is true that application of knowledge management has resulted in tremendous savings to banks on the score of human resource as they have not been required to increase the staff in proportion their businesses have gone up. Even so, it may be noted that there exists variance among different banks in so far as rewarding of employees are concerned for knowledge sharing, accounting techniques for measuring intellectual capital, existence of specific training and development programmes emphasizing knowledge management, etc.

5.19 Wide variety of information as available in the publications of Reserve Bank of India, Report/Publications of Other Commercial Banks/ Bank Websites, Reports of other national and international financial institutions is used and ways of accessing this information include : Direct Reading of these Publications, Searching Bank Websites, Interacting with the Operative and Managerial Staff, Consulting Books and Journals, Attending Variegated Events as organized by Banks. Respondents further pointed out that Internet and Intranet are assuming potential source of providing comprehensive body of relevant information. In respect to the impact of use of information, while they were not very categorical, yet majority of them admitted that the information made available / utilized has increased their level of confidence and analytical skills and competence. Further, it has helped in straightening the operational procedures, improving the information systems, developing websites and in encouraging knowledge sharing initiatives. However, it should be a matter of concern that banks have not been able to disseminate adequate information about themselves as per the expectations of different stakeholders in general and clients in particular for variety of reasons.

5.20 To secure information in regard to 'Business Process Analysis,' the author attempted to find out as to how and on what bases policy decisions are taken by top managements of the selected banks. It was found that while in the case of public banks the experiences of the members of the boards and the expert knowledge dominated the most of the policy decisions, it has not been so in case of other banks. Accordingly, decisions are taken after taking into account the strategies of competitive banks and perceived expectations of customers in the case of both private and foreign sector banks which is surely a preferred practice.

5.21 The structure has been found most subservient for practicing knowledge management in ICICI and Citi Bank and the same is quite close to it in case of STAN and HDFC Banks. Howbeit, it is least befitting is case of SBI and PNB. The other findings are : (a) the position of CKO (or an alternate designation) is missing in the organizational charts of all the banks covered by this study ; (b) knowledge management, as a formal programme, is yet to be designed and implemented in any of the bank under review. Yet evidences are available which indirectly prove that these banks admit the usefulness of intellectual capital in managing their affairs for a better worth. These evidences have been in the form of emphasis on learning and innovativeness, a distinct department of Product and Service Innovation, and use of CRM, ERP, Data Warehousing, etc., and (c) outsourcing of delivery and other non core functions. It would be interesting to note here that having realized the cost advantage accruing to private banks due to their outsourcing binge, the Finance Ministry, Govt. of India has quite recently given its approval to two public sector banks to go ahead for outsourcing their non core work like, salary payment and recruitment. The Finance Ministry officials feels that outsourcing of non core functions would help the nationalized banks in making more efficient use of their work force for sanctioning loans and recovering of bed debts particularly in a situation where some of them are complaining of staff shortage in certain pockets. However, it may be reiterated in the context that private banks have been using direct sales agents for a host of activities ranging from giving loans to issue credit cards and accepting deposits ; although, it is also true that they had to scale down their dependence on outsourced staff following a directive from the Reserve Bank of India : "outsourcing of core services cannot be permitted but a lot of other work can be outsourced and this can help reduce costs for the nationalized banks".[1] On the whole the present Govt. policy is not to force any bank to embrace the outsourcing culture but it is merely for creating an environment for the banks who wants to exercise this option.[2]

SECTION : 2

RECOMMENDATIONS

5.22 On the basis of our major findings and the critical analysis thereof, the entire recommendations can broadly be placed in following major sub-heads.

Strategy and Structure

5.23 Since there exists no explicit and well defined practice of integrating strategic actions related to perusing of knowledge into the overall business strategy of the banks, it would be appropriate if the horizon of formulation of Business Strategy is broadened so as to allow the formal integration of Knowledge Management into the Business Strategy of Banks. Thus, the first step in the formulation of strategy could be the 'Knowledge Survey' which may be followed by Vision, Mission and other stages involved in the formulation phase of the Strategic Management Process.

5.24 The organizational structures of banks need to be re oriented with a view to take care of such vital aspects as : (a) adequate space for creation of Knowledge Management System in the concerned bank – a system that may permit appointing of Learning Officers, Information Officers, Knowledge Officers aside assisting group and team structure for promotion of knowledge sharing and learning ; (b) may enable the employees working at varied levels to make use of internal knowledge fully and in a transparent manner so that there is a strong conducive environment for pushing Knowledge Management across the board ; (c) alongside (a) and (b), facilitate the replacement of the existing Basel Capital Accord, which presumes allocation of capital by one size-fit approach, by a risk-based approach to capital allocation as internal risk based approach would need substantial investments in technology and development of MIS tools (Knowledge System and Expert Systems). For faster assessment of risks and putting in place the counter safeguards, the structure of knowledge management system should also be subservient to key decision making areas like, Risk Management, Credit Management, Forex Management, etc. Needless to mention here that the banks shall have to develop internationally accepted technological evaluation tools for managing the operational risks effectively by pooling relevant data for the preceding five to seven years period ; (d) allow setting up of Research and Market Intelligence Units so as to be operationally innovative and satisfying to the customers ; and, (e) remain updated in respect to market developments and interact on a continual basis with the industry and trade organizations / associations, farming community, academic/ research institutions and initiate studies, pilot projects etc. for evolving better financial modules/products.

5.25 The structure of the banks may ideally allow them to be flexible so as to permit outsourcing some of their marketing and delivery functions aside affecting warranted changes at branch level. Thus they may appoint direct selling agents (DSA) for marketing their products like credit and debit cards, smart cards and other innovative products/services. Outsourcing of several functions, as indicated here may in fact help them in augmenting their fee-based income. Further, the extent of flexibility be adequate enough not only to provide freedom to the banks to outsource some of its functions but also allow them to opt for consolidations *via* strategic alliances / partnerships which would help them achieve economies of scale in their operations and augment capital base. This measure may strengthen the competitiveness of banks by shedding out their non-core business portfolios in favour of potentially profitable areas. This may lead to emergence of niche players in different functional areas and business segments such as housing, cards, mutual funds, insurance, sharing of infrastructure including ATM networks, etc. A word of caution may, however, be added here. If consolidations are taken beyond limits, it may lead to misuse of dominant market positions, and delay in decision-making. Rapid entry to foreign markets without sufficient knowledge of local economic conditions may increase vulnerability of individual banks.

Process-Reengineering and Product Innovation

5.26 A continual and afresh look to the banking processes, and if need be process-reengineering, is called for in all banks so as to enable them to provide value added and innovative products/ services to their customers. In the times ahead, product innovation and creation of brand equity for specialized products will be a major determining factor for the bank's share and value of its businesses in the market.

5.27 The investors with varying risk profiles and looking for better yields may prefer new products such as forex and investment linked deposits. Banks' efforts towards innovations should, however, be not restricted to product and service offerings. They should perceive the customers as an important source of database which may ultimately strengthen their marketing efforts in a big way.

5.28 At the national level, there is a move to look at small and medium enterprises (SME) as a group from the view point of policy thrust and encouragement. Indeed SME sector is soon going to emerge as a group of industries which are likely to be more competitive, efficient and knowledge-based. SMEs will be dominating in industry segments such as Pharmaceuticals, Information Technology and Biotechnology. With SME sector emerging as a vibrant sector of the Indian economy, flow of credit to this sector would go up significantly. Hence, banks will have to sharpen their skills for meeting the financial needs of this segment. Even a few of them may emerge as niche players in handling SME finance. In any case, flow of credit to this sector will be purely guided by commercial considerations. Therefore, for SMEs, banks should explore the option of E-banking channels to develop web-based relationship banking models, which are customer-driven and more cost effective.

Legal and Technology Infrastructure

5.29 Having optimized the business processes, organizational structure, possible strategic alliances/consolidations, charting out the niche operational areas/products/services, the warranted level of technology infrastructure needs to be created alongside its constant and continual upgradation. Application of technology would surely help banks in reducing their operational costs in the long run, although initial investments are likely to be sizeable ; spending on IT by banking and financial services industry in USA is approximately 7 per cent of their total revenue as against bare 1 per cent by Indian commercial banks. Obviously, therefore, we expect that spending on IT by Indian Banking System is likely to go up significantly. In regard to creation of technology infrastructure, two tips may be considered. One, the requirement of investments being huge, banks may explore the possibilities of partnerships either among themselves and/or with IT enabling companies. Two, technology applications usually have high degree of obsolescence. Hence, it would be worthwhile for banks to consider the proposition of sharing of technology and skills both at national and global level.

5.30 Technology infrastructure of banks would enable them to find out faster, more precise and accurate operational solutions in the spheres of deposit mobilization, credit dispensation, investments and other specialized portfolios that could be taken up down the lines in their conscious efforts to specialize more and more and provide customer-centric products/services. This apart, banks would also be able to develop effective tools for appraising and monitoring the credit proposals. Further, banks would be enabled to go in for larger volumes of retail business/es. One point may seriously be considered in the context. The technology infrastructure should not remain concentrated at the corporate office level. It must engross the branches of the banks too as branch managers constitute an important chain who can revolutionize the functioning of banks with the help of knowledge management. In addition, there is a need for harmonious relationships with the Inspection/Audit Departments of the bank, the Controlling Offices, the policy formulating departments, system specialists and even major customers.

5.31 The legal environment is likely to be more complex in years to come. Innovative financial products and services offered through internet, softwares developed for risk management, etc.

may become patentable. In such an environment some of the banks may like to make licensing as a potential source of earning.

Human and Social Issues :

5.32 With greater use of technology and outsourcing of services in different areas, the human resource management would also require a paradigm shift in its approach. On account of nearly total computerization/strategic alliances/ consolidation/shedding of non-core business, a part of the existing work force may be rendered surplus. Banks may either go for VRS to shed their excess flab or think in terms of re deployment for strengthening existing marketing efforts and/or create newer arms for potential areas. The requirement of staff may be in highly specialized fields and for technology-oriented tasks/ activities. The specialist may be required in such fields as Treasury Management, Credit & Risk Management, Information Technology, and in tune with the segmentation and product/ service innovations. The recruitment of manpower has to match with global quality and standards. With commitment shifting from organization to profession, there could be larger lateral movement of banking personnel. Development of human resources *via* training and continual education mode may assume renewed importance. E-learning may be required to be widely used internally. Adequate opportunities for attending workshops/conferences/seminars both in and outside the country would be the need of the hour. Short-term Exchange Programmes of the staff between banks, as well as other financial intermediaries can also help in this direction. Existing Training Modules may be revamped. Benchmarks could also be evolved in respect to varied training programmes. Merit and performance based promotions may need to be institutionalized in order to inject dynamism and youthfulness in the workforce. In order to institutionalize talent management, the priority has to be assigned to spot, recognize and nurture the talent from within. Finding out the ways and means of integrating and sustaining of talent in banks is of critical importance. With the age profile of staff undergoing changes, banks will also be required to focus on the development of leadership qualities among its employees, aside preparing a feasible succession plan.

MODEL FRAMEWORK FOR PRACTICING KNOWLEDGE MANAGEMENT

5.33 On the basis of this study and the literature surveyed on the subject, we have also attempted to develop a model framework for practicing knowledge management effectively. This framework would not only assists us in precisely mapping, evaluating and comparing the existing level of growth that has actually taken place in a bank at a given point of time but possibly also in affecting and controlling the process of growth as it relates to the primary tasks of knowledge workers and other aspects of knowledge management for optimizing the results. Basically it is a four step model, namely, (i) Stages of Knowledge Growth ; (ii) Knowledge Management Team ; (iii) Building up of an Information Technology structure for Knowledge Management ; and, (iv) Knowledge Management System.

First : Stages of Knowledge Growth[3]

5.34 Identify Where does your bank stand ?

	Know-Stage	*Know-Chart*	*Location of Knowledge*	*Work Process*	*Learning Method*
0	Total Ignorance	Cannot tell the good state from the bad	Undefined	Undefined	Undefined
1	Pure Art	Pure Art	In the expert's head; so tacit that it can not even be articulated	Rely on trial and error	Keep repeating processes. Hope for some patterns to emerge
2	Awareness	List of possibly relevant variable exists	In the expert's head (tacit); however the expert can express it in words, diagrams, etc., although in a very limited way.	Experts can dictate conditions for processes to work well. Some degree of randomness still exists; Start with methods that might have worked in earlier problems	Experts instead of all other people. Keep repeating processes. Hope for some patterns to emerge.
3	Measure	Pre-technological	You are able to decide which variable are more important by noting their correlation with desirable outputs	Patterns begin to emerge; experts will, however differ in their opinions on why successful processes were successful?	Same as above. You can be more creative and tweak processes to see changes.

First : Stages of Knowledge Growth[3] (...Contd.)

4	Control of the mean	Scientific Method Feasible	Written and embodied in hardware/software to some extent	Some parts of the knowledge underlying the process can be explicated, codified and written down	Keep good records of what was done, what happened and the final outcomes.
5	Process Capability	Local repeatable recipe	A local recipe based on experience is developed; it often works, but not always, the notion of following a procedure to obtain desirable results begins to emerge. The recipe might or might not be formally written down in its entirely.	A semi-reliable recipe emerges. Some steps in the recipe might still be random or inconsistent. Work processes are tackled using this somewhat repeatable.	Use the records kept in the preceding stages and determine statistic patterns that work.
6	Process characterization	Tradeoffs to reduce costs: a well-developed recipe along with a limited knowledge of how contingencies are to be handled now exists.	Knowledge is well documented in the recipe; a methodology is developed; it almost always works, applying the process in almost a mechanical task of applying the recipe.	Very mechanized highly automated; uses a time-proven methodology.	Use the proven methodology. Continuous application of the methodology (recipe) will allow weaknesses and problems in the recipe to emerge.
7	Know Why	Science; automation is possible; a formal or informal quantitative model is developed	Most of the relevant knowledge is documented; most of tacit knowledge is converted to explicit; almost all knowledge can be codified and built into computer software. Strong knowledge of how contingencies can be dealt with now exists.	Codified in computer software and process manuals	More of the above; this is as good as it gets.
8	Complete knowledge	Nirvana	Rarely possible	No need for knowledge management or knowledge manager. Knowledge Management becomes a natural part of the firm or group; it is done perfectly; unlikely to ever be achieved.	This stage might never be reached; you will need know when you are here; occasional variations resulting in the inability to apply processes from the preceding stage push it to back stage.

Second: Knowledge Management-Team[4]

5.35 A multi-disciplinary team should be created from at least from the following functional areas:

- ***Corporate Strategist***: Sets goals, determines optimal performance levels, brings the big picture perspective into the analysis.
- ***Senior Management:*** Bank's visionary and long-term planner brings long term Knowledge Management Vision which is analyzed alongside the business strategy.
- ***Risk Management***: Ability to gauge the risks and take appropriate position.
- ***HR Manager***: Brings good understanding of employee skills and their distribution within the bank.
- ***Marketer***: Provides a fair picture of actual market performance of the bank and the possible implication of its knowledge assets on the marketability of the firm's products and services at new price-service function points.
- ***IS/IT Expert***: Brings in knowledge, skills and expertise for mobilizing the technology implementation aspects of KM strategy.
- ***Credit Expert***: Experts in analyzing the project proposals for securitinization.
- ***Knowledge Managers or Chief Knowledge Officer (CKO)***: The middle role that integrates inputs from all other participants on the knowledge audit team in a consensual, unbiased and fair manner.

Third : Building up of an Information Technology Structure for Knowledge Management

5.36 The discussion may be divided into two parts. First, Information Technology Architecture for Knowledge Management, and Second, Key Knowledge Management Enabling Technologies. The information technology architecture for knowledge management is displayed in Graph 5.1.

Graph 5.1

KM - IT ARCHITECTURE

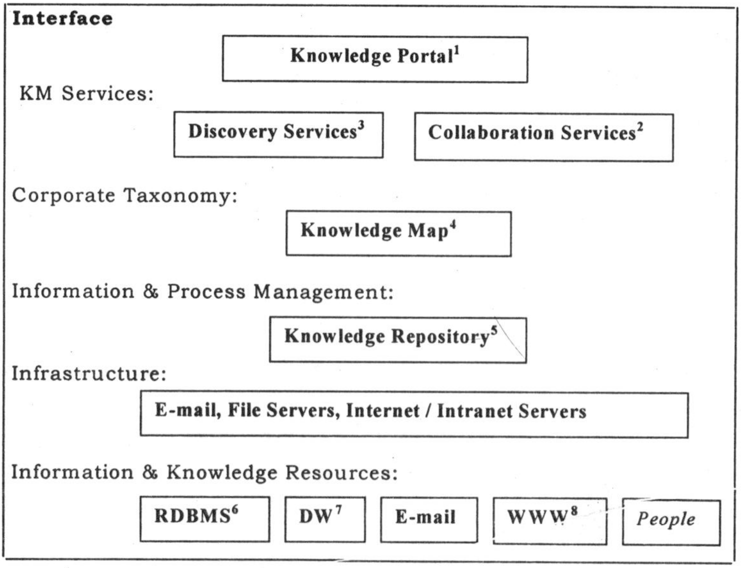

1. Interface between user and knowledge management system
2. Dissemination of knowledge (groupware & workflow system)
3. Retrieval System
4. Existing organizational knowledge combined with an information retrieval machine.
5. The heart of the architecture model and administers the knowledge management system serves as a classification and automatic indexing tool.
6. Relational Database Management System
7. Data Warehousing
8. World Wide Web

Key Knowledge Management Enabling Technologies

- ***B2E Enterprise Information Portal (EIP)*** : Provides a single point access to all relevant information and applications, while also functioning as a gateway for best practices etc. to groups of interested communities. EIP can also function as a platform for knowledge networks.

- ***Federated Search:*** The ability to search across all structured (database) and unstructured (documents, records, e-mails, video and audio file, etc.) sources of information *via* a single technology (search engine).
- ***Taxonomy, Classification, Indexing of information sources:*** Indexing of information sources and establishment and/or automation of information taxonomy for industry specific or organizational specific information.
- ***Document / Information Management System:*** Organization and archiving of documents, e-mails, files, illustrations, policies, procedures, records, audio files, video files, etc.
- ***Collaborative e-commerce application environment and/or workspaces***: Enable organization to easily create virtual team rooms, and/or communities of best practice by allowing team members to collaboratively develop and store documents, tasks and schedules in a secure virtual environment.
- ***Simultaneous Collaboration***: Allow workgroups and project team members to share information in real time.
- ***Business Process Management Community of interest building:*** Facilitates best practices and interested communities by leveraging an EIP front end with threaded discussion groups and collaborative technologies through and EIP.
- ***Intelligent agents, Web Crawlers, Knowbots***: Enable relevant information derived from automated searching to be pushed to the desktop or added to a repository.
- ***Network news and threaded discussion groups***: One of the first technologies of the web to be employed as KM system for sharing information on projects and other topics. Can also serve as a key technology for facilitating e-meetings.
- ***Chat/Internet Messaging***: A real-time person to person interaction.

Four: KM System[5]

5.37 The primary knowledge management enabling technologies are as described in the preceding paragraph. The interaction of knowledge at enterprise wise (co.) levels is indicated by C; at group or task team level by G; and at individual level by I. The corresponding technology enablers are exemplified in each quadrant in Graph 5.2.

Technology Enabled Knowledge Processes

5.38 On the basis of above description, it can be concluded that it involves primarily the five technology enabled knowledge processes as detailed hereunder :

- **Find Knowledge:** Knowledge bases in consulting firms; search and retrieval tools that scan both journal and informal sources of knowledge; employee skills, yellow pages.
- **Create new knowledge**: Capture of Collaborative decision making processes; Decision Support System tools; rational capture tools; Notes databases; decision repositories; externalization tools.
- **Package and Assemble Knowledge**: Customized publishing tools; information refinery tools; push technology; customized discussion groups.
- **Apply Knowledge**: Search, retrieval, and storage tools to help organize and classify both formal and informal knowledge.
- **Reuse or Revalidation of Knowledge**: Customer support knowledge bases; consulting firm discussion databases; past project record databases and Community of Practice.

5.39 With a view to facilitate any specific commercial bank to find out as to where it stands in terms of initiating and transcribing the process of knowledge management into its functioning a Knowledge Management Matrix has been devised and the same can be employed as an Assessment Toolkit for the purpose.

Graph 5.2
KM SYSTEM

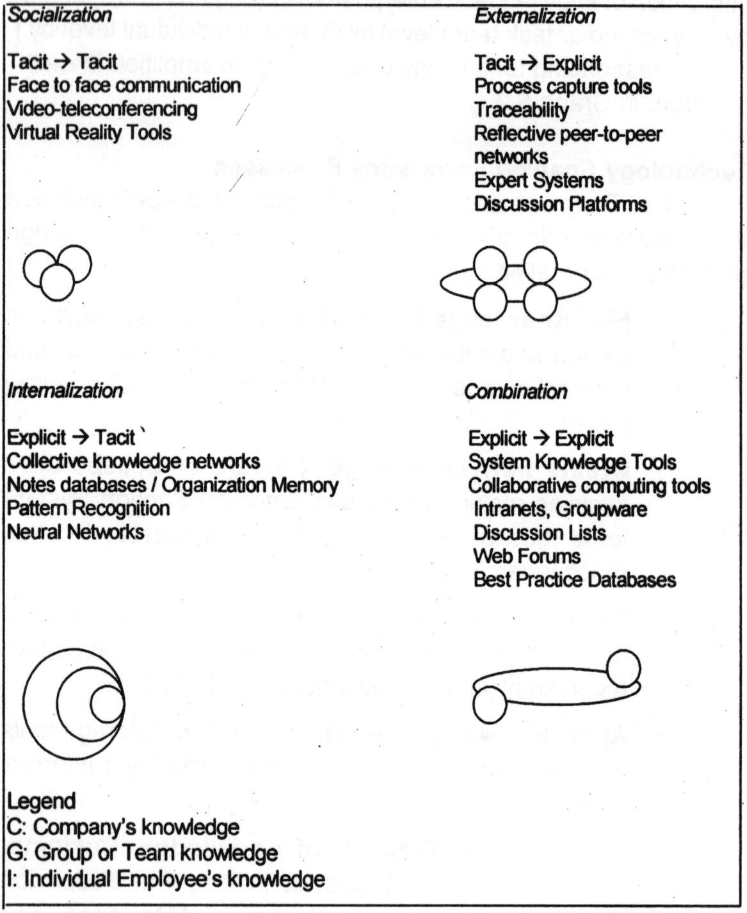

KMM', as designed may be perused in Appendix IV. Among other things, The KMM, we thrust, would stimulate discussion about the knowledge management in different Indian commercial banking units besides opening up of an opportunity for accelerating the process of practicing knowledge management for those which are already in.

NOTES

1. The Times of India, New Delhi, Friday, July 21, 2006, p.15.
2. Ibid.
3. Bohn, R.E., "Measuring and Managing Technical Knowledge", Sloan Management Review, Vol 36, Fall (1994), pp.61-73
4. Jeroen Kemp; Marc Pudlatz; Philippe Perez; Aracelli, Munoz Ortega, " KM Terminology and Approaches", European KM Forum IST Project No 2000-26393, p55.
5. Nonaka, I, and S. Reinmoeller, "The Art of knowledge: Systems to capitalize on Market knowledge, European Management Journal, Vol 16, No. 6(1998), pp.673-684

Appendix-1

Tables

3.1 through 3.16

TABLE 3.1 : LIST OF SCHEDULED COMMERCIAL BANKS
(AS ON MARCH 31, 2003) *(Contd... 156)*

Sr. No.	*Name of Public Bank*	*Sr. No.*	*Name of Private Bank*	*Sr. No.*	*Name of Foreign Bank*
(1)	**(2)**	**(3)**	**(4)**	**(5)**	**(6)**
1	Allahabad Bank	1	Bank of Rajasthan Ltd.	1	ABN-AMRO Bank
2	Andhra Bank	2	Bharat Overseas Bank Ltd.	2	Abu Dhabi Commercial Bank
3	Bank of Baroda	3	Catholic Syrian Bank Ltd.	3	American Express Bank
4	Bank of India	4	City Union Bank Ltd.	4	Antwerp Diamond Bank
5	Bank of Maharashtra	5	Development Credit Bank Ltd.	5	Arab Bangladesh Bank Ltd.
6	Canara Bank	6	Dhanalakshmi Bank Ltd.	6	Bank Internasional Indonesia
7	Central Bank of India	7	Federal Bank Ltd.	7	Bank Muscat S.A.O.G.
8	Corporation Bank	8	ING Vysya Bank Ltd.	8	Bank of America
9	Dena Bank	9	Jammu & Kashmir Bank Ltd.	9	Bank of Bahrain & Kuwait B.S.C.
10	Indian Bank	10	Karnataka Bank Ltd.	10	Bank of Ceylon
11	Indian Overseas Bank	11	Karur Vysya Bank Ltd.	11	Bank of Nova Scotia
12	Oriental Bank of Commerce	12	Lakshmi Vilas Bank Ltd.	12	Bank of Tokyo-Mitsubishi Ltd.
13	Punjab & Sind Bank	13	Lord Krishna Bank Ltd.	13	Barclays Bank PLC

TABLE 3.1 : LIST OF SCHEDULED COMMERCIAL BANKS *(AS ON MARCH 31, 2003)* *(Contd... 157)*

Sr. No.	*Name of Public Bank*	*Sr. No.*	*Name of Private Bank*	*Sr. No.*	*Name of Foreign Bank*
(1)	**(2)**	**(3)**	**(4)**	**(5)**	**(6)**
14	Punjab National Bank	14	South Indian Bank Ltd.	14	BNP Paribas
15	Syndicate Bank	15	United Western Bank Ltd.	15	Chohung Bank
16	UCO Bank	16	Bank of Punjab Ltd.	16	Citibank
17	Union Bank of India	17	Centurion Bank Ltd.	17	Credit Agricole Indosuez
18	United Bank of India	18	HDFC Bank Ltd.	18	Credit Lyonnais
19	Vijaya Bank	19	ICICI Bank Ltd.	19	Deutsche Bank AG
20	State Bank of India	20	IDBI Bank Ltd.	20	Development Bank of Singapore
21	State Bank of Bikaner & Jaipur	21	IndusInd Bank Ltd.	21	HSBC Ltd.
22	State Bank of Hyderabad	22	Kotak Mahindra Bank Ltd.	22	ING Bank
23	State Bank of Indore	23	UTI Bank Ltd.	23	JPMorgan Chase Bank
24	State Bank of Mysore			24	Krung Thai Bank Public Co.
25	State Bank of Patiala			25	Mashreqbank psc
26	State Bank of Saurashtra			26	Mizuho Corporate Bank Ltd.

TABLE 3.1 : LIST OF SCHEDULED COMMERCIAL BANKS (AS ON MARCH 31, 2003)

Sr. No.	Name of Public Bank	Sr. No.	Name of Private Bank	Sr. No.	Name of Foreign Bank
(1)	(2)	(3)	(4)	(5)	(6)
27	State Bank of Travancore			27	Oman International Bank
				28	Oversea-Chinese Banking
				29	Societe Generale
				30	Standard Chartered Bank
				31	State Bank of Mauritius Ltd.
				32	Sumitomo Mitsui Banking
				33	The Toronto-Dominion Bank
				34	UFJ Bank Ltd.

Source : RBI : Trend and Progress Report for the Year 2003.

TABLE 3.2 : AMOUNT OF NET PROFITS, TOTAL INCOME AND TOTAL ASSETS OF PUBLIC SECTOR BANKS
(AS ON MARCH 31, 2003) *(Contd... 159)*

(Amount in Rupees Crores)

Sr. No.	*Name of the Bank*	*Net Profit (Amount)*	*Total Income (Amount)*	*Total Assets (Amount)*
(1)	**(2)**	**(3)**	**(4)**	**(5)**
1	**Allahabad Bank**	166	3094	28051
2	**Andhra Bank**	403	2274	24678
3	**Bank of Baroda**	772	6097	76418
4	**Bank of India**	851	7570	76627
5	**Bank of Maharashtra**	222	2442	24923
6	**Canara Bank**	1019	8170	82055
7	**Central Bank of India**	306	5626	57105
8	**Corporation Bank**	416	2634	26272
9	**Dena Bank**	114	2209	20162

TABLE 3.2 : AMOUNT OF NET PROFITS, TOTAL INCOME AND TOTAL ASSESTS OF PUBLIC SECTOR BANKS
(AS ON MARCH 31, 2003) *(Contd... 160)*

(Amount in Rupees Crores)

Sr. No.	*Name of the Bank*	*Net Profit (Amount)*	*Total Income (Amount)*	*Total Assets (Amount)*
(1)	**(2)**	**(3)**	**(4)**	**(5)**
10	**Indian Bank**	189	3056	35375
11	**Indian Overseas Bank**	416	3671	41155
12	**Oriental Bank of Commerce**	457	3835	33988
13	**Punjab & Sind Bank**	04	1591	14491
14	**Punjab National Bank**	842	8735	86222
15	**Syndicate Bank**	344	3370	34435
16	**UCO Bank**	207	3402	34914
17	**Union Bank of India**	553	5130	51060
18	**United Bank of India**	305	2547	24271
19	**Vijaya Bank**	197	2016	19079

TABLE 3.2 : AMOUNT OF NET PROFITS, TOTAL INCOME AND TOTAL ASSETS OF PUBLIC SECTOR BANKS (AS ON MARCH 31, 2003)

(Amount in Rupees Crores)

Sr. No.	Name of the Bank	Net Profit (Amount)	Total Income (Amount)	Total Assets (Amount)
(1)	(2)	(3)	(4)	(5)
20	State Bank of India	3105	36827	375877
21	State Bank of Bikaner & Jaipur	203	1778	18038
22	State Bank of Hyderabad	301	2528	26132
23	State Bank of Indore	200	1288	11376
24	State Bank of Mysore	65	1192	11336
25	State Bank of Patiala	322	2109	21289
26	State Bank of Saurashtra	82	1026	10874
27	State Bank of Travancore	171	1884	19033

Source : RBI : Trend and Progress Report for the Year 2003.

TABLE 3.3: RANKING OF PUBLIC SECTOR BANKS

S.No.	*Name of the Bank*	*Net Profit*	*Income*	*Total Assets*	*Median*
(1)	**(2)**	**(3)**	**(4)**	**(5)**	**(6)**
1	State Bank of India	01	01	01	01
2	Punjab National Bank	04	02	02	02
3	Canara Bank	02	03	03	0.3
4	Bank of India	03	04	04	04
5	Bank of Baroda	05	05	05	05
6	Central Bank of India	13	06	06	06
7	Union Bank of India	06	07	07	07
8	Indian Overseas Bank	08	09	08	08
9	Oriental Bank of Commerce	07	08	12	08
10	UCO Bank	17	10	10	10
11	Syndicate Bank	11	11	11	11
12	Allahabad Bank	23	12	13	13
13	Indian Bank	21	13	09	13
14	Corporation Bank	09	14	14	14
15	State Bank of Hyderabad	15	16	15	15
16	United Bank of India	14	15	18	15
17	Bank of Maharashtra	16	17	16	16
18	Andhra Bank	10	18	17	17
19	State Bank of Patiala	12	20	19	19
20	Dena Bank	24	19	20	20
21	Vijaya Bank	20	21	21	21
22	State Bank of Travancore	22	22	22	22
23	State Bank of Bikaner & Jaipur	18	23	23	23
24	Punjab & Sind Bank	27	24	24	24
25	State Bank of Indore	19	25	25	25
26	State Bank of Mysore	26	26	26	26
27	State Bank of Saurashtra	25	27	27	27

Source: Computed by Author

TABLE 3.4 : STATEMENT SHOWING THE FREQUENCY OF THE RANKS RELATED TO PUBLIC SECTOR BANKS

(Status of Frequency Distribution of the Secured Ranks) *(Contd....163)*

Sr. No.	Name of the Bank	1	2	3	4	5	6	7	8	9	10	11	12	13	14
1.	State Bank of India	3													
2.	Punjab National Bank		2		1										
3.	Canara Bank		1	2											
4.	Bank of India			1	2										
5.	Bank of Baroda					3									
6.	Central Bank of India						2							1	
7.	Union Bank of India						1	2							
8.	Indian Overseas Bank								2	1					
9.	Oriental Bank of Commerce							1	1				1		
10.	UCO Bank										2				
11.	Syndicate Bank											3			
12.	Allahabad Bank												1	1	
13.	Indian Bank									1				1	
14.	Corporation Bank									1					2

TABLE 3.4 : STATEMENT SHOWING THE FREQUENCY OF THE RANKS RELATED TO PUBLIC SECTOR BANKS

(Status of Frequency Distribution of the Secured Ranks) *(Contd...164)*

Sr. No.	Name of the Bank	15	16	17	18	19	20	21	22	23	24	25	26	27
1.	State Bank of India													
2.	Punjab National Bank													
3.	Canara Bank													
4.	Bank of India													
5.	Bank of Baroda													
6.	Central Bank of India													
7.	Union Bank of India													
8.	Indian Overseas Bank													
9.	Oriental Bank of Commerce													
10.	UCO Bank			1										
11.	Syndicate Bank													
12.	Allahabad Bank									1				
13.	Indian Bank							1						
14.	Corporation Bank													

TABLE 3.4 : STATEMENT SHOWING THE FREQUENCY OF THE RANKS RELATED TO PUBLIC SECTOR BANKS

(Status of Frequency Distribution of the Secured Ranks) (Contd...165)

Sr. No.	Name of the Bank	1	2	3	4	5	6	7	8	9	10	11	12	13	14
15.	State Bank of Hyderabad														
16.	United Bank of India														1
17.	Bank of Maharashtra														
18.	Andhra Bank										1				
19.	State Bank of Patiala												1		
20.	Dena Bank														
21.	Vijaya Bank														
22.	State Bank of Travancore														
23.	State Bank of Bikaner & Jaipur														
24.	Punjab & Sind Bank														
25.	State Bank of Indore														
26.	State Bank of Mysore														
27.	State Bank of Saurashtra														

TABLE 3.4 : STATEMENT SHOWING THE FREQUENCY OF THE RANKS RELATED TO PUBLIC SECTOR BANKS

(Status of Frequency Distribution of the Secured Ranks)

Sr. No.	Name of the Bank	15	16	17	18	19	20	21	22	23	24	25	26	27
15.	State Bank of Hyderabad	2	1											
16.	United Bank of India	1			1									
17.	Bank of Maharashtra		2	1										
18.	Andhra Bank			1	1									
19.	State Bank of Patiala					1	1							
20.	Dena Bank					1	1				1			
21.	Vijaya Bank						1	2						
22.	State Bank of Travancore								3					
23.	State Bank of Bikaner & Jaipur				1					2				
24.	Punjab & Sind Bank										2			1
25.	State Bank of Indore					1						2		
26.	State Bank of Mysore												3	
27.	State Bank of Saurashtra											1		2

TABLE 3.5 : STATEMENT SHOWING THE WEIGHTS ASSIGNED TO THE PUBLIC SECTOR BANKS

Sr. No.	*Name of the Bank*	*Rank*	*Weight*	*Normalized Weight*	*Calculated Weight*
(1)	(2)	(3)	(4)	(5)	(6)
1.	State Bank of India	01	27	0.0705	0.2115
2.	Punjab National Bank	02	26	0.0679	0.1984
3.	Canara Bank	03	25	0.0653	0.1984
4.	Bank of India	04	24	0.0627	0.1906
5.	Bank of Baroda	05	23	0.0601	0.1802
6.	Central Bank of India	06	22	0.0574	0.1567
7.	Union Bank of India	07	21	0.0548	0.1671
8.	Indian Overseas Bank	08	20	0.0522	0.1514
9.	Oriental Bank of Commerce	08	20	0.0522	0.1488
10.	UCO Bank	10	18	0.0470	0.1253
11.	Syndicate Bank	11	17	0.0444	0.1332
12.	Allahabad Bank	13	16	0.0418	0.0966
13.	Indian Bank	13	16	0.0418	0.1123
14.	Corporation Bank	14	14	0.0366	0.1253
15.	State Bank of Hyderabad	15	13	0.0339	0.1018
16.	United Bank of India	15	13	0.0339	0.0992
17.	Bank of Maharashtra	16	12	0.0313	0.0992
18.	Andhra Bank	17	11	0.0287	0.1070
19.	State Bank of Patiala	19	09	0.0235	0.0862
20.	Dena Bank	20	08	0.0209	0.0548
21.	Vijaya Bank	21	07	0.0183	0.0574
22.	State Bank of Travancore	22	06	0.0157	0.0470
23.	State Bank of Bikaner & Jaipur	23	05	0.0131	0.0548
24.	Punjab & Sind Bank	24	04	0.0104	0.0157
25.	State Bank of Indore(N.A)	25	03	0.0078	0.0444
26.	State Bank of Mysore	26	02	0.0052	0.0157
27.	State Bank of Saurashtra	27	01	0.0026	0.0131
		Total	**383**	**1.0000**	**2.9922**

TABLE 3.6 : OVERALL RANKING OF PUBLIC SECTOR BANKS

Sr. No.	*Name of the Bank*	*Overall Rank*
(1)	(2)	(3)
1.	State Bank of India	01
2.	Punjab National Bank	02
3.	Canara Bank	02
4.	Bank of India	04
5.	Bank of Baroda	05
6.	Union Bank of India	06
7.	Central Bank of India	07
8.	Indian Overseas Bank	08
9.	Oriental Bank of Commerce	09
10.	Syndicate Bank	10
11.	Corporation Bank	11
12.	UCO Bank	11
13.	Indian Bank	13
14.	Andhra Bank	14
15.	State Bank of Hyderabad	15
16.	Bank of Maharashtra	16
17.	United Bank of India	16
18.	Allahabad Bank	18
19.	State Bank of Patiala	19
20.	Vijaya Bank	20
21.	Dena Bank	21
22.	State Bank of Bikaner & Jaipur	21
23.	State Bank of Travancore	23
24.	State Bank of Indore	24
25.	Punjab & Sind Bank	25
26.	State Bank of Mysore	25
27.	State Bank of Saurashtra	27

TABLE 3.7 : AMOUNT OF NET PROFITS, TOTAL INCOME AND TOTAL ASSETS OF PRIVATE SECTOR BANKS (As on March 31, 2003)

(Amount in Rupees Crores)

S. No.	Name of the Bank	Net Profit (Amount)	Total Income (Amount)	Total Assets (Amount)
(1)	(2)	(3)	(4)	(5)
1	Bank of Rajasthan Ltd.	68	6130	599
2	Bharat Overseas Bank Ltd.	29	2440	212
3	Catholic Syrian Bank Ltd.	45	3863	472
4	City Union Bank Ltd.	33	2630	289
5	Development Credit Bank Ltd.	35	4412	446
6	Dhanalakshmi Bank Ltd.	15	2106	259
7	Federal Bank Ltd.	105	12201	1346
9	ING Vysya Bank Ltd.	86	11597	1263
10	Jammu & Kashmir Bank Ltd.	338	16794	1715
11	Karnataka Bank Ltd.	110	9265	1051
12	Karur Vysya Bank Ltd.	125	6179	648
13	Lakshmi Vilas Bank Ltd.	34	3197	355
14	Lord Krishna Bank Ltd.	23	1858	223
19	South Indian Bank Ltd.	72	7629	838
21	United Western Bank Ltd.	28	5972	622
22	Bank of Punjab Ltd.	32	4287	488
23	Centurion Bank Ltd.	-25	3385	451
25	HDFC Bank Ltd.	388	30424	2496
26	ICICI Bank Ltd.	1206	106812	12527
27	IDBI Bank Ltd.	71	7929	763
28	IndusInd Bank Ltd.	90	9901	1001
29	Kotak Mahindra Bank Ltd.	45	2153	255
30	UTI Bank Ltd.	192	19613	1875

Source: RBI: Trend and Progress Report for the Year 2003.

TABLE 3.8 : RANKING OF PRIVATE SECTOR BANKS

S. No.	Name of the Bank	Net Profit	Income	Total Assets	Median
(1)	(2)	(3)	(4)	(5)	(6)
1	ICICI Bank Ltd.	01	01	01	01
2	HDFC Bank Ltd.	02	02	02	02
3	UTI Bank Ltd.	04	03	03	03
4	Jammu & Kashmir Bank Ltd.	03	04	04	04
5	Federal Bank Ltd.	07	05	05	05
6	ING Vysya Bank Ltd.	09	06	06	06
7	Karnataka Bank Ltd.	06	08	07	07
8	IndusInd Bank Ltd.	08	07	08	08
9	IDBI Bank Ltd.	11	09	10	10
10	South Indian Bank Ltd.	10	10	09	10
11	Karur Vysya Bank Ltd.	05	11	11	11
12	Bank of Rajasthan Ltd.	12	12	13	12
13	United Western Bank Ltd.	20	13	12	13
14	Bank of Punjab Ltd.	18	15	14	15
15	Catholic Syrian Bank Ltd.	13	16	15	15
16	Development Credit Bank Ltd.	15	14	17	15
17	Centurion Bank Ltd.	23	17	16	17
18	Lakshmi Vilas Bank Ltd.	16	18	18	18
19	City Union Bank Ltd.	17	19	19	19
20	Bharat Overseas Bank Ltd.	19	20	23	20
21	Kotak Mahindra Bank Ltd.	14	21	21	21
22	Dhanalakshmi Bank Ltd.	22	22	20	22
23	Lord Krishna Bank Ltd.	21	23	22	22

Source: Computed by Author

TABLE 3.9 : STATEMENT SHOWING THE FREQUENCY OF THE RANKS RELATED TO PRIVATE SECTOR BANKS

(Status of Frequency Distribution of the Secured Ranks)

Sr. No	Name of the Bank	1	2	3	4	5	6	7	8	9	10	11	12	13	14	15	16	17	18	19	20	21	22	23
1.	ICICI Bank Ltd.	3																						
2.	HDFC Bank Ltd.		3																					
3.	UTI Bank Ltd.			2	1																			
4.	Jammu & Kashmir Bank Ltd.			1	2																			
5.	Federal Bank Ltd.					2		1																
6.	ING Vysya Bank Ltd.						2			1														
7.	Karnataka Bank Ltd.						1	1	1															
8.	IndusInd Bank Ltd.							1	2															
9.	IDBI Bank Ltd.									1	1	1												
10.	South Indian Bank Ltd.									1	2													
11.	Karur Vysya Bank Ltd.					1						2												
12.	Bank of Rajasthan Ltd.												2	1										
13.	United Western Bank Ltd.												1	1							1			
14.	Bank of Punjab Ltd.														1	1			1					
15.	Catholic Syrian Bank Ltd.													1		1	1							
16.	Development Credit Bank Ltd.														1	1		1						
17.	Centurion Bank Ltd.																1	1						1
18.	Lakshmi Vilas Bank Ltd.																2		1					
19.	City Union Bank Ltd.																	1		2				
20.	Bharat Overseas Bank Ltd.																			1	1			1
21.	Kotak Mahindra Bank Ltd.														1							2		
22.	Dhanalakshmi Bank Ltd.																				1		2	
23.	Lord Krishna Bank Ltd.																					1	1	1

TABLE 3.10 : STATEMENT SHOWING THE WEIGHTS ASSIGNED TO THE PRIVATE SECTOR BANKS

Sr. No.	Name of the Bank	Rank	Weight	Normalized Weight	Calculated Weight
(1)	(2)	(3)	(4)	(5)	(6)
1.	ICICI Bank Ltd.	01	23	0.0833	0.2500
2.	HDFC Bank Ltd.	02	22	0.0797	0.2391
3.	UTI Bank Ltd.	03	21	0.0761	0.2246
4.	Jammu & Kashmir Bank Ltd.	04	20	0.0725	0.2210
5.	Federal Bank Ltd.	05	19	0.0688	0.1993
6.	ING Vysya Bank Ltd.	06	18	0.0652	0.1812
7.	Karnataka Bank Ltd.	07	17	0.0616	0.1848
8.	IndusInd Bank Ltd.	08	16	0.0580	0.1775
9.	IDBI Bank Ltd.	10	14	0.0507	0.1486
10.	South Indian Bank Ltd.	10	14	0.0507	0.1522
11.	Karur Vysya Bank Ltd.	11	13	0.0471	0.1630
12.	Bank of Rajasthan Ltd.	12	12	0.0435	0.1268
13.	United Western Bank Ltd.	13	11	0.0399	0.0978
14.	Bank of Punjab Ltd.	15	09	0.0326	0.0870
15.	Catholic Syrian Bank Ltd.	15	09	0.0326	0.1051
16.	Development Credit Bank Ltd.	15	09	0.0326	0.0906
17.	Centurion Bank Ltd.	17	07	0.0254	0.0652
18.	Lakshmi Vilas Bank Ltd.	18	06	0.0217	0.0870
19.	City Union Bank Ltd.	19	05	0.0181	0.0616
20.	Bharat Overseas Bank Ltd.	20	04	0.0145	0.0399
21.	Kotak Mahindra Bank Ltd.	21	03	0.0109	0.0543
22.	Dhanalakshmi Bank Ltd.	22	02	0.0072	0.0290
23.	Lord Krishna Bank Ltd.	22	02	0.0072	0.0254
			276	1.0000	

TABLE 3.11 : OVERALL RANKING OF PRIVATE SECTOR BANKS

Sr. No.	*Name of the Bank*	*Overall Rank*
(1)	(2)	(3)
1.	ICICI Bank Ltd.	01
2.	HDFC Bank Ltd.	02
3.	UTI Bank Ltd.	03
4.	Jammu & Kashmir Bank Ltd.	04
5.	Federal Bank Ltd.	05
6.	Karnataka Bank Ltd.	06
7.	ING Vysya Bank Ltd.	07
8.	IndusInd Bank Ltd.	08
9.	Karur Vysya Bank Ltd.	09
10.	South Indian Bank Ltd.	10
11.	IDBI Bank Ltd.	11
12.	Bank of Rajasthan Ltd.	12
13.	Catholic Syrian Bank Ltd.	13
14.	United Western Bank Ltd.	14
15.	Development Credit Bank Ltd.	15
16.	Bank of Punjab Ltd.	16
17.	Lakshmi Vilas Bank Ltd.	16
18.	Centurion Bank Ltd.	18
19.	City Union Bank Ltd.	19
20.	Kotak Mahindra Bank Ltd.	20
21.	Bharat Overseas Bank Ltd.	21
22.	Dhanalakshmi Bank Ltd.	22
23.	Lord Krishna Bank Ltd.	23

TABLE 3.12 : AMOUNT OF NET PROFITS, TOTAL INCOME AND TOTAL ASSETS OF FOREIGN SECTOR BANKS
(AS ON MARCH 31, 2003)

(Amount in Rupees Crores)

S. No.	*Name of the Bank*	*Net Profit (Amount)*	*Total Assets (Amount)*	*Total Income (Amount)*
(1)	(2)	(3)	(4)	(5)
1	ABN-AMRO Bank	146	9384	996
2	Abu Dhabi Commercial Bank	03	1910	196
3	American Express Bank	-28	3171	518
4	Antwerp Diamond Bank N.V.	01	248	12
5	Arab Bangladesh Bank Ltd.	03	92	08
6	Bank Internasional Indonesia	02	85	05
7	Bank Muscat S.A.O.G.	00	255	28
8	Bank of America	85	4913	435
9	Bank of Bahrain & Kuwait B.S.C.	07	691	72
10	Bank of Ceylon	00	179	14
11	Bank of Nova Scotia	18	2332	265
12	Bank of Tokyo-Mitsubishi Ltd.	29	1072	135
13	Barclays Bank PLC	29	738	126
14	BNP Paribas	-14	2721	281
16	Chohung Bank	04	153	20
17	Citibank	391	25240	2735
18	Credit Agricole Indosuez	04	986	91
19	Credit Lyonnais	09	1439	160
20	Deutsche Bank AG	171	5843	688
21	Development Bank of Singapore	07	336	40
22	HSBC Ltd.	150	20910	1962
23	ING Bank N.V.	-30	229	31
24	JPMorgan Chase Bank	19	615	56
25	Krung Thai Bank Public Co.	00	55	04
26	Mashreqbank psc	12	366	54
27	Mizuho Corporate Bank Ltd.	01	312	30
28	Oman International Bank	-10	573	34
29	Oversea-Chinese Banking	00	38	02
30	Societe Generale	-09	559	40
32	Standard Chartered Bank	855	29312	2847
33	State Bank of Mauritius Ltd.	04	401	36
34	Sumitomo Mitsui Banking	-46	647	74
35	The Toronto-Dominion Bank	01	54	04
36	UFJ Bank Ltd.	01	359	25

Source : RBI :Trend and Progress Report for the Year 2003.

TABLE 3.13 : RANKING OF FOREIGN SECTOR BANKS

S.No.	*Name of the Bank*	*Net Profit*	*Income*	*Total Assets*	*Median*
(1)	(2)	(3)	(4)	(5)	(6)
1	Standard Chartered Bank	01	01	01	01
2	Citibank	02	02	02	02
3	HSBC Ltd.	04	03	03	03
4	ABN-AMRO Bank N.V.	05	04	04	04
5	Deutsche Bank AG	03	05	05	05
6	Bank of America	06	06	07	06
7	American Express Bank	32	07	06	07
8	BNP Paribas	31	08	08	08
9	Bank of Nova Scotia	10	09	09	09
10	Abu Dhabi Commercial Bank	18	10	10	10
11	Credit Lyonnais	12	11	11	11
12	Bank of Tokyo-Mitsubishi Ltd.	08	12	12	12
13	Barclays Bank PLC	07	14	13	13
14	Credit Agricole Indosuez	17	13	14	14
15	Bank of Bahrain & Kuwait B.S.C.	13	15	16	15
16	Sumitomo Mitsui Banking	34	16	15	16
17	JPMorgan Chase Bank	09	17	17	17
18	Mashreqbank psc	11	21	18	18
19	Societe Generale	29	19	19	19
20	Development Bank of Singapore	14	23	20	20
21	State Bank of Mauritius Ltd.	15	20	21	20
22	Oman International Bank	30	18	22	22
23	UFJ Bank Ltd.	21	22	26	22
24	Mizuho Corporate Bank Ltd.	22	24	24	24
25	Bank Muscat S.A.O.G.	26	25	25	25
26	Antwerp Diamond Bank N.V.	23	26	29	26
27	Chohung Bank	16	29	27	27
28	ING Bank N.V.	33	27	23	27
29	Bank of Ceylon	25	28	28	28
30	Arab Bangladesh Bank Ltd.	19	30	30	30
31	Bank Internasional Indonesia	20	31	31	31
32	Krung Thai Bank Public Co.	28	32	33	32
33	The Toronto-Dominion Bank	24	33	32	32
34	Oversea-Chinese Banking	27	34	34	34

TABLE 3.14: STATEMENT SHOWING THE FREQUENCY OF THE RANKS RELATED TO FOREIGN SECTOR BANKS

(Status of Frequency Distribution of the Secured Ranks) (Contd...176)

Sr. No.	Name of the Bank	1	2	3	4	5	6	7	8	9	10	11	12	13	14	15	16	17	18	19	20	21	22	23	24	25	26	27	28	29	30	31	32	33	34
1.	Standard Chartered Bank	3																																	
2.	Citibank		3																																
3.	HSBC Ltd.			2	1																														
4.	ABN-AMRO Bank N.V.				2	1																													
5.	Deutsche Bank AG			1		2																													
6.	Bank of America						2	1																											
7.	American Express Bank						1	1																									1		
8.	BNP Paribas								2																							1			
9.	Bank of Nova Scotia									2	1																								
10.	Abu Dhabi Commercial Bank										2								1																
11.	Credit Lyonnais											2	1																						
12.	Bank of Tokyo-Mitsubishi Ltd.								1				2																						
13.	Barclays Bank PLC							1						1	1																				
14.	Credit Agricole Indosuez													1	1			1																	
15.	Bank of Bahrain & Kuwait B.S.C.													1		1	1																		

TABLE 3.14: STATEMENT SHOWING THE FREQUENCY OF THE RANKS RELATED TO FOREIGN SECTOR BANKS

(Status of Frequency Distribution of the Secured Ranks)

Sr. No.	Name of the Bank	1	2	3	4	5	6	7	8	9	10	11	12	13	14	15	16	17	18	19	20	21	22	23	24	25	26	27	28	29	30	31	32	33	34
16.	Sumitomo Mitsui Banking															1	1																		1
17.	JPMorgan Chase Bank									1								2																	
18.	Mashreqbank psc											1							1			1													
19.	Societe Generale																			2										1					
20.	Development Bank of Singapore														1						1			1											
21.	State Bank of Mauritius Ltd.															1					1	1													
22.	Oman International Bank																		1				1								1				
23.	UFJ Bank Ltd.																					1	1				1								
24.	Mizuho Corporate Bank Ltd.																						1		2										
25.	Bank Muscat S.A.O.G.																									2	1								
26.	Antwerp Diamond Bank N.V.																							1			1			1					
27.	Chohung Bank																1											1		1					
28.	ING Bank N.V.																							1				1						1	
29.	Bank of Ceylon																									1			2						
30.	Arab Bangladesh Bank Ltd.																			1											2				
31.	Bank Internasional Indonesia																				1											2			
32.	Krung Thai Bank Public Co.																												1				1	1	
33.	The Toronto-Dominion Bank																								1								1	1	
34.	Oversea-Chinese Banking																											1							2

TABLE 3.15 : STATEMENT SHOWING THE WEIGHTS ASSIGNED TO THE FOREIGN SECTOR BANKS

Sr. No.	Name of the Bank	Rank	Weight	Normalized Weight	Calculated Weight
(1)	(2)	(3)	(4)	(5)	(6)
1	Standard Chartered Bank	01	34	0.0567	0.1700
2	Citibank	02	33	0.0550	0.1650
3	HSBC Ltd.	03	32	0.0533	0.1583
4	ABN-AMRO Bank N.V.	04	31	0.0517	0.1533
5	Deutsche Bank AG	05	30	0.0500	0.1533
6	Bank of America	06	29	0.0483	0.1433
7	American Express Bank	07	28	0.0467	0.1000
8	BNP Paribas	08	27	0.0450	0.0967
9	Bank of Nova Scotia	09	26	0.0433	0.1283
10	Abu Dhabi Commercial Bank	10	25	0.0417	0.1117
11	Credit Lyonnais	11	24	0.0400	0.1183
12	Bank of Tokyo-Mitsubishi Ltd.	12	23	0.0383	0.1217
13	Barclays Bank PLC	13	22	0.0367	0.1183
14	Credit Agricole Indosuez	14	21	0.0350	0.1017
15	Bank of Bahrain & Kuwait B.S.C.	15	20	0.0333	0.1017
16	Sumitomo Mitsui Banking	16	19	0.0317	0.0667
17	JPMorgan Chase Bank	17	18	0.0300	0.1033
18	Mashreqbank psc	18	17	0.0283	0.0933
19	Societe Generale	19	16	0.0267	0.0650
20	Development Bank of Singapore	20	15	0.0250	0.0817
21	State Bank of Mauritius Ltd.	20	15	0.0250	0.0800
22	Oman International Bank	22	13	0.0217	0.0583
23	UFJ Bank Ltd.	22	13	0.0217	0.0617
24	Mizuho Corporate Bank Ltd.	24	11	0.0183	0.0583
25	Bank Muscat S.A.O.G.	25	10	0.0167	0.0483
26	Antwerp Diamond Bank N.V.	26	09	0.0150	0.0483
27	Chohung Bank	27	08	0.0133	0.0567
28	ING Bank N.V.	27	08	0.0133	0.0400
29	Bank of Ceylon	28	07	0.0117	0.0433
30	Arab Bangladesh Bank Ltd.	30	05	0.0083	0.0433
31	Bank Internasional Indonesia	31	04	0.0067	0.0383
32	Krung Thai Bank Public Co.	32	03	0.0050	0.0233
33	The Toronto-Dominion Bank	32	03	0.0050	0.0283
34	Oversea-Chinese Banking	34	01	0.0017	0.0167
			600	1.0000	

TABLE 3.16 : OVERALL RANKING OF FOREIGN SECTOR BANKS

Sr. No.	*Name of the Bank*	*Overall Rank*
(1)	**(2)**	**(3)**
1.	Standard Chartered Bank	01
2.	Citibank	02
3.	HSBC Ltd.	03
4.	ABN-AMRO Bank N.V.	04
5.	Deutsche Bank AG	04
6.	Bank of America	06
7.	Bank of Nova Scotia	07
8.	Bank of Tokyo-Mitsubishi Ltd.	08
9.	Barclays Bank PLC	09
10.	Credit Lyonnais	09
11.	Abu Dhabi Commercial Bank	11
12.	JPMorgan Chase Bank	12
13.	Bank of Bahrain & Kuwait B.S.C.	13
14.	Credit Agricole Indosuez	13
15.	American Express Bank	14
16.	BNP Paribas	15
17.	Mashreqbank psc	16
18.	Development Bank of Singapore	17
19.	State Bank of Mauritius Ltd.	18
20.	Sumitomo Mitsui Banking	19
21.	Societe Generale	20
22.	UFJ Bank Ltd.	21
23.	Mizuho Corporate Bank Ltd.	22
24.	Oman International Bank	22
25.	Chohung Bank	24
26.	Antwerp Diamond Bank N.V.	25
27.	Bank Muscat S.A.O.G.	25
28.	Arab Bangladesh Bank Ltd.	27
29.	Bank of Ceylon	27
30.	ING Bank N.V.	29
31.	Bank Internasional Indonesia	30
32.	The Toronto-Dominion Bank	31
33.	Krung Thai Bank Public Co.	32
34.	Oversea-Chinese Banking	33

Appendix - II

- Schedule - 1
- Schedule - 2

Schedule – 1

*[For Respondents belonging to the
Top Managements of chosen Commercial Banks]*

Name of the Respondent : ____________________

Designation and Address : ____________________

1. **Are you aware about the 'Knowledge Management'? Tick Mark (√) the appropriate answer.**
   Yes / No

2. **If 'Yes' to (1) above, should you like to elaborate your perception about the phrase 'Knowledge Management'?**

____

____

3. **In your opinion what would be the distinct benefits in practicing knowledge management in a Bank? Mention the benefits in order of your priority.**

(i) ____________________

(ii) ____________________

(iii) ____________________

(iv) ____________________

4. **Is knowledge management is being practiced in your bank? Tick Mark (√) the appropriate answer.**
   Yes / No

5. If 'Yes' to (4) above, narrate the status of practice of KM in your bank

a. Describe the formal policy decision taken, if any.

____

____

____

b. Give details of the structure created

____

____

____

c. Details of the budget provided for the purpose (may mention such details for the period 1998-2003)

____

____

____

d. Engagement of an outside Consultant

____

____

____

e. Outsourcing of this function as a whole or part thereof to some IT enabling Organization

____

____

____

6. Does your bank have a Strategic Business Plan? Tick Mark (√) the appropriate answer.

Yes / No

7. If 'Yes' to (6) above, was it prepared in consultation with the different managerial and operating staff of the bank? Tick Mark (√) the appropriate answer

Yes / No

8. State the Bank's Statement pertaining to its:

i. Vision

____

____

ii. Mission

____

____

iii. Objective/s

____

____

iv. Action Plan

____

____

9. Describe the nature of information that is usually considered while taking policy decision by the Board of Directors

i. Experience of the members of the board
ii. Experience / Opinion of other employees
iii. Clients Feedback
iv. Competitive Firms (National / Global)
v. Experts Knowledge

10. Is there any formal mechanism of storing / sharing the data / information / knowledge. If 'yes', describe the same in brief

i. MIS Division
ii. Constitution of Standing/Adhoc Committee / Task Force / Groups
iii. Re-designing of Job-Profile
iv. Organizing of Conferences / Workshops / Seminars / Training Programs
v. Appointment of Full Time / Part Time Consultants/Advisor
vi. Holding of Brainstorming Sessions

11. Does your Bank Reward Employee for knowledge sharing? Tick Mark (√) the appropriate answer.
Yes / No

12. If 'Yes' to (11) above, provide the details of the reward system.

____
____
____
____

13. Does your Bank provide Training and Development Programs that emphasize Knowledge Management and Sharing? Tick Mark (√) the appropriate answer.
Yes / No

14. Please rank the following sources of Intellectual Capital as per the importance attached by your Bank:

Intellectual Capital	*Extremely Important*	*Somewhat Important*	*Not Important*
Customer Relations			
Patents			
HR			

15. What kind of Performance Appraisal System do you follow in your Bank for assessing the performance of your employees? Tick Mark (√) the appropriate answer.

i. Skill Rating
ii. Ongoing Feedback
iii. Multiple Raters
iv. Peer Evaluation
v. Behaviorally Based Measures
vi. Post Appraisal Interview
vii. Others (Please Specify)

16. Are the different departments of your Bank are interacting among themselves? Check (√) the relevant answer/s.

i. As an effective team
ii. Closely with regular communication

iii. Reasonably well, making occasionally errors
iv. Acceptable, with room for improvement

17. Does your bank have a process for scanning the external environment for new ideas, information etc. Tick Mark (√) the appropriate answer.
Yes / No

18. If 'Yes' to (17) above, then briefly describe the nature of information gathered by such a scanning.

____

____

____

19. Describe the process, the Bank adopts for updating the information about its Competitors.

____

____

____

____

20. How the data / information / knowledge shared and distributed among its different components? Check (√) the relevant answer/s.
i. By Papers
ii. By Groupware System
iii. By Informal Communication
iv. By Formal Communication

21. What are the main issues involved in managing knowledge as per your opinion / experience / observation? Check (√) the concerned answer/s.
i. Sharing knowledge internally
ii. Acquiring knowledge externally
iii. Updating knowledge
iv. Re-using the knowledge
v. Creating new knowledge
vi. Applying knowledge to some benefit
vii. Encouraging the generation of knowledge internally

22. Please Rank (√) as per your Opinion / Experience / Observation the areas of 'Knowledge' in your Bank.

Areas of Essentials of Knowledge	*Very Important*	*Important*	*Somewhat important*	*Low importance*	*Not important*
Gaining competitive advantage					
Developing new products / services					
Identifying new markets					
Improving efficiency					
Improving market share					
Growth Revenue					
Survival					

23. Do you have a system for documenting people experiences (i.e. employees, customers, externals)? Tick Mark (√) the appropriate answer.

Yes / No

24. If 'Yes' to (23) above, check (√) the appropriate answer/s.

i. Regular Database
ii. Newsletter/Articles
iii. Project Manuals
iv. By Researchers

25. Do you have a process for measuring customer satisfaction? Tick Mark (√) the appropriate answer.

Yes / No

26. Do we have the system in place for gathering, presenting and utilizing the feedback from the customers? Tick Mark (√) the appropriate answer.

Yes / No

27. If 'Yes' to (26) above, briefly describe this system?

____

____

____

28. Do we have the 'Single Counter / Window' information service for the benefit of customers? Tick Mark (√) the appropriate answer.

Yes / No

29. **If 'Yes' to (28) above, briefly describe the nature of Counter / Window.**

____

____

____

30. **How frequently you have been developing new process/s for launching a new financial product / service? Kindly narrate the answer taking different new financial product / service.**

____

____

____

(a) **Describe the nature of documentation done for your new product / service.**

____

____

____

____

____

(b) **Also answer the level of documentation done by checking the following answers.**

(i) Everything is Documented

(ii) Most Things are Documented

(iii) Certain Things are Documented

31. **Kindly mention the Current Status of your Bank in respect of the following?**

	Done	*Next 6 months*	*Later*
*CRM Systems			
*ERP Systems			
*SCM Systems			
*KM Systems			
Sharing Best Practices			
Training Programs			
Knowledge Policies			
Incentive (Team Based / Individual)			
Build & Develop Community of practice			
Appoint *CIO / *CKO			
Measure Intellectual Capital			

* CRM (Customer Relationship Management), ERP(Enterprise Resource Planning), CIO(Chief Information Officer), CKO(Chief Knowledge Officer) SCM (Supply Chain Management), KM (Knowledge Management)

32. What kind of IT Tools / Systems are used in your bank? Check (√) the appropriate answer/s.

(i) MS-Office
(ii) Lotus Notes
(iii) Document Management System
(iv) Groupware
(v) Databases
(vi) Data Warehousing
(vii) Data Mining
(viii) ERP Systems
(ix) Internet / Intranet
(x) Decision Support System
(xi) CRM System
(xii) Workflow Management System
(xiii) Business Intelligence
(xiv) Artificial Intelligence
(xv) Extranet

33. In what manner the Technology Support would enhance the Capabilities of your Bank? Check (√) the concerned answer/s.

(i) Ease of Use
(ii) Access to data
(iii) Security of Data
(iv) Quality of Reporting
(v) Sophistication of data analysis
(vi) Decentralized Access
(vii) Flexibility of Reporting
(viii) Web-based
(ix) Low Cost

34. In order to achieve your Business Objectives over the next three to five years, what would be the focus of your Bank? Check (√) the concerned answer/s.

(i) Customer needs Focused
(ii) To be the Market Driven
(iii) Developing and Marinating the Competitive Edge
(iv) Technology Focused

(v) Continuous Improvement in the Performance Parameters of the Bank

35. Check (√) the problems that your Bank is facing in managing knowledge.

(i) Excessive Availability of Knowledge
(ii) KM needs Costly Infrastructure
(iii) Inappropriate Human Resources in terms of their Attitude and Skills
(iv) Any Other (Please Specify)

Schedule – 2

[For Respondents Belonging to Middle Level Managements of the chosen Commercial Banks, Management Consultancy Firms, including IT Companies, Researchers and Academicians]

A. HR Issues

Respondents may record their response from out of the five responses indicated hereunder on the Likert's Five Points Scale to the vital statements related to HR issues ; the relevant numerical may be mentioned in the appropriate space provided for the purpose.

Not at all true = 1
Rarely true = 2
Sometimes true = 3
Mostly true = 4
Almost always true = 5

Sr. No.	*Statements*	*Response (Mention the Relevant Numerical)*
1	Vision and Mission statement directing the business leadership.	
2	There is a clear agreement where and how Knowledge Management (KM) will be practiced in the organization.	
3	Our banking markets are clear, customer requirements defined and competitive advantage leveraged and identified and these are embedded in the mission, vision and objectives of our business units and shared and understood throughout the unit	
4	We form strategic alliances with other Banks that balance our competencies in the market.	
5	We have a strong tie-up with corporate and management consulting firms for continuous sharing information / knowledge.	
6	We outsource skills and expertise to other social and economic development organizations	
7	We participate in industry-based research groups to help us decide whether we need to acquire new knowledge.	
8	Few instruments are, important for successfully implementing and applying Knowledge Management.	

Sr. No.	Statements	Response (Mention the Relevant Numerical)
	a) Creating a knowledge friendly corporate culture b) Integrating knowledge processes /into business processes c) Providing information technologies d) Motivating and qualifying employees	
9.	Knowledge management expectations achieves the following: a) Better Decision making b) Better customer handling c) Faster response to key business issues d) Improved employee skills e) Improved productivity f) Increased profits g) Increased innovation h) Create additional business opportunities i) Improved new product development	

Background Information of Respondent

1) Name :
2) Designation :
3) Contact Number :

B. Strategic Issues

Respondents may record their response from out of the five responses indicated hereunder on the Likert's Five Points Scale to the vital statements related to Strategic issues ; the relevant numerical may be mentioned in the appropriate space provided for the purpose.

Not at all true = 1
Rarely true = 2
Sometimes true = 3
Mostly true = 4
Almost always true = 5

Sr. No.	Statements	Response (Mention the Relevant Numerical)
1	Our bank have a range of well-organized and integrated techniques for transferring knowledge, meetings, email, bulletin boards, online-forums and databases	

Sr. No.	*Statements*	*Response (Mention the Relevant Numerical)*
2	Information is ready and easy available at one place.	
3	Information Technology helps us in: - a) Improving Productivity b) Greatly reduced time to management in MIS c) Better Risk Management d) Efficient Tracking of NPAs e) Better Regulatory Compliance f) Swifter reaction of market changes and customer needs g) Reduction in Transaction costs	
4	The physical environment is designed to encourage and facilitate learning and knowledge sharing.	
5	Please mark the status of technology support tools as a) Corporate Intranet – Extranet b) Distributed to Centralized Computing c) Messaging or E-mail Systems d) Decision Support Systems e) Data Warehousing/ Data Marts f) CRM g) Integrated Core Banking System, with capability for online real time transaction processing h) Search Engines – Intelligent Agents – Information Retrieval Systems i) Online Chat j) Video-conferencing k) Communities of Practice l) Net Banking/ATM/Mobile Banking m) Automated Treasury and Risk Management System n) Business Process Management o) Workflow Management System	
6	The electronic and physical spaces where we store our knowledge kept up to date.	
7	We have a formal policy that insures we share technology and ideas across unit	
8	Training on new systems focuses on how these technologies can be used to improve the quality and efficiency.	
9	Access the utility of IT tools in the following patterns. a) Management of documents b) Using existing information c) Improving collaboration d) Providing better transparency e) Bringing together and consolidating information	
10	In what manner the Technology Support would enhance the Capabilities of your Bank a) Ease of Use b) Access to data c) Security of Data d) Quality of Reporting e) Sophistication of data analysis f) Flexibility of Reporting g) Web-based h) Low Cost	

Background Information of Respondent

1) Name :
2) Designation :
3) Contact Number :

C. Operational Issues

Respondents may record their response from out of the five responses indicated hereunder on the Likert's Five Points Scale to the vital statements related to Operational issues ; the relevant numerical may be mentioned in the appropriate space provided for the purpose.

Not at all true = 1
Rarely true = 2
Sometimes true = 3
Mostly true = 4
Almost always true = 5

Sr. No.	*Statements*	*Response (Mention the Relevant Numerical)*
1	Our bank reward employee for sharing knowledge	
2	We have accounting techniques to measure intellectual capital	
3	Our bank provides training and development programs that emphasize knowledge management and sharing of other developmental programs	
4	Employees engaged in cross training in other areas outside their current area	
5	Training in the critical skills required in each unit is provided	
6	Training opportunity are made available to all individuals	
7	Appreciations and acknowledgements are freely given	
8	Employees have the competencies needed in our bank to take us towards the ideal state.	
9	People are sufficiently motivated for sharing and using knowledge in the bank	
10	The willingness to share knowledge among the employees is very high.	
11	Everyone in our organization can explain the basics about or financials	
12	Supervisors generally consult their workers whenever every problem crops up	
13	Employees are encouraged for suggesting new ideas about the work	
14	Concepts of team spirit and cooperation are followed in the organization	
15	Banks actively recruits for qualified talent	
16	The organizational values are communicated and are practiced in the organization.	
17	Our bank has been awarded in the national/international market by quality concerns.	
18	Outstanding performance is recognized	
19	Proper Suggestions are given to the employee when they commit any mistake.	
20	Career development activities are conducted with each individual	

Background Information of Respondent

1) Name :
2) Designation :
3) Contact Number :

D. Technology Issues :

Respondents may record their response from out of the five responses indicated hereunder on the Likert's Five Points Scale to the vital statements related to Technology Issues ; the relevant numerical may be mentioned in the appropriate space provided for the purpose.

Not at all true = 1
Rarely true = 2
Sometimes true = 3
Mostly true = 4
Almost always true = 5

Sr. No.	*Statements*	*Response (Mention the Relevant Numerical)*
1	Our Bank share information with the customers.	
2	Our Bank using incentive for fostering knowledge sharing	
3	Historical data is using for project planning and estimating.	
4	We use standard templates for opening an account, internet banking, ATM, credit card etc.	
5	Routine knowledge is well documented.	
6	Our bank is adopting new ideas	
7	Measurement systems do not encourage individual and organizational creativity.	
8	A defined process for knowledge sharing (contribution) and knowledge reuse (implementation).	
9	New products and services are introduced quickly with the technology	
10	People have complete explanations when they make information requests.	
11	We have a defined process for measuring customer satisfaction	
12	Groups and individuals routinely document and share information about their achievement.	
13	People only request information when they really need it.	
14	We have established ways for people to document and share information.	
15	Office space is used as a symbol of status in our bank.	
16	Information is shared across all levels of the organization.	
17	Involving our customers in the process of creating and developing new products and services is a well-established practice in our bank	
18	We have a process for scanning the external environment for new ideas, information etc.	
19	There is a process to ensure that competitor information is kept up to date.	
20	The available knowledge improves your effectiveness in performing your tasks.	

Background Information of Respondent

1) Name :
2) Designation :
3) Contact Number :

E. Structural Issues

Respondents may record their response from out of the five responses indicated hereunder on the Likert's Five Points Scale to the vital statements related to Structural issues ; the relevant numerical may be mentioned in the appropriate space provided for the purpose.

Not at all true = 1
Rarely true = 2
Sometimes true = 3
Mostly true = 4
Almost always true = 5

Sr. No	*Statements*	*Response (Mention the Relevant Numerical)*
1.	Our bank has a designation of knowledge management practices (e.g. Chief Knowledge Officer, Chief Learning Officer, Chief Information Officer, Knowledge Manager, and Knowledge Associate. Etc.)	
2.	Collective banking knowledge communicated and supported as an important and essential requirement of employee's work in the bank	
3.	The organizational structure of our bank is able to make internal knowledge transparent.	
4.	Our top management is pushing hardest to have some knowledge programme	
5.	Some special units in our bank are responsible for KM	
6.	Employees are eager to share ideas and information.	
7.	Management personnel are regularly interested in how the business is doing.	
8.	Different department and disciplines are interacting at some intervals.	
9.	Our efforts in effective innovation and new-use recognized and rewarded	
10.	Our learning process often includes gathering feedback from customers.	

Sr. No	*Statements*	*Response (Mention the Relevant Numerical)*
11.	It is very easy to talk to other project teams among the various units.	
12.	There is a complete freedom for the project teams.	
13.	People follow clear guidelines and instructions about work	
14.	My immediate supervisor keeps me informed about what is going on	
15.	Workers in my branch share information about what is going on	
16.	My coworkers openly discuss what they need of one another	
17.	Top management keeps everyone in the organization informed about what is happening.	
18.	The sharing of information across banking units is open and easy.	
19.	Employees can get what they need from the banking units.	
20.	It is the goal of the banking for all employees to be as open in sharing information as possible.	

Background Information of Respondent

1) Name :
2) Designation :
3) Contact Number :

Appendix - III

Tables
4.1 through 4.28

Table 4.1: Statement Showing Recent Studies conducted in different countries of the world for Evaluating Technical Efficiency *via* DEA Technique

Authors	Country of Study and Number of Banks	Input Variables	Output Variables
(1)	2)	(3)	(4)
Sherman and Gold (1985)	USA (14)	• Labour • Expenses • Space	• Number of transactions
Parkan (1987)	Canada (35)	• Labour • Expenses • Space • Rent • Terminals	• Number of Transactions • Customer Response • Error corrections
Oral and Yolalan (1990)	Turkey (20)	• Labour • Terminals • Number of accounts • Credit applications	• Number of Transactions
Bhattacharya, Lovell and Sahay (1997)	India (74)	• Interest Expense • Operating Expense	• Advances • Deposits • Investments
Schaffnit, Rosen and Paradi (1997)	Canada (291)	• Personnel (Teller, Typing, Accounting, Supervision, and Credit)	• Transactions (Counter Transactions, Counter Sales, Security Transactions, Deposit Sales, Commercial Loan Sales, and Personal Loan Sales) • Maintenance (Commercial and Personal Loan Accounts)

Table 4.2 : DEA- Outputs/Inputs Variables of Indicators

Growth Indicators	
Outputs:	1. Advances Growth 2. Investment Growth 3. Deposits Growth 4. Commission Fee Growth 5. Net Profit Growth
Inputs:	1. Staff Expense to Operating Expense 2. Spread to Total Assets 3. Net NPAs to Net Advances
Productivity Indicators	
Outputs:	1. Business Per Branch 2. Business Per Employee 3. Operating Profit Per Employee
Inputs:	1. Staff Expenses to Operating Expenses
Profitability Indicators	
Outputs:	1. Return on Assets 2. Return on Equity 3. Non-Interest Income to Gross Income 4. Net Profit Margin 5. Net Profit to Deposits
Inputs:	1. Net Profit to Spread 2. Staff Expenses to Operating Expenses

Table 4.3 : Statement Showing the Growth Indicators of Public Sector Banks (Year 2003-04) *(Contd... 204)*

(Figures are in Percentages)

		Indicators of Outputs				Indicators of Inputs			
S. No	Name of the Pubic Sector Bank	Growth in Advances	Growth in Income	Growth in Deposits	Growth in Net Profit	Growth in Staff Expense to Operating Expense	Spread to Total Assets	Net NPAs to Net Advances	Technical Efficiency Score in Percentages
(1)	(2)	(3)	(4)	(5)	(6)	(7)	(8)	(9)	(10)
1	Allahabad Bank	22.31	10.46	23.62	179.16	58.28	3.13	2.37	1
2	Andhra Bank	11.92	3.81	8.92	15.02	62.18	3.37	0.93	0.369
3	Bank of Baroda	0.72	6.89	9.95	25.13	69.38	3.02	2.99	0.377
4	Bank of India	7.56	0.23	10.16	18.49	66.94	2.59	4.50	0.336
5	Bank of Maharashtra	23.38	9.27	19.26	37.17	66.24	2.40	2.46	0.839
6	Canara Bank	17.71	11.14	19.77	31.32	67.13	2.69	2.89	0.721
7	Central Bank of India	-1.53	7.14	9.27	102.31	75.98	3.35	5.57	0.558
8	Corporation Bank	15.47	3.18	6.75	21.19	49.58	3.31	1.80	0.52
9	Dena Bank	11.57	6.50	11.27	101.84	67.88	2.67	9.40	0.667
10	Indian Bank	15.08	11.69	12.69	114.87	81.24	2.85	2.71	0.849

Table 4.3 : Statement Showing the Growth Indicators of Public Sector Banks (Year 2003-04) *(Contd... 205)*

(Figures are in Percentages)

S. No	Name of the Pubic Sector Bank	Indicators of Outputs				Indicators of Inputs			Technical Efficiency Score in Percentages
		Growth in Advances	Growth in Income	Growth in Deposits	Growth in Net Profit	Growth in Staff Expense to Operating Expense	Spread to Total Assets	Net NPAs to Net Advances	
(1)	(2)	(3)	(4)	(5)	(6)	(7)	(8)	(9)	(10)
11	Indian Overseas Bank	16.32	12.21	13.04	23.23	74.23	3.38	2.85	0.558
12	Oriental Bank of Commerce	25.54	4.86	19.67	50.14	56.85	3.55	0.00	1
13	Punjab & Sind Bank	2.34	-3.58	3.16	100.23	80.10	3.29	9.62	0.53
14	Punjab National Bank	17.39	10.43	15.96	31.64	69.77	3.54	0.98	0.554
15	Syndicate Bank	26.63	14.57	38.89	26.15	75.70	3.03	2.58	1
16	UCO Bank	29.54	9.39	25.21	109.85	76.59	2.73	3.65	1
17	United Bank of India	8.32	1.21	8.21	3.24	76.57	3.02	3.75	0.262
18	Vijaya Bank	39.97	22.26	23.47	109.25	66.61	3.48	0.91	1
19	State Bank of India	14.65	3.38	7.60	18.55	69.74	0.27	3.48	1

Table 4.3 : Statement Showing the Growth Indicators of Public Sector Banks (Year 2003-04)

(Figures are in Percentages)

S. No	Name of the Pubic Sector Bank	Indicators of Outputs				Indicators of Inputs			Technical Efficiency Score in Percentages
		Growth in Advances	Growth in Income	Growth in Deposits	Growth in Net Profit	Growth in Staff Expense to Operating Expense	Spread to Total Assets	Net NPAs to Net Advances	
(1)	(2)	(3)	(4)	(5)	(6)	(7)	(8)	(9)	(10)
20	State Bank of Bikaner & Jaipur	26.92	16.14	18.20	48.32	68.47	3.54	1.24	0.723
21	State Bank of Hyderabad	22.26	15.48	17.76	26.48	63.86	2.75	0.65	0.875
22	State Bank of Indore	23.60	9.19	13.04	12.95	62.92	3.48	0.00	0.969
23	State Bank of Mysore	19.88	5.00	22.97	52.15	71.68	3.30	2.96	0.689
24	State Bank of Patiala	21.77	19.42	25.76	33.64	62.63	3.06	0.00	1
25	State Bank of Saurashtra	12.73	16.02	17.94	91.66	59.88	3.15	0.00	1
26	State Bank of Travancore	21.39	17.26	-19.24	43.00	70.01	2.85	1.39	0.929
	Mean								**0.743**

Source : RBI : Trend and Progress Report for the year 2003-04

Table 4.4: Statement Showing the Growth Indicators of Private Sector Banks (Year 2003-04) *(Contd... 207)*

(Figures are in Percentages)

S. No	Name of the Private Sector Bank	Indicators of Outputs				Indicators of Inputs			Technical Efficiency Score in Percentages
		Growth in Advances	Growth in Income	Growth in Deposits	Growth in Net Profit	Growth in Staff Expense to Operating Expense	Spread to Total Assets	Net NPAs to Net Advances	
(1)	(2)	(3)	(4)	(5)	(6)	(7)	(8)	(9)	(10)
1	Bank of Rajasthan Ltd.	9.47	13.48	39.75	0.88	64.01	2.25	2.99	0.668
2	Bharat Overseas Bank Ltd.	20.68	8.63	15.00	22.87	45.98	3.03	2.26	0.259
3	Catholic Syrian Bank Ltd.	29.07	0.80	10.67	25.18	72.10	2.84	4.65	0.367
4	City Union Bank Ltd.	27.38	19.24	22.84	70.80	55.53	3.02	6.37	0.445
5	Dhanalakshmi Bank Ltd.	5.38	-3.91	17.30	16.38	63.31	2.84	6.68	0.222
6	Federal Bank Ltd.	23.85	10.70	23.10	29.75	63.01	2.79	2.89	0.353
7	Ganesh Bank of Kurundwad Ltd.	-1.08	-4.07	10.82	16.10	60.88	1.13	1.59	0.378

Table 4.4: Statement Showing the Growth Indicators of Private Sector Banks (Year 2003-04) *(Contd... 208)*

(Figures are in Percentages)

S. No	Name of the Private Sector Bank	Indicators of Outputs				Indicators of Inputs			Technical Efficiency Score in Percentages
		Growth in Advances	Growth in Income	Growth in Deposits	Growth in Net Profit	Growth in Staff Expense to Operating Expense	Spread to Total Assets	Net NPAs to Net Advances	
(1)	(2)	(3)	(4)	(5)	(6)	(7)	(8)	(9)	(10)
8	ING Vysya Bank Ltd.	25.57	1.95	14.06	-31.66	48.49	1.85	2.60	0.496
9	Jammu & Kashmir Bank Ltd.	15.90	6.32	27.17	20.30	57.43	2.92	1.48	0.353
10	Karnataka Bank Ltd.	19.70	6.47	13.45	20.93	61.01	2.02	4.98	0.35
11	Karur Vysya Bank Ltd.	20.30	11.39	15.42	28.86	50.27	4.18	2.32	0.249
12	Lakshmi Vilas Bank Ltd.	15.59	4.96	18.96	20.17	58.35	2.18	5.40	0.322
13	Lord Krishna Bank Ltd.	22.17	5.20	38.95	14.22	38.69	1.30	6.05	1

Table 4.4: Statement Showing the Growth Indicators of Private Sector Banks (Year 2003-04)

(Figures are in Percentages)

S. No	Name of the Private Sector Bank	Indicators of Outputs				Indicators of Inputs			Technical Efficiency Score in Percentages
		Growth in Advances	Growth in Income	Growth in Deposits	Growth in Net Profit	Growth in Staff Expense to Operating Expense	Spread to Total Assets	Net NPAs to Net Advances	
(1)	(2)	(3)	(4)	(5)	(6)	(7)	(8)	(9)	(10)
14	Nainital Bank Ltd.	36.62	15.28	13.47	61.00	76.54	3.87	0.00	1
15	Ratnakar Bank Ltd.	10.89	-8.66	11.35	-12.07	60.70	2.73	5.58	0.155
16	Sangli Bank Ltd.	14.10	-3.11	10.82	3.15	74.45	2.63	6.56	0.192
17	South Indian Bank Ltd.	16.16	9.27	20.68	16.54	67.59	2.16	4.55	0.402
18	United Western Bank Ltd.	19.04	176.56	19.27	12.58	61.94	17.45	8.95	1
19	Bank of Punjab Ltd.	30.96	-3.25	15.25	16.31	13.20	2.65	4.69	0.872
20	HDFC Bank Ltd.	50.95	21.35	35.90	31.45	25.20	3.16	0.16	1
21	ICICI Bank Ltd.	16.55	-4.53	41.39	35.73	21.24	1.50	2.21	1
22	IDBI Bank Ltd.	71.07	24.10	66.57	86.27	26.42	2.55	0.83	1
23	IndusInd Bank Ltd.	46.08	33.01	30.27	190.63	23.20	2.10	2.72	1
24	UTI Bank Ltd.	30.40	13.42	23.51	44.82	28.92	2.34	1.29	0.526
	Mean								**0.567**

Table 4.5: Statement Showing the Growth Indicators of Foreign Sector Banks (Year 2003-04) *(Contd...210)*

(Contd...210)

(Figures are in Percentages)

S. No	Name of the Foreign Sector Bank	Indicators of Outputs				Indicators of Inputs			Technical Efficiency Score in Percentage
		Growth in Advances	Growth in Income	Growth in Deposits	Growth in Net Profit	Growth in Staff Expense to Operating Expense	Spread to Total Assets	Net NPAs to Net Advances	
(1)	(2)	(3)	(4)	(5)	(6)	(7)	(8)	(9)	(10)
1	ABN-AMRO Bank N.V.	22.94	482.73	16.61	33.38	27.61	4.23	0.88	0.409
2	Abu Dhabi Commercial Bank	-38.77	-66.81	2.68	206.67	38.52	0.83	27.39	1
3	Antwerp Diamond Bank N.V.	69.21	211.93	20.17	555.56	37.64	2.99	0.00	1
4	Bank of America NA	-7.24	402.89	2.86	-24.66	42.20	2.30	0.00	0.186
5	Bank of Bahrain & Kuwait B.S.C.	-13.90	280.76	-9.02	-88.68	40.18	1.06	17.73	0.104
6	Bank of Nova Scotia	38.32	40.68	16.88	-1.05	36.80	1.41	9.07	0.528
7	Bank of Tokyo-Mitsubishi Ltd.	-2.59	25.08	0.25	186.47	59.86	4.82	0.10	0.211

Table 4.5 : Statement Showing the Growth Indicators of Foreign Sector Banks (Year 2003-04) *(Contd... 211)*

(Figures are in Percentages)

S. No	Name of the Foreign Sector Bank	Indicators of Outputs				Indicators of Inputs			Technical Efficiency Score in Percentage
		Growth in Advances	Growth in Income	Growth in Deposits	Growth in Net Profit	Growth in Staff Expense to Operating Expense	Spread to Total Assets	Net NPAs to Net Advances	
(1)	(2)	(3)	(4)	(5)	(6)	(7)	(8)	(9)	(10)
8	Chinatrust Commercial Bank	22.61	-30.00	-4.00	-46.13	30.81	6.85	5.76	0.332
9	Chohung Bank	-40.65	-99.47	6.70	10.11	28.15	3.73	0.80	0.069
10	Citibank N.A.	20.83	3399.36	15.35	46.02	24.97	4.58	1.40	0.662
11	Credit Lyonnais	-22.30	-79.93	-6.24	12.95	50.06	1.63	2.60	0.042
12	Deutsche Bank AG	30.51	2162.87	30.20	59.79	37.00	0.84	0.00	1
13	HSBC Ltd.	18.04	6752.02	27.10	161.98	37.08	2.73	0.70	1
14	JPMorgan Chase Bank	0.00	1334.07	111.00	-15.68	53.38	4.12	0.00	1

Table 4.5 : Statement Showing the Growth Indicators of Foreign Sector Banks (Year 2003-04)

(Figures are in Percentages)

S. No	Name of the Foreign Sector Bank	Indicators of Outputs				Indicators of Inputs			Technical Efficiency Score in Percentage
		Growth in Advances	Growth in Income	Growth in Deposits	Growth in Net Profit	Growth in Staff Expense to Operating Expense	Spread to Total Assets	Net NPAs to Net Advances	
(1)	(2)	(3)	(4)	(5)	(6)	(7)	(8)	(9)	(10)
15	Krung Thai Bank Public Co.	32.82	-93.57	3.00	-288.10	24.22	5.28	0.00	0.736
16	Mashreqbank psc	-57.85	22.93	-5.97	-48.69	29.38	2.41	0.00	0.013
17	Mizuho Corporate Bank Ltd.	-3.11	-31.01	-64.13	643.16	44.18	4.52	0.00	1
18	Societe Generale	96.79	1101.21	222.46	-269.19	43.77	1.88	1.37	1
19	Sonali Bank (N.A.)	-8.89	-99.80	-1.14	147.92	53.75	1.41	1.47	0.559
20	Standard Chartered Bank	23.85	8886.48	10.81	-30.22	28.44	4.23	0.52	1
21	State Bank of Mauritius Ltd.	5.35	-41.06	14.90	36.34	34.83	2.98	4.64	0.147
	Mean								0.571

Table 4.6 : Statement Showing Productivity Indicators of Public Sector Banks (Year 2003-04) *(Contd...213)*

(Figures are in Percentages)

S. No	Name of the Pubic Sector Bank	Indicators of Outputs		Indicators of Inputs		Technical Efficiency Score in Percentages
		Business Per Branch (Rs in Lakhs)	Business Per Employee (Rs in Lakhs)	Profit Per Employee (Rs in Lakhs)	Staff Expense to Operating Expense	
(1)	(2)	(3)	(4)	(5)	(6)	(7)
1	Allahabad Bank	2326.95	215.00	2.40	58.28	0.5
2	Andhra Bank	3162.05	277.35	3.54	62.18	0.605
3	Bank of Baroda	3909.55	252.51	2.43	69.38	0.532
4	Bank of India	4383.31	266.72	2.37	66.94	0.618
5	Bank of Maharashtra	2957.20	268.65	2.15	66.24	0.55
6	Canara Bank	5183.10	297.58	2.81	67.13	0.729
7	Central Bank of India	2444.49	181.51	1.59	75.98	0.324
8	Corporation Bank	5252.22	365.56	4.70	49.58	1
9	Dena Bank	2544.54	274.00	2.23	67.88	0.547
10	Indian Bank	3149.86	189.00	1.86	81.24	0.366
11	Indian Overseas Bank	4003.72	232.51	2.10	74.23	0.509

Table 4.6 : Statement Showing Productivity Indicators of Public Sector Banks (Year 2003-04) *(Contd. 214)*

(Figures are in Percentages)

S. No	Name of the Pubic Sector Bank	Indicators of Outputs		Indicators of Inputs		Technical Efficiency Score in Percentages
		Business Per Branch (Rs in Lakhs)	Business Per Employee (Rs in Lakhs)	Profit Per Employee (Rs in Lakhs)	Staff Expense to Operating Expense	
(1)	(2)	(3)	(4)	(5)	(6)	(7)
12	Oriental Bank of Commerce	5271.83	416.00	5.05	56.85	0.992
13	Punjab & Sind Bank	2512.39	205.08	0.09	80.10	0.347
14	Punjab National Bank	3294.52	228.22	1.88	69.77	0.446
15	Syndicate Bank	3383.19	240.31	1.62	75.70	0.431
16	UCO Bank	3316.94	249.00	1.73	76.59	0.441
17	United Bank of India	2299.52	169.00	1.76	76.57	0.299
18	Vijaya Bank	3492.41	249.39	3.54	66.61	0.561
19	State Bank of India	5253.58	210.56	1.78	69.74	0.711

Table 4.6 : Statement Showing Productivity Indicators of Public Sector Banks (Year 2003-04)

(Figures are in Percentages)

S. No	Name of the Pubic Sector Bank	Indicators of Outputs		Indicators of Inputs		Technical Efficiency Score in Percentages
		Business Per Branch (Rs in Lakhs)	Business Per Employee (Rs in Lakhs)	Profit Per Employee (Rs in Lakhs)	Staff Expense to Operating Expense	
(1)	(2)	(3)	(4)	(5)	(6)	(7)
20	State Bank of Bikaner & Jaipur	2945.18	169.82	2.31	68.47	0.406
21	State Bank of Hyderabad	3925.08	265.86	2.87	63.86	0.58
22	State Bank of Indore	-	230.77	3.46	62.92	0.58
23	State Bank of Mysore	2786.92	162.81	1.82	71.68	0.367
24	State Bank of Patiala	4760.32	305.24	3.69	62.63	0.717
25	State Bank of Saurashtra	3718.51	193.16	2.40	59.88	0.586
26	State Bank of Travancore	3985.08	271.78	2.04	70.01	0.537
	Mean					0.549

Source : RBI : Trend and Progress Report for the year 2003-04

Table 4.7: Statement Showing Productivity Indicators of Private Sector Banks (Year 2003-04) *(Contd...216)*

(Figures are in Percentages)

S. No	Name of the Private Sector Bank	Indicators of Outputs		Indicators of Inputs		Technical Efficiency Score in Percentages
		Business Per Branch (Rs in Lakhs)	Business Per Employee (Rs in Lakhs)	Profit Per Employee (Rs in Lakhs)	Staff Expense to Operating Expense	
(1)	(2)	(3)	(4)	(5)	(6)	(7)
1	Bank of Rajasthan Ltd.	2763.35	199.93	1.67	64.01	0.066
2	Bharat Overseas Bank Ltd.	4598.87	370.00	3.41	45.98	0.169
3	Catholic Syrian Bank Ltd.	1858.10	182.16	1.95	72.10	0.053
4	City Union Bank Ltd.	3353.91	286.80	4.09	55.53	0.109
5	Dhanalakshmi Bank Ltd.	1926.53	248.63	1.32	63.31	0.083
6	Federal Bank Ltd.	4748.26	327.00	2.14	63.01	0.109
7	Ganesh Bank of Kurundwad Ltd.	1018.10	126.21	0.57	60.88	0.044
8	ING Vysya Bank Ltd.	4540.04	324.34	1.24	48.49	0.141
9	Jammu & Kashmir Bank Ltd.	6529.51	345.00	5.74	57.43	0.127

Table 4.7: Statement Showing Productivity Indicators of Private Sector Banks (Year 2003-04) *(Contd...217)*

(Figures are in Percentages)

S. No	*Name of the Private Sector Bank*	*Indicators of Outputs*		*Indicators of Inputs*		*Technical Efficiency Score in Percentages*
		Business Per Branch (Rs in Lakhs)	*Business Per Employee (Rs in Lakhs)*	*Profit Per Employee (Rs in Lakhs)*	*Staff Expense to Operating Expense*	
(1)	**(2)**	**(3)**	**(4)**	**(5)**	**(6)**	**(7)**
10	Karnataka Bank Ltd.	3665.33	320.23	3.10	61.01	0.11
11	Karur Vysya Bank Ltd.	4245.61	330.00	5.65	50.27	0.139
12	Lakshmi Vilas Bank Ltd.	2232.02	276.00	2.11	58.35	0.099
13	Lord Krishna Bank Ltd.	3089.29	308.94	2.38	38.69	0.168
14	Nainital Bank Ltd.	1630.02	124.56	2.02	76.54	0.034
15	Ratnakar Bank Ltd.	1473.92	198.36	1.58	60.70	0.069
16	Sangli Bank Ltd.	1312.88	95.70	0.61	74.45	0.027
17	South Indian Bank Ltd.	3006.47	306.00	2.39	67.59	0.095
18	United Western Bank Ltd.	4275.07	290.00	0.96	61.94	0.098
19	Bank of Punjab Ltd.	5900.32	444.54	3.09	13.20	0.708

Table 4.7 : Statement Showing Productivity Indicators ofPrivate Sector Banks (Year 2003-04)

(Figures are in Percentages)

S. No	Name of the Private Sector Bank	Indicators of Outputs		Indicators of Inputs		Technical Efficiency Score in Percentages
		Business Per Branch (Rs in Lakhs)	Business Per Employee (Rs in Lakhs)	Profit Per Employee (Rs in Lakhs)	Staff Expense to Operating Expense	
(1)	(2)	(3)	(4)	(5)	(6)	(7)
20	HDFC Bank Ltd.	16323.18	866.00	8.98	25.20	0.723
21	ICICI Bank Ltd.	31149.31	1010.00	12.03	21.24	1
22	IDBI Bank Ltd.	18760.29	1080.31	9.12	26.42	0.86
23	IndusInd Bank Ltd.	30665.32	1079.95	30.37	23.20	1
24	UTI Bank Ltd.	16476.55	808.00	8.07	28.92	0.588
	Mean					**0.276**

Source : RBI : Trend and Progress Report for the year 2003-04

Table 4.8 : Statement Showing Productivity Indicators of Foreign Banks (Year 2003-04) *(Contd... 219)*

(Figures are in Percentages)

S. No	Name of the Foreign Bank	Indicators of Outputs		Indicators of Inputs		Technical Efficiency Score in Percentages
		Business Per Branch (Rs in Lakhs)	Business Per Employee (Rs in Lakhs)	Profit Per Employee (Rs in Lakhs)	Staff Expense to Operating Expense	
(1)	(2)	(3)	(4)	(5)	(6)	(7)
1.	ABN-AMRO Bank N.V.	78456.38	891.45	15.22	27.61	0.497
2.	Abu Dhabi Commercial Bank	99178.00	1407.67	12.68	38.52	0.547
3.	Antwerp Diamond Bank N.V.	34219.00	1723.61	32.85	37.64	0.728
4.	Bank of America NA	232425.50	1747.56	24.12	42.20	0.962
5.	Bank of Bahrain & Kuwait B.S.C.	73699.00	784.00	1.00	40.18	0.321
6.	Bank of Nova Scotia	123776.33	1678.52	9.96	36.80	0.683
7.	Bank of Tokyo-Mitsubishi Ltd.	100628.00	582.27	48.58	59.86	0.506
8.	Chinatrust Commercial Bank	15208.00	800.45	7.69	30.81	0.389
9.	Chohung Bank	10421.00	744.38	29.62	28.15	0.662
10.	Citibank N.A.	142897.00	1666.92	28.33	24.97	1
11.	Credit Lyonnais	36090.25	1401.56	9.41	50.06	0.419
12.	Deutsche Bank AG	92611.20	1099.23	65.23	37.00	1
13.	HSBC Ltd.	72088.75	820.91	6.32	37.08	0.34

Table 4.8 : Statement Showing Productivity Indicators of Foreign Banks (Year 2003-04)

(Figures are in Percentages)

S. No	Name of the Foreign Bank	Indicators of Outputs		Indicators of Inputs		Technical Efficiency Score in Percentages
		Business Per Branch (Rs in Lakhs)	Business Per Employee (Rs in Lakhs)	Profit Per Employee (Rs in Lakhs)	Staff Expense to Operating Expense	
(1)	(2)	(3)	(4)	(5)	(6)	(7)
14.	JPMorgan Chase Bank	39178.00	259.33	28.74	53.38	0.305
15.	Krung Thai Bank Public Co.	3200.00	291.03	7.12	24.22	0.22
16.	Mashreqbank psc	14833.00	865.85	50.53	29.38	0.979
17.	Mizuho Corporate Bank Ltd.	23305.00	527.80	16.05	44.18	0.25
18.	Societe Generale	29164.50	1017.00	25.40	43.77	0.43
19.	Sonali Bank (N.A.)	3428.00	74.54	2.57	53.75	0.031
20.	Standard Chartered Bank	50846.82	780.11	13.37	28.44	0.413
21.	State Bank of Mauritius Ltd.	14727.33	1523.00	20.00	34.83	0.655
	Mean					**0.54**

Source : RBI : Trend and Progress Report for the year 2003-04

Table 4.9 : Statement Showing the Profitability Indicators of Public Sector Banks (Year 2003-04) *(Contd... 221)*

(Figures are in Percentages)

S. No	Name of the Pubic Sector Bank	Indicators of Outputs				Indicators of Inputs			Technical Efficiency Score in Percentages
		Return on Assets	Return on Equity	Non-Interest Income to Gross Income	Net Profit Margin	Net Profit to Deposits	Staff Expense to Operating Expense	Net Profit to Spread	
(1)	(2)	(3)	(4)	(5)	(6)	(7)	(8)	(9)	(10)
1	Allahabad Bank	1.34	34.00	21.93	13.56	1.47	58.28	42.68	1
2	Andhra Bank	1.72	36.10	23.34	15.95	2.02	62.18	50.90	1
3	Bank of Baroda	1.20	20.32	21.85	12.29	1.33	69.38	37.60	0.948
4	Bank of India	1.25	26.71	23.62	13.29	1.42	66.94	45.80	0.908
5	Bank of Maharashtra	0.95	25.21	17.43	11.41	1.15	66.24	39.46	0.83
6	Canara Bank	1.34	28.47	22.83	14.74	1.55	67.13	49.88	0.887
7	Central Bank of India	0.98	22.90	16.00	10.25	1.11	75.98	29.13	0.95
8	Corporation Bank	1.96	19.62	19.01	18.55	2.17	49.58	52.30	1
9	Dena Bank	1.11	19.89	26.24	9.80	1.26	67.88	38.92	1
10	Indian Bank	1.21	7.61	21.89	11.88	1.33	81.24	36.32	0.912

Table 4.9 : Statement Showing the Profitability Indicators of Public Sector Banks (Year 2003-04) *(Contd...222)*

(Figures are in Percentages)

S. No	Name of the Pubic Sector Bank	Indicators of Outputs				Indicators of Inputs			Technical Efficiency Score in Percentages
		Return on Assets	Return on Equity	Non-Interest Income to Gross Income	Net Profit Margin	Net Profit to Deposits	Staff Expense to Operating Expense	Net Profit to Spread	
(1)	(2)	(3)	(4)	(5)	(6)	(7)	(8)	(9)	(10)
11	Indian Overseas Bank	1.08	28.96	16.48	11.41	1.24	74.23	32.06	1
12	Oriental Bank of Commerce	1.70	28.67	17.94	17.06	1.92	56.85	47.13	1
13	Punjab & Sind Bank	0.06	1.92	16.68	0.58	0.07	80.10	1.80	1
14	Punjab National Bank	1.08	24.52	19.35	11.49	1.26	69.77	30.59	1
15	Syndicate Bank	1.67	24.92	20.11	11.24	1.02	75.70	30.38	1
16	UCO Bank	1.13	29.10	16.80	11.70	1.11	76.59	36.45	0.912
17	United Bank of India	1.25	16.07	19.60	12.22	1.38	76.57	40.37	0.837
18	Vijaya Bank	1.91	38.32	21.32	16.68	1.96	66.61	49.10	1

Table 4.9 : Statement Showing the Profitability Indicators of Public Sector Banks (Year 2003-04)

(Figures are in Percentages)

S. No	Name of the Pubic Sector Bank	Indicators of Outputs				Indicators of Inputs			Technical Efficiency Score in Percentages
		Return on Assets	Return on Equity	Non-Interest Income to Gross Income	Net Profit Margin	Net Profit to Deposits	Staff Expense to Operating Expense	Net Profit to Spread	
(1)	(2)	(3)	(4)	(5)	(6)	(7)	(8)	(9)	(10)
19	State Bank of India	0.94	19.67	19.99	9.67	1.16	69.74	32.91	0.886
20	State Bank of Bikaner & Jaipur	1.49	29.39	23.80	14.60	1.93	68.47	42.08	1
21	State Bank of Hyderabad	1.25	26.99	24.22	13.05	1.57	63.86	45.31	0.948
22	State Bank of Indore	1.73	32.94	25.64	16.08	2.17	62.92	49.90	1
23	State Bank of Mysore	1.28	34.83	24.36	12.62	1.59	71.68	38.81	1
24	State Bank of Patiala	1.60	27.39	25.03	17.09	1.91	62.63	52.34	0.992
25	State Bank of Saurashtra	1.38	25.47	24.68	13.66	1.66	59.88	43.93	1
26	State Bank of Travancore	1.02	29.68	21.27	11.07	1.54	70.01	35.79	1
	Mean								**0.962**

Source : RBI : Trend and Progress Report for the year 2003-04

Table 4.10 : Statement Showing the Profitability Indicators of Private Sector Banks (Year 2003-04) *(Contd...224)*

(Figures are in Percentages)

S. No	Name of the Private Sector Bank	Indicators of Outputs				Indicators of Inputs			Technical Efficiency Score in Percentages
		Return on Assets	Return on Equity	Non-Interest Income to Gross Income	Net Profit Margin	Net Profit to Deposits	Staff Expense to Operating Expense	Net Profit to Spread	
(1)	(2)	(3)	(4)	(5)	(6)	(7)	(8)	(9)	(10)
1	Bank of Rajasthan Ltd.	0.82	22.46	26.04	10.15	0.93	64.01	36.36	0.81
2	Bharat Overseas Bank Ltd.	1.25	22.45	13.75	15.24	1.42	45.98	41.12	0.859
3	Catholic Syrian Bank Ltd.	1.31	33.83	24.96	11.87	1.46	72.10	46.22	0.904
4	City Union Bank Ltd.	1.86	31.03	19.40	16.64	2.00	55.53	59.25	0.852
5	Dhanalakshmi Bank Ltd.	0.71	13.74	23.34	7.01	0.81	63.31	25.19	0.851
6	Federal Bank Ltd.	0.90	23.14	19.99	9.15	1.01	63.01	32.31	0.832
7	Ganesh Bank of Kurundwad Ltd.	0.86	10.43	19.57	5.99	0.66	60.88	54.37	0.435
8	ING Vysya Bank Ltd.	0.45	8.12	28.22	4.58	0.56	48.49	24.17	1
9	Jammu & Kashmir Bank Ltd.	1.92	28.66	16.55	22.29	2.18	57.43	65.55	0.766

Table 4.10 : Statement Showing the Profitability Indicators of Private Sector Banks (Year 2003-04) *(Contd... 225)*

(Figures are in Percentages)

S. No	Name of the Private Sector Bank	Indicators of Outputs				Indicators of Inputs			Technical Efficiency Score in Percentages
		Return on Assets	Return on Equity	Non-Interest Income to Gross Income	Net Profit Margin	Net Profit to Deposits	Staff Expense to Operating Expense	Net Profit to Spread	
(1)	(2)	(3)	(4)	(5)	(6)	(7)	(8)	(9)	(10)
9	Jammu & Kashmir Bank Ltd.	1.92	28.66	16.55	22.29	2.18	57.43	65.55	0.766
10	Karnataka Bank Ltd.	1.34	20.78	24.16	11.90	1.42	61.01	62.33	0.573
11	Karur Vysya Bank Ltd.	2.43	25.35	10.29	22.31	2.72	50.27	54.19	1
12	Lakshmi Vilas Bank Ltd.	1.19	19.61	23.30	11.01	1.25	58.35	49.20	0.639
13	Lord Krishna Bank Ltd.	1.33	20.54	29.03	11.24	1.14	38.69	77.73	0.549
14	Nainital Bank Ltd.	1.58	19.62	15.72	14.69	1.61	76.54	36.94	0.893
15	Ratnakar Bank Ltd.	1.12	17.87	15.40	10.97	1.18	60.70	37.93	0.692
16	Sangli Bank Ltd.	0.64	14.56	18.41	7.34	0.65	74.45	23.15	0.812
17	South Indian Bank Ltd.	1.00	23.56	25.69	9.21	1.02	67.59	42.11	0.718

Table 4.10 : Statement Showing the Profitability Indicators of Private Sector Banks (Year 2003-04)

(Figures are in Percentages)

S. No	Name of the Private Sector Bank	Indicators of Outputs				Indicators of Inputs			Technical Efficiency Score in Percentages
		Return on Assets	Return on Equity	Non-Interest Income to Gross Income	Net Profit Margin	Net Profit to Deposits	Staff Expense to Operating Expense	Net Profit to Spread	
(1)	(2)	(3)	(4)	(5)	(6)	(7)	(8)	(9)	(10)
18	United Western Bank Ltd.	0.43	10.62	7.74	1.80	0.48	61.94	2.49	1
19	Bank of Punjab Ltd.	0.85	16.15	28.03	7.84	0.89	13.20	28.89	1
20	HDFC Bank Ltd.	1.45	20.61	15.85	16.82	1.68	25.20	38.08	1
21	ICICI Bank Ltd.	1.31	20.93	25.63	13.69	2.40	21.24	87.14	1
22	IDBI Bank Ltd.	1.02	27.24	22.20	13.99	1.32	26.42	40.01	1
23	IndusInd Bank Ltd.	1.74	37.37	25.91	19.69	2.34	23.20	82.70	1
24	UTI Bank Ltd.	1.42	27.08	25.39	13.09	1.33	28.92	49.24	0.93
	Mean								**0.838**

Source : RBI : Trend and Progress Report for the year 2003-04

Table 4.11 : Statement Showing the Profitability Indicators of Foreign Banks (Year 2003-04) *(Contd...227)*

(Figures are in Percentages)

S. No	Name of the Foreign Sector Bank	Indicators of Outputs				Indicators of Inputs			Technical Efficiency Score in Percentages
		Return on Assets	Return on Equity	Non-Interest Income to Gross Income	Net Profit Margin	Net Profit to Deposits	Staff Expense to Operating Expense	Net Profit to Spread	
(1)	(2)	(3)	(4)	(5)	(6)	(7)	(8)	(9)	(10)
1	ABN-AMRO Bank N.V.	1.84	18.66	33.26	17.08	3.33	27.61	43.37	1
2	Abu Dhabi Commercial Bank	0.50	14.33	4.89	5.62	0.53	38.52	59.26	0.43
3	Antwerp Diamond Bank N.V.	1.18	4.99	14.41	24.79	13.28	37.64	39.28	1
4	Bank of America NA	1.26	9.60	22.51	17.75	4.04	42.20	54.65	0.627
5	Bank of Bahrain & Kuwait B.S.C.	0.12	0.90	26.65	1.54	0.19	40.18	11.42	1
6	Bank of Nova Scotia	0.64	6.86	25.81	9.45	1.06	36.80	40.80	0.694
7	Bank of Tokyo-Mitsubishi Ltd.	6.96	22.40	50.53	52.57	14.27	59.86	144.49	1
8	Chinatrust Commercial Bank	1.15	3.45	9.63	10.41	2.33	30.81	16.84	1
9	Chohung Bank	1.93	6.55	30.38	28.40	6.95	28.15	51.62	1
10	Citibank N.A.	3.55	23.70	28.01	18.05	2.79	24.97	42.16	1

Table 4.11 : Statement Showing the Profitability Indicators of Foreign Banks (Year 2003-04)

(Figures are in Percentages)

S. No	Name of the Foreign Sector Bank	Indicators of Outputs				Indicators of Inputs			Technical Efficiency Score in Percentages
		Return on Assets	Return on Equity	Non-Interest Income to Gross Income	Net Profit Margin	Net Profit to Deposits	Staff Expense to Operating Expense	Net Profit to Spread	
(1)	(2)	(3)	(4)	(5)	(6)	(7)	(8)	(9)	(10)
11	Credit Lyonnais	0.70	4.08	22.46	7.01	1.04	50.06	42.76	0.497
12	Deutsche Bank AG	3.17	31.04	66.77	30.11	10.77	37.00	375.71	1
13	HSBC Ltd.	0.91	8.33	33.28	18.58	2.42	37.08	56.98	0.777
14	JPMorgan Chase Bank	2.34	7.62	35.64	27.69	4.10	53.38	56.80	0.891
15	Krung Thai Bank Public Co.	1.37	2.00	4.62	22.83	4.79	24.22	26.16	1
16	Mashreqbank psc	1.76	11.64	6.67	16.48	2.18	29.38	73.43	0.65
17	Mizuho Corporate Bank Ltd.	2.41	6.04	13.28	30.54	13.78	44.18	53.28	1
18	Societe Generale	2.14	10.34	40.48	30.14	3.63	43.77	108.70	0.784
19	Sonali Bank (N.A.)	3.34	25.41	75.62	21.02	4.16	53.75	238.00	1
20	Standard Chartered Bank	1.74	21.56	21.70	18.51	2.99	28.44	41.06	0.988
21	State Bank of Mauritius Ltd.	1.33	4.88	32.82	13.09	3.19	34.83	44.36	0.889
	Mean								0.868

Source : RBI : Trend and Progress Report for the year 2003-04

Table 4.12 : Statement Showing the Business Performance Ratios of Public Sector Banks (Year 2003-04) *(Contd... 229)*

(Figures are in Percentages)

Sr. No.	Name of Public Sector Banks	NPA to Net Advances	Total CRAR	Profit Per Employee	Business Per Employee	Ratio of operating profits to total assets	Return on Assets	Return on Equity	Cost of Deposits	Cost of Borrowings	Cost of Funds	Return on Advancements	Return on Investment
(1)	(2)	(3)	(4)	(5)	(6)	(7)	(8)	(9)	(10)	(11)	(12)	(13)	(14)
1	Allahabad Bank	2.37	12.52	2.46	215	2.79	1.34	34.04	5.41	1.6	5.4	9.49	9.33
2	Andhra Bank	0.93	13.71	3.54	277.35	3.6	1.72	36.1	5.63	3.46	5.54	10.09	9.13
3	Bank of Baroda	2.99	13.91	2.43	252.51	3.08	1.2	20.32	4.83	6.49	4.85	7.9	8.6
4	Bank of India	4.50	13.01	2.35	266.72	2.78	1.25	26.71	4.56	7.39	4.73	7.48	8.03
5	Bank of Maharashtra	2.46	11.88	2.16	268.65	2.37	0.95	25.21	5.58	0.72	5.5	8.06	9.83
6	Canara Bank	2.89	12.66	2.97	297.58	3.15	1.34	28.47	5.2	3.16	5.19	8.67	9.04
7	Central Bank of India	5.57	12.43	1.58	181.51	2.54	0.98	22.9	5.2	3.81	5.2	9.52	9.25
8	Corporation Bank	1.80	20.12	4.98	365.56	3.27	1.96	19.62	5.3	2.11	5.18	7.64	10.24
9	Dena Bank	9.40	9.48	2.23	274	3.23	1.11	19.89	6.15	1.25	6.07	9.16	9.52
10	Indian Bank	2.71	12.82	1.85	189	2.15	1.21	7.61	5.24	7.57	5.27	8.88	9.23
11	Indian Overseas Bank	2.85	12.49	2.1	232.51	3	1.08	28.96	5.26	5.4	5.26	9.8	9.38
12	Oriental Bank of Commerce	0.00	14.47	5.1	416	4.09	1.7	28.67	5.46	0.81	5.35	9	10.35
13	Punjab & Sind Bank	9.62	11.06	0.09	205.08	1.01	0.06	1.92	5.63	5.8	5.63	10.01	9.75
14	Punjab National Bank	0.98	13.1	1.88	228.22	3.31	1.08	24.52	4.8	1.37	4.76	8.86	9.67
15	Syndicate Bank	2.58	11.49	1.62	240.31	2.58	1.67	24.92	4.42	2.47	4.41	8.61	8.63

Table 4.12 : Statement Showing the Business Performance Ratios of Public Sector Banks (Year 2003-04) *(Contd... 230)*

(Figures are in Percentages)

Sr. No.	Name of Public Sector Banks	NPA to Net Advances	Total CRAR	Profit Per Employee	Business Per Employee	Ratio of operating profits to total assets	Return on Assets	Return on Equity	Cost of Deposits	Cost of Borrowings	Cost of Funds	Return on Advan-cements	Return on Investment
(1)	(2)	(3)	(4)	(5)	(6)	(7)	(8)	(9)	(10)	(11)	(12)	(13)	(14)
16	UCO Bank	3.65	11.88	1.79	249	2.41	1.13	29.14	5.18	4.53	5.17	8.84	8.52
17	Union Bank of India	2.87	12.32	2.78	286.48	2.71	1.22		5.52	0.45	5.45	8.79	9.27
18	United Bank of India	3.75	17.04	1.76	169	2.45	1.25	16.07	5.82	0.72	5.81	8.75	9.95
19	Vijaya Bank	0.91	14.11	3.73	249.39	4.01	1.91	38.32	5.53	0.3	5.45	10.28	9.44
20	State Bank of India	3.48	13.53	1.77	210.56	2.44	0.94	19.67	5.9	1.42	5.74	7.62	8.78
21	State Bank of Bikaner & Jaipur	1.24	12.93	2.44	169.82	3.56	1.49	29.39	5.81	1.43	5.68	8.99	10.22
22	State Bank of Hyderabad	0.65	14.29	2.87	265.86	3.57	1.25	26.99	5.9	2.66	5.81	8.93	8.86
23	State Bank of Indore	0.00	12.39	3.45	230.77	4.36	1.73	32.94	5.75	0.17	5.56	8.57	9.96
24	State Bank of Mysore	2.96	11.53	1.82	162.81	3.39	1.28	34.83	5.64	0.91	5.51	9.65	9.37
25	State Bank of Patiala	0.00	13.56	3.69	305.24	4.17	1.60	27.39	5.21	2.26	5.14	8.33	8.31
26	State Bank of Saurashtra	0.00	14.53	2.4	193.16	3.82	1.38	25.47	5.73	0.8	5.49	8.46	9.63
27	State Bank of Travancore	1.39	11.36	2.16	271.78	3.26	1.02	29.68	5.59	0.56	5.54	8.55	8.8

Source : RBI : Trend and Progress Report for the year 2003-04

Table 4.12 : Statement Showing the Business Performance Ratios of Public Sector Banks (Year 2003-04) *(Contd...231)*

(Figures in Percentages)

Sr. No.	Name of Public Sector Banks	Cash Deposit Ratio	Credit Deposit Ratio	Investment Deposit Ratio	Ratio of Deposits to Total Liabilities	Ratio of Priority Sector Advances to Total Advanced	Ratio of Interest Income to Total Assets	Ratio of Net Interest Margin to Total Assets	Ratio of Non-Interest Income to Total Assets
(1)	(2)	(15)	(16)	(17)	(18)	(19)	(20)	(21)	(22)
1	Allahabad Bank	6.85	48.74	49.42	90.7	41.93	8.51	3.46	2.39
2	Andhra Bank	8.91	56.17	44.97	84.94	37.19	8.62	3.52	2.62
3	Bank of Baroda	4.19	48.79	52.1	85.73	27.88	7.61	3.18	2.13
4	Bank of India	5.96	64.58	38.26	83.67	28.26	7.18	2.73	2.22
5	Bank of Maharashtra	17.16	44.36	52.72	82.1	35.29	7.71	2.7	1.63
6	Canara Bank	7.98	55.17	41.45	86.74	33.9	7.72	2.95	2.28
7	Central Bank of India	6.13	40.79	56.17	88.26	43.52	8.41	3.52	1.6
8	Corporation Bank	7.31	59.89	46.07	79.55	35.85	7.94	3.48	1.86
9	Dena Bank	6.72	51.29	53.06	82.8	40.54	8.2	2.8	2.92
10	Indian Bank	9.34	46.4	54.84	77.76	38.2	7.16	3	2.01
11	Indian Overseas Bank	10.44	48.92	48.63	87.66	39.13	8.49	3.62	1.67
12	Oriental Bank of Commerce	7.38	55.17	47.08	86.99	38.05	8.8	3.88	1.92
13	Punjab & Sind Bank	7.82	44.2	49.67	90.88	47.18	8.67	3.34	1.73
14	Punjab National Bank	7.67	53.72	47.92	85.91	43.91	8.25	3.84	1.98

Table 4.12 : Statement Showing the Business Performance Ratios of Public Sector Banks (Year 2003-04)

(Figures in Percentages)

Sr. No.	Name of Public Sector Banks	Cash Deposit Ratio	Credit Deposit Ratio	Investment Deposit Ratio	Ratio of Deposits to Total Liabilities	Ratio of Priority Sector Advances to Total Advanced	Ratio of Interest Income to Total Assets	Ratio of Net Interest Margin to Total Assets	Ratio of Non-Interest Income to Total Assets
(1)	(2)	(15)	(16)	(17)	(18)	(19)	(20)	(21)	(22)
15	Syndicate Bank	10.58	48.48	42.07	90.18	32.57	7.56	3.5	1.9
16	UCO Bank	5.97	52.56	44.88	89.6	31.75	7.87	3.04	1.59
17	Union Bank of India	4.75	58.2	44.39	86.7	39.37	8.26	3.17	1.52
18	United Bank of India	4.67	34.99	61.15	88.06	33.91	8.27	3.12	2.02
19	Vijaya Bank	4.17	52.56	51.57	87.3	40.28	8.99	3.88	2.44
20	State Bank of India	5.98	49.57	58.28	78.13	27.04	7.77	2.85	1.94
21	State Bank of Bikaner & Jaipur	8.06	54.96	53.89	77.22	43.86	8.22	3.74	2.57
22	State Bank of Hyderabad	7.5	48.7	61.91	79.15	39.51	7.8	2.96	2.49
23	State Bank of Indore	5.3	61.49	52.11	79.87	46.32	8.57	3.71	2.95
24	State Bank of Mysore	6.41	56.9	49.5	80.56	36.52	8.42	3.62	2.71
25	State Bank of Patiala	4.84	58.23	49.44	83.55	39.39	7.84	3.41	2.62
26	State Bank of Saurashtra	6.88	49.09	54.77	83.15	42.67	8.25	3.41	2.7
27	State Bank of Travancore	4.86	56.45	54.65	82.16	37.22	8.09	3.18	2.18

Source : RBI : Trend and Progress Report for the year 2003-04

Table 4.13 : Statement Showing the Business Performance Ratios of Private Sector Banks (Year 2003-04) *(Contd... 233)*

(Figures are in Percentages)

Sr. No.	Name of Private Sector Banks	NPA to Net Advances	Total CRAR	Profit Per Employee	Business Per Employee	Ratio of operating profits to total assets	Return on Assets	Return on Equity	Cost of Deposits	Cost of Borrowings	Cost of Funds	Return on Advan-cements
(1)	(2)	(3)	(4)	(5)	(6)	(7)	(8)	(9)	(10)	(11)	(12)	(13)
1	Bank of Punjab Ltd.	4.69	12.64	444.54	2.53	2.26	0.85	16.15	4.98	5.68	5	8.66
2	Bank of Rajasthan Ltd.	2.99	11.18	199.93	1.67	2.54	0.82	22.46	4.86	0.96	4.8	8.48
3	Bharat Overseas Bank Ltd.	2.26	16.25	370	3.41	2.16	1:25	22.45	4.76	5.16	4.76	8.27
4	Catholic Syrian Bank Ltd.	4.65	11.23	182.16	1.96	3.02	1.31	33.83	6.2	1.84	6.19	10.24
5	Centurion Bank Ltd.	4.43	4.41	392.84	-9.46	0.35	-3.16	-57.02	6.17	4.65	6.14	14.11
6	City Union Bank Ltd.	6.37	13.36	286.8	4.09	4.05	1.86	31.03	6.94	2.74	6.9	11.46
7	Development Credit Bank	4.87	14.14	480.45	1.21	1.1	0.37	6.47	5.6	4.92	5.56	8.53
8	Dhanalakshmi Bank Ltd.	6.68	13.56	248.63	1.32	2.94	0.71	13.74	5.84	2.42	5.8	10.32
9	Federal Bank Ltd.	2.89	11.48	327	2.14	3.2	0.9	23.14	5.92	1.61	5.88	10.26
10	Ganesh Bank of Kurundwad Ltd.	10.59	11.94	126.21	0.81	0.82	0.86	10.43	8.01	13.09	8.02	12.01
11	Global Trust Bank Ltd.	27.99	0	624.95	-66.7	-1.06	-11.28	-303.8	5.73	5.74	5.73	8.8
12	HDFC Bank Ltd.	0.16	11.66	866	9.39	2.77	1.45	20.61	3.93	6.25	4.12	7.52
13	ICICI Bank Ltd.	2.21	10.36	1,010.00	12	2.04	1.31	20.93	5.2	0.71	3.59	10.53
14	IDBI Bank Ltd.	0.83	10.38	1,080.31	8.2	2.72	1.02	27.24	3.68	4.68	3.82	8.32
15	IndusInd Bank Ltd.	2.72	12.75	1,079.95	14.98	3.56	1.74	37.37	5.05	7.33	5.31	10.59
16	ING Vysya Bank Ltd.	2.6	11.05	324.34	1.15	2.11	0.45	8.12	5.89	1.11	5.47	8.83
17	Jammu & Kashmir Bank Ltd.	1.48	16.88	345	6	3.31	1.92	28.66	5.26	5.83	5.27	9.5

Table 4.13 : Statement Showing the Business Performance Ratios of Private Sector Banks (Year 2003-04)

(Figures are in Percentages)

Sr. No.	Name of Private Sector Banks	NPA to Net Advances	Total CRAR	Profit Per Employee	Business Per Employee	Ratio of operating profits to total assets	Return on Assets	Return on Equity	Cost of Deposits	Cost of Borrowings	Cost of Funds	Return on Advan-cements
(1)	(2)	(3)	(4)	(5)	(6)	(7)	(8)	(9)	(10)	(11)	(12)	(13)
18	Karnataka Bank Ltd.	4.98	13.03	320.23	3.1	3.32	1.34	20.78	7.03	4.17	6.98	9.73
19	Karur Vysya Bank Ltd.	2.32	17.11	330	5.65	3.23	2.43	25.35	6.04	6.25	6.05	9.8
20	Kotak Mahindra Bank Ltd.	0.17	15.25	354.28	10.25	2.18	2.4	13	1.2	3.95	1.48	10.04
21	Lakshmi Vilas Bank Ltd.	5.4	13.79	276	2.11	2.59	1.19	19.61	6.34	6.64	6.35	9.5
22	Lord Krishna Bank Ltd.	6.05	16.68	308.94	2.37	2.16	1.33	20.54	6.49	21.95	6.5	8.61
23	Nainital Bank Ltd.	0	18.54	124.56	1.91	2.54	1.58	19.62	5.18	18.54	5.18	11.43
24	Ratnakar Bank Ltd.	5.58	16.65	198.36	1.58	1.79	1.12	17.87	6.28	10.76	6.29	11.74
25	Sangli Bank Ltd.	6.56	13.68	95.7	0.62	1.47	0.64	14.56	4.65	5.2	4.65	8.18
26	SBI Commercial & International Bank Ltd.	18.31	30.43	570.69	17.12	4.82	3.67	20.1	5.98	0.8	5.94	11.73
27	South Indian Bank Ltd.	4.55	11.32	306	2.39	2.87	1	23.56	6.15	0.38	6.08	9.17
28	Tamilnad Mercantile Bank Ltd.	5	21.07	292.43	3.69	3.46	1.59	18.47	6.59	1.56	6.53	11.45
29	United Western Bank Ltd.	8.95	10.13	290	0.96	2.03	0.43	10.62	5.43	6.61	5.44	7.86
30	UTI Bank Ltd.	1.29	11.21	808	8.07	3.14	1.42	27.08	4.93	3.12	4.87	9.28

Source : *RBI : Trend and Progress Report for the year 2003-04*

Table 4.13 : Statement Showing the Business Performance Ratios of Private Sector Banks (Year 2003-04) *(Contd...235)*

(Figures are in Percentages)

Sr. No.	Name of Public Sector Banks	Return on Investment	Cash Deposit Ratio	Credit Deposit Ratio	Investment Deposit Ratio	Ratio of Deposits to Total Liabilities	Ratio of Priority Sector Advances to Total Advanced	Ratio of Interest Income to Total Assets	Ratio of Net Interest Margin to Total Assets	Ratio of Non-Interest Income to Total Assets
(1)	(2)	(14)	(15)	(16)	(17)	(18)	(19)	(20)	(21)	(22)
1	Bank of Punjab Ltd.	9.62	7.8	56.89	38	85.48	18.85	7.45	2.81	2.9
2	Bank of Rajasthan Ltd.	8.04	4.4	32.83	58.78	87.59	32.14	6.9	2.6	2.43
3	Bharat Overseas Bank Ltd.	9.48	5.12	56.3	37.89	87.74	21.01	7.55	3.25	1.2
4	Catholic Syrian Bank Ltd.	9.53	4.33	48.92	46.87	90.09	26.89	8.74	2.99	2.91
5	Centurion Bank Ltd.	8.38	8.62	51.39	33.15	85.35	28.83	9.63	3.75	1.82
6	City Union Bank Ltd.	9.65	7.13	54.34	44.93	89.2	38.49	9.49	3.31	2.28
7	Development Credit Bank	6.82	6.19	54.52	46.58	82.97	35.07	7.19	1.95	1.8
8	Dhanalakshmi Bank Ltd.	9.03	6.66	52.82	41.51	88.18	27.19	8.4	3.05	2.56
9	Federal Bank Ltd.	8.68	5.39	57.14	40.87	89.17	31.32	8.73	3.09	2.18
10	Ganesh Bank of Kurundwad Ltd.	7.97	7.22	46.68	37.21	93.74	62.7	8.68	1.19	2.11
11	Global Trust Bank Ltd.	4.06	10.07	35.09	33.11	88.84	27.87	4.76	-1.09	2.17

Table 4.13 : Statement Showing the Business Performance Ratios of Private Sector Banks (Year 2003-04) *(Contd...236)*

(Figures are in Percentages)

Sr. No.	Name of Public Sector Banks	Return on Investment	Cash Deposit Ratio	Credit Deposit Ratio	Investment Deposit Ratio	Ratio of Deposits to Total Liabilities	Ratio of Priority Sector Advances to Total Advanced	Ratio of Interest Income to Total Assets	Ratio of Net Interest Margin to Total Assets	Ratio of Non-Interest Income to Total Assets
(1)	(2)	(14)	(15)	(16)	(17)	(18)	(19)	(20)	(21)	(22)
12	HDFC Bank Ltd.	8.1	8.36	58.35	63.33	71.88	14.08	7.01	3.68	1.32
13	ICICI Bank Ltd.	6.22	7.94	91.17	62.76	54.39	23.4	7.67	1.62	2.64
14	IDBI Bank Ltd.	7.24	7.6	73.63	38.95	77.28	38.1	7.04	3.16	2.01
15	IndusInd Bank Ltd.	8	11.92	69.75	35.46	74.24	32.19	7.89	2.54	2.76
16	ING Vysya Bank Ltd.	7.01	5.97	67.25	38.99	79.39	30.61	7.45	1.97	2.93
17	Jammu & Kashmir Bank Ltd.	8.75	8.22	49.75	45.29	76.66	21.17	8.01	3.26	1.59
18	Karnataka Bank Ltd.	8.7	4.13	49.62	51.87	83.17	40.92	8.55	2.15	2.72
19	Karur Vysya Bank Ltd.	13.22	5.53	68.06	36.76	88.94	37.5	9.75	4.47	1.12
20	Kotak Mahindra Bank Ltd.	2.5	2.84	47.03	64.65	88	41.84	4.96	2.93	1.64
21	Lakshmi Vilas Bank Ltd.	8.51	6.99	61.86	40.6	86.25	37.55	8.15	2.38	2.48
22	Lord Krishna Bank Ltd.	8.23	8.84	48.37	45.31	88.74	36.29	7.46	1.52	3.05
23	Nainital Bank Ltd.	9.71	6.88	31.04	54.09	88.8	56.49	8.64	4.08	1.61

Table 4.13 : Statement Showing the Business Performance Ratios of Private Sector Banks (Year 2003-04)

(Figures are in Percentages)

Sr. No.	Name of Public Sector Banks	Return on Investment	Cash Deposit Ratio	Credit Deposit Ratio	Investment Deposit Ratio	Ratio of Deposits to Total Liabilities	Ratio of Priority Sector Advances to Total Advanced	Ratio of Interest Income to Total Assets	Ratio of Net Interest Margin to Total Assets	Ratio of Non-Interest Income to Total Assets
(1)	(2)	(14)	(15)	(16)	(17)	(18)	(19)	(20)	(21)	(22)
24	Ratnakar Bank Ltd.	8.42	13.61	48.38	36.13	87.72	22.42	8.38	2.86	1.53
25	Sangli Bank Ltd.	6.58	4.97	34.86	58.08	93.32	15.12	7.08	2.75	1.6
26	SBI Commercial & International Bank Ltd.	7.72	5.88	32.29	38.32	76.31	12.03	7.33	2.5	
27	South Indian Bank Ltd.	8.88	4.89	50.69	47.85	89.47	30.75	8.06	2.37	2.79
28	Tamilnad Mercantile Bank Ltd.	11.72	5.08	48	53.44	86.54	45.14	10.96	4.4	1.38
29	United Western Bank Ltd.	8.26	5.55	58.23	37.53	90.07	34.1	7.06	1.86	2.03
30	UTI Bank Ltd.	8.17	18.03	44.68	37.19	86.77	26.23	7.25	2.58	2.47

Source : RBI : Trend and Progress Report for the year 2003-04

Table 4.14 : Statement Showing the Business Performance Ratios of Foreign Banks (Year 2003-04) *(Contd...238)*

(Figures are in Percentages)

Sr. No.	Name of Foreign Banks	NPA to Net Advances	Total CRAR	Profit Per Employee	Business Per Employee	Ratio of operating profits to total assets	Return on Assets	Return on Equity	Cost of Deposits	Cost of Borrowings	Cost of Funds	Return on Advancements	Return on Investment
(1)	(2)	(3)	(4)	(5)	(6)	(7)	(8)	(9)	(10)	(11)	(12)	(13)	(14)
1	ABN-AMRO Bank N.V.	0.88	13.48	15.22	891.45	3.58	1.84	18.66	1.61	6.4	3.28	7.95	8.32
2	Abu Dhabi Commercial Bank	27.39	14.22	12.68	1,407.67	0.71	0.5	14.33	8.06	13.93	8.08	10.5	9.75
3	American Express Bank	5.68	10.74	-1.67	284.91	3.05	-0.69	-9.49	6.41	4.51	6.26	15.88	8.22
4	Antwerp Diamond Bank N.V.	0	53.22	32.85	1,723.61	3.07	1.18	4.99	0.71	1.26	1.14	5.82	7.51
5	Arab Bangladesh Bank Ltd.	0.37	111.34	12.9	221.45	6.26	3.67	7.1	1.27	8.64	1.46	8.34	4.48
6	Bank Internasional Indonesia	72.15	133.94	-1.56	326.47	0.04	-0.33	-0.31	4.28	3.73	4.07	10.8	13.64
7	Bank of America	0	22.92	24.12	1,747.56	2.39	1.26	9.6	4.12	3.88	3.97	5.15	7.53
8	Bank of Bahrain & Kuwait B.S.C.	17.73	21.06	1	784	1.23	0.12	0.9	5.69	4.86	5.52	6.32	6.36
9	Bank of Ceylon	21.85	45.26	2.66	637.48	3.15	0.36	1.38	6.66	0.13	5.07	10.93	6.36
10	Bank of Nova Scotia	9.07	13.78	9.96	1,678.52	2.23	0.64	6.86	5.44	1.34	4.09	4.88	7.16

Table 4.14 : Statement Showing the Business Performance Ratios of Foreign Banks (Year 2003-04) *(Contd...239)*

(Figures are in Percentages)

Sr. No.	Name of Foreign Banks	NPA to Net Advances	Total CRAR	Profit Per Employee	Business Per Employee	Ratio of operating profits to total assets	Return on Assets	Return on Equity	Cost of Deposits	Cost of Borrowings	Cost of Funds	Return on Advancements	Return on Investment
(1)	(2)	(3)	(4)	(5)	(6)	(7)	(8)	(9)	(10)	(11)	(12)	(13)	(14)
11	Bank of Tokyo-Mitsubishi Ltd.	0.1	32.78	48.58	582.27	8.46	6.96	22.4	2.72	0.26	2.63	8.19	6.05
12	Barclays Bank PLC	0	37.16	211.4	270.79	10.97	5.2	19.43	1.39	3.23	2.57	5.03	5.65
13	BNP Paribas	2.7	21.7	-3.99	921.94	1.23	-0.44	-4.42	4.25	3.17	3.94	6.74	8.45
14	Calyon Bank	1.01	24.51	8.63	1,006.21	-0.22	0.51	3.04	0.78	36.56	5.62	8.08	10.91
15	Chinatrust Commercial Bank	5.76	39.98	7.69	800.45	4.56	1.15	3.45	5.55	1.27	4.79	10.38	12.49
16	Chohung Bank	0.8	54.43	29.62	744.38	4.74	1.93	6.55	1.34	0.4	1.04	6.64	7.54
17	Citibank N.A.	1.4	11.11	28.33	1,666.92	4.5	3.55	23.7	4.16	2.53	3.91	9.93	10.91
18	Credit Lyonnais	2.6	21.7	9.41	1,401.56	1.53	0.7	4.08	8.64	2.21	8.39	8.03	10.16
19	Development Bank of Singapore	0	55.49	-27.6	1,669.70	2.52	-1.69	-5.44	3.44	8	4.35	9.54	4.63
20	Deutsche Bank AG	0	14.42	65.23	1,099.23	7	3.17	31.04	1.48	5.25	3.83	5.01	6.14
21	HSBC Ltd.	0.7	14.54	6.32	820.91	2.49	0.91	8.33	3.45	6.67	3.98	8.4	6.58
22	ING Bank N.V.	0.09	56.91	-5.21	0	0.41	-0.05	-0.07	22.31	0	2.16	6.21	0.6

Table 4.14 : Statement Showing the Business Performance Ratios of Foreign Banks (Year 2003-04) *(Contd...240)*

(Figures are in Percentages)

Sr. No.	Name of Foreign Banks	NPA to Net Advances	Total CRAR	Profit Per Employee	Business Per Employee	Ratio of operating profits to total assets	Return on Assets	Return on Equity	Cost of Deposits	Cost of Borrowings	Cost of Funds	Return on Advan-cements	Return on Investment
(1)	(2)	(3)	(4)	(5)	(6)	(7)	(8)	(9)	(10)	(11)	(12)	(13)	(14)
23	JP Morgan Chase Bank	0	34.83	28.74	259.33	3.96	2.34	7.62	2.29	1.22	1.98	0	7.87
24	Krung Thai Bank Public Co.	0	115.98	7.12	291.03	1.67	1.37	2	1.73	0.52	1.71	9.81	6.91
25	Mashreqbank psc	0	54.71	50.53	865.85	1.78	1.76	11.64	9.05	3.03	8.98	21.79	11.02
26	Mizuho Corporate Bank Ltd.	0	36.09	16.05	527.8	2.87	2.41	6.04	2.71	4.07	3.33	7.47	5.52
27	Oman International Bank	61.37	16.48	-5.61	1,233.79	-0.16	0.49	-1.36	6.68	4.82	6.51	6.09	7.31
28	Societe Generale	1.37	32.71	25.4	1,017.00	2.97	2.14	10.34	2.46	4.41	3.31	5.08	5.06
29	Sonali Bank (N.A.)	1.47	60.55	2.57	74.54	6.17	3.34	25.41	2.02	0	2.02	8.85	8.55
30	Standard Chartered Bank	0.52	10.87	13.37	780.11	4.33	1.74	21.56	3.77	3.83	3.78	10.47	8.8
31	State Bank of Mauritius Ltd.	4.64	35.08	20	1,523.00	5.42	1.33	4.88	5.62	5.8	5.69	6.33	10.55
32	Sumitomo Mitsui Banking	12.78	52.3	-70.55	297.32	4.17	-13.71	-41.57	3.13	4.56	3.87	10.83	6.01
33	UFJ Bank Ltd.	0	121.69	17.35	535.72	3.6	1.75	2.7	2.22	0.48	1.8	6.91	4.74

Source : RBI : Trend and Progress Report for the year 2003-04

Table 4.14 : Statement Showing the Business Performance Ratios of Foreign Banks (Year 2003-04) *(Contd...241)*

(Figures are in Percentages)

Sr. No.	*Name of Foreign Banks*	*Cash Deposit Ratio*	*Credit Deposit Ratio*	*Investment Deposit Ratio*	*Ratio of Deposits to Total Liabilities*	*Ratio of Priority Sector Advances to Total Advanced*	*Ratio of Interest Income to Total Assets*	*Ratio of Net Interest Margin to Total Assets*	*Ratio of Non-Interest Income to Total Assets*
(1)	(2)	(15)	(16)	(17)	(18)	(19)	(20)	(21)	(22)
1	ABN-AMRO Bank N.V.	8.69	114.35	49.82	55.2	28.25	7.62	4.49	3.8
2	Abu Dhabi Commercial Bank	4.53	9.23	74.55	92.82	15.26	8.45	0.84	0.43
3	American Express Bank	4.9	45.28	29.13	81.93	11.97	9.31	3.87	6.7
4	Antwerp Diamond Bank N.V.	29.61	669.97	215.63	8.85	99.64	5.43	4.01	0.92
5	Arab Bangladesh Bank Ltd.	2.66	38.21	32.75	40.83	31.12	4.31	3.62	4.7
6	Bank International Indonesia	15.15	26.73	96.48	12.47	19.52	3.95	3.16	0.14
7	Bank of America	14.59	192.5	86.93	31.1	31.88	5.59	2.34	1.62
8	Bank of Bahrain & Kuwait B.S.C.	4.94	70.11	73.18	63.07	13.72	5.75	1.05	2.09
9	Bank of Ceylon	19.47	62.24	44.21	50.25	62.84	5.44	2.15	2.64
10	Bank of Nova Scotia	6.1	119.19	45.6	54.35	37.2	5.17	1.61	1.8
11	Bank of Tokyo-Mitsubishi Ltd.	5.52	73.86	55.81	48.81	0.83	6.88	5.06	7.03

Table 4.14 : Statement Showing the Business Performance Ratios of Foreign Banks (Year 2003-04) *(Contd...242)*

(Figures are in Percentages)

Sr. No.	*Name of Foreign Banks*	*Cash Deposit Ratio*	*Credit Deposit Ratio*	*Investment Deposit Ratio*	*Ratio of Deposits to Total Liabilities*	*Ratio of Priority Sector Advances to Total Advanced*	*Ratio of Interest Income to Total Assets*	*Ratio of Net Interest Margin to Total Assets*	*Ratio of Non-Interest Income to Total Assets*
(1)	(2)	(15)	(16)	(17)	(18)	(19)	(20)	(21)	(22)
12	Barclays Bank PLC	9.31	2.86	499.24	6.48	0	2.86	2.17	11.15
13	BNP Paribas	5.55	75.69	57.65	57.99	24.98		2.74	1.55
14	Calyon Bank	5.17	9.37	66.34	72.14	3.67	6.95	2.37	-0.78
15	Chinatrust Commercial Bank	5.9	142.92	39.21	49.44	30.25	9.95	6.82	1.06
16	Chohung Bank	8.47	74.99	66.79	27.69	0	5.52	4.36	2.41
17	Citibank N.A.	17.09	74.56	32.69	69.15	22.51	8.31	4.94	3.24
18	Credit Lyonnais	4.14	54.84	56.44	67.3	7.78	7.58	1.6	2.19
19	Development Bank of Singapore	2.85	28.96	65.36	61.64	21.29	6.27	3.4	0.6
20	Deutsche Bank AG	13.22	82.85	89.92	29.46	23.49	4.17	1.01	8.38
21	HSBC Ltd.	4.49	59.18	63.89	64.16	14.72	6.11	2.99	3.05
22	ING Bank N.V.	0	0	0	0	0	1.09	0.29	1.9
23	JP Morgan Chase Bank	56.47	0	75.39	56.95	0	5.74	4.35	3.18

Table 4.14 : Statement Showing the Business Performance Ratios of Foreign Banks (Year 2003-04)

(Figures are in Percentages)

Sr. No.	Name of Foreign Banks	Cash Deposit Ratio	Credit Deposit Ratio	Investment Deposit Ratio	Ratio of Deposits to Total Liabilities	Ratio of Priority Sector Advances to Total Advanced	Ratio of Interest Income to Total Assets	Ratio of Net Interest Margin to Total Assets	Ratio of Non-Interest Income to Total Assets
(1)	(2)	(15)	(16)	(17)	(18)	(19)	(20)	(21)	(22)
24	Krung Thai Bank Public Co.	4.96	93.91	51.19	28.87	34.65	5.86	5.35	0.28
25	Mashreqbank psc	3.57	6.24	73.9	81.29	60.05	9.71	2.33	0.69
26	Mizuho Corporate Bank Ltd.	10.01	354.73	63.55	17.49	0.31	6.63	4.38	1.01
27	Oman International Bank	8.3	6.09	49.48	54.12	35.53	3.84	-0.34	1.21
28	Societe Generale	5.37	41.42	111.38	56.18	13.26	4.58	2.13	3.11
29	Sonali Bank (N.A.)	11.52	19.7	22.1	80.85	1.82	3.82	1.38	11.77
30	Standard Chartered Bank	5.19	80.97	50.52	58.08	24.61	7.93	4.56	2.2
31	State Bank of Mauritius Ltd.	6.03	145.86	62.14	41.38	18.8	7.05	3.1	3.44
32	Sumitomo Mitsui Banking	15.04	132.1	132.49	24.89	15.14	7.61	5.55	1.04
33	UFJ Bank Ltd.	10.61	153.65	73.78	19.24	17.07	4.9	4.24	1.12

Source : RBI : Trend and Progress Report for the year 2003-04

Table 4.15 : Descriptives

TOTAL SCORE

	N	Mean	Std. Deviation	Std. Error	95% Confidence Interval for Mean		Minimum	Maximum
					Lower Bound	Upper Bound		
PUBLIC	10	127.6000	4.1952	1.3266	124.5989	130.6011	119.00	134.00
PRIVATE	10	166.6000	7.0269	2.2221	161.5732	171.6268	158.00	178.00
FOREIGN	10	167.4000	6.9474	2.1970	162.4301	172.3699	159.00	178.00
Total	30	153.8667	19.8177	3.6182	146.4666	161.2667	119.00	178.00

Table 4.16: Test of Homogeneity of Variances

TOTAL SCORE

Levene Statistic	df1	df2	Sig.
2.098	2	27	.142

Table 4.17: ANOVA

TOTAL SCORE

	Sum of Squares	df	Mean Square	F	Sig.
Between Groups	10352.267	2	5176.133	134.743	.000
Within Groups	1037.200	27	38.415		
Total	11389.467	29			

Table 4.18 : STATEMENT SHOWING THE BANKWISE DETAILS OF THE TOTAL SCORES SECURED IN RESPECT TO AVAILABILITY OF INFORMATION TECHNOLOGY INFRASTRUCTURE

Sr. No.	Name of the Bank	**Sum of Total Score Secured** (Out of 100)
1	**SBI**	**130**
2	**PNB**	**125**
3	**ICICI**	**168**
4	**HDFC**	**165**
5	**CITI**	**172**
6	**STAN**	**162**

Table 4.19 : TOTAL SCORES SECURED BY DIFFERENT BANKS IN REGARD TO INTEGRATION OF KNOWLEDGE MANAGEMENT INTO BUSINESS STRATEGIES

Sr. No.	*Name of the Bank*	*Sum of Total Score Secured (Out of 100)*
1	SBI	78
2	PNB	73
3	ICICI	85
4	HDFC	83
5	CITI	84
6	STAN	83

Table 4.20

Descriptives

TOTAL SCORE

	N	Mean	Std. Deviation	Std. Error	95% Confidence Interval for Mean		Minimum	Maximum
					Lower Bound	Upper Bound		
PUBLIC	10	75.5000	2.4608	.7782	73.7396	77.2604	72.00	79.00
PRIVATE	10	83.8000	3.1198	.9866	81.5682	86.0318	80.00	89.00
FOREIGN	10	83.6000	3.1693	1.0022	81.3328	85.8672	78.00	88.00
Total	30	80.9667	4.8458	.8847	79.1572	82.7761	72.00	89.00

Table 4.21

ANOVA

TOTAL SCORE

	Sum of Squares	df	Mean Square	F	Sig.
Between Groups	448.467	2	224.233	26.040	.000
Within Groups	232.500	27	8.611		
Total	680.967	29			

Table 4.22

Test of Homogeneity of Variances

TOTAL SCORE

Levene Statistic	df1	df2	Sig.
.295	2	27	.747

Table 4.23

ANOVA

TOTAL SCORE

	Sum of Squares	df	Mean Square	F	Sig.
Between Groups	1308.200	2	654.100	18.532	.000
Within Groups	953.000	27	35.296		
Total	2261.200	29			

Table 4.24

Test of Homogeneity of Variances

TOTAL SCORE

Levene Statistic	df1	df2	Sig.
1.818	2	27	.182

Table 4.25

TOTAL SCORES SECURED BY SELECTED BANKS IN RESPECT TO MANAGING OF HUMAN RESOURCES

Sr. No.	Name of the Bank	Sum of Total Score Secured (Out of 100)
1	SBI	52
2	PNB	62
3	ICICI	73
4	HDFC	63
5	CITI	72
6	STAN	74

Table 4.26

ANOVA

	Sum of Squares	df	Mean Square	F	Sig.
Between Groups	**2496.600**	**2**	**1248.300**	**193.036**	**.000**
Within Groups	**174.600**	**27**	**6.467**		
Total	2671.200	29			

Table 4.27

Test of Homogeneity of Variances

Levene Statistic	df1	df2	Sig.
1.125	**2**	**27**	**.339**

Table 4.28

Sr. No.	Name of the Bank	**Sum of Total Score Secured (Out of 100)**
1	**SBI**	**57**
2	**PNB**	**55**
3	**ICICI**	**73**
4	**HDFC**	**72**
5	**CITI**	**81**
6	**STAN**	**77**

Table 4.29

Sr. No.	Name of the Bank	**Sum of Total Score Secured (Out of 100)**
1	**SBI**	**52**
2	**PNB**	**52**
3	**ICICI**	**77**
4	**HDFC**	**75**
5	**CITI**	**77**
6	**STAN**	**76**

APPENDIX - IV

Knowledge Management Matrix - Assessment Toolkit

The structure of the KMM covers the check-list which could be used for collecting the relevant data that is required for ascertaining the present status of knowledge management in a given commercial bank. It is divided into six sections, namely, financial, technology, strategy, people, process and structure. Each section is assigned weightage as per their significance as indicated to the author by the banking experts. Thus the total weightage of 400 has been assigned to financial section followed by 200 for technology, 100 for strategy, 100 for people, 100 for process and 100 for structure. Thus the total weightage adds up to 1000. To this, it may be added that each section contains list of different statements which are required to be evaluated concerning with the bank under investigation. The number of statements covers almost all the relevant variables. The responses to each statement have been presented on a five point Likert scale. For the purpose of interpretation, we have to encircle the relevant numerical of the response. And then compute the total scores of each section ; add them up and then reach to overall scores in respect to different sections of this matrix. Higher the score, better would be the bank performance related to the relevant process.

Instructions

For each section, read each of the statement and figures. Consider the Bank that you are evaluating and decide the response that would realistically describe the situation of the banking unit under investigation.

If the statement is strongly agreed, -circle 5
If the statement is agreed, -circle 4
If the statement is neither agreed nor disagreed, -circle 3
If the statement is disagreed, -circle 2
If the statement is strongly disagreed, -circle 1

Financial Analysis

To analyze the technical efficiency among all the selected banks in different time periods for evaluating the performance on profitability, growth, and productivity.

Technique: Data Envelopment Analysis
Weightage: 300

- o Profitability Indicator (100)
- o Growth Indicator (100)
- o Productivity Indicator (100)

To analyze the various business performance indicators, for bank's strategy it needs to follow for long term sustainability.

Weightage: 100
Technique: Ratio Analysis

Top Performance indicators of commercial banks operating in India are available in the annual RBI publication "Report on Trend and Progress in Banking in India". RBI provides numerous indicators, (ratios) which covers two aspects of performance, i.e. productivity and profitability of banks. Bank productivity is indicated through capital structure, asset structure and business generated though employee strength. Different performance indicators and ratios are being used in the checklist, where we rank them from the concerned public, private and foreign sectors. Like in Public sector banks, there are 27 banks has to evaluated for identify their rank and then it has been put it into the checklist of the concerned banking like: (If Rank is in between 1-6 than it's a Very Strong (VS), 7 – 12 than it is a Strong (S), 13-18 – Not so Strong, 19-24 – Weak, Above 24 is Very Weak). The same is being applied in the private and foreign sector banks with their respective total, which has been divided into a Likert scale of 5 to 1 with Very Strong to Very Weak bank.

Very Strong (5)	Strong (4)	Not so Strong (3)	Weak (2)	Very Weak (1)

1. NPA	5	4	3	2	1
2. Total CARR	5	4	3	2	1
3. Profit Per Employee	5	4	3	2	1
4. Business Per Employee	5	4	3	2	1
5. Return on Investment	5	4	3	2	1
6. Return on Advancements	5	4	3	2	1
7. Cost of funds	5	4	3	2	1
8. Cost of Borrowings	5	4	3	2	1
9. Cost of Deposits	5	4	3	2	1
10. Return on Equity	5	4	3	2	1
11. Return on Assets	5	4	3	2	1

12. Ratio of Operating Profit to Total Assets	5	4	3	2	1
13. Cash : Deposit Ratio	5	4	3	2	1
14. Credit Deposit Ratio	5	4	3	2	1
15. Investment Deposit Ratio	5	4	3	2	1
16. Ratio of Deposits to Total Liabilities	5	4	3	2	1
17. Ratio of Priority Sector advances to Total Advances	5	4	3	2	1
18. Ratio of Interest Income to Total Assets	5	4	3	2	1
19. Ratio of Non-Interest Income to Total Assets	5	4	3	2	1
20. Ratio of Net-Interest Margin to total assets	5	4	3	2	1

Section I score

Calculating your score

Number of Strongly Agreed	* 5	=
Number of Agreed	* 4	=
Number of Neither Agree nor disagreed	* 3	=
Number of Disagreed	* 2	=
Number of Strongly Disagreed	* 1	=

Your Total Score

Total Point Score Possible 400

Your percent score

(Your point score divided by 400)

Strategy (100)

Strongly Agreed (5)	Agreed (4)	Neither Agreed nor disagreed (3)	Disagreed (2)	Strongly Disagreed (1)

1. Vision and mission statement directing the business leadership	5 4 3 2 1
2. There is an agreement where and how Knowledge Management (KM) will be practiced.	a) Yes, the agreement focuses on a clearly defined subject and/or on a business division (e.g. creating a knowledge map for the loans department) – (5) b) Yes, the agreement focuses on a general reformation of the banking knowledge base (e.g. identifying and storing all employees skills and making them available by the intranet) (4)

	c) Yes, the agreement wants to roll our banking process into a knowledge based bank in all of its parts (e.g. applying a special KM framework) (3) d) Our understanding is quit vague and there are many different opinion on how to approach KM (2) e) There is no common agreement at all (1)

3. Our banking markets clear, customer requirement defined and competitive advantage leveraged and identified and these embedded in the mission, vision and objectives of our business units and shared and understand throughout the unit	5	4	3	2	1
4. We form strategic alliances with other Banks that balance our competencies in the market.	5	4	3	2	1
5. We have a strong tie-up with corporate and management consulting firms to continuous sharing information / knowledge	5	4	3	2	1
6. We outsource skills and expertise to other social and economic development organizations	5	4	3	2	1
7. We participate in industry-based research groups to help us decide whether we need to acquire new knowledge	5	4	3	2	1
8. A Few instruments are, important for successfully implementing and applying Knowledge Management.					
a) Creating a knowledge friendly corporate culture	5	4	3	2	1
b) Integrating knowledge processes /into business processes	5	4	3	2	1
c) Providing information technologies	5	4	3	2	1
d) Motivating and qualifying employees	5	4	3	2	1
9. Knowledge management expectations achieves the following:					
a) Better Decision making	5	4	3	2	1
b) Better customer handling	5	4	3	2	1
c) Faster response to key business issues	5	4	3	2	1
d) Improved employee skills					
e) Improved productivity	5	4	3	2	1
f) Increased profits	5	4	3	2	1
g) Increased innovation	5	4	3	2	1
h) Create additional business opportunities	5	4	3	2	1
i) Improved new product development	5	4	3	2	1
	5	4	3	2	1

Section II score

Calculating your score

Number of Strongly Agree	*	5	=
Number of Agree	*	4	=
Number of Neither Agree nor disagree	*	3	=
Number of Disagree	*	2	=
Number of Strongly Disagree	*	1	=

Your Total Score

Total Point Score Possible 100

Your percent score

(Your point score divided by 100)

Technology (200)

Strongly Agreed (5)	Agreed (4)	Neither Agreed nor disagreed (3)	Disagreed (2)	Strongly Disagreed (1)

1. Our bank have a range of well-organized and integrated techniques for transferring knowledge, meetings, email, bulletin boards, online-forums and databases.	5 4 3 2 1
2. Information is ready and easy available at one place	5 4 3 2 1
3. Information Technology helps us in:	
o Improving Productivity	5 4 3 2 1
o Greatly reduced time to management in MIS	5 4 3 2 1
o Better Risk Management	5 4 3 2 1
o Efficient Tracking of NPAs	5 4 3 2 1
o Better Regulatory Compliance	5 4 3 2 1
o Swifter reaction of market changes and customer needs	5 4 3 2 1
o Reduction in Transaction costs	5 4 3 2 1
4. The physical environment is designed to encourage and facilitate learning and knowledge sharing	5 4 3 2 1

5. Please mark the status of technology support tools as	
▪ Corporate Intranet – Extranet	5 4 3 2 1
▪ Distributed to Centralized Computing	5 4 3 2 1
▪ Messaging or E-mail Systems	
▪ Decision Support Systems	5 4 3 2 1
▪ Data Warehousing/ Data Marts	5 4 3 2 1
▪ CRM	5 4 3 2 1
▪ Integrated Core Banking System, with capability for online real time transaction processing	5 4 3 2 1 5 4 3 2 1
▪ Search Engines – Intelligent Agents – Information Retrieval Systems	5 4 3 2 1
▪ Online Chat	
▪ Video-conferencing	5 4 3 2 1
▪ Communities of Practice	5 4 3 2 1
▪ Net Banking/ATM/Mobile Banking	5 4 3 2 1
▪ Automated Treasury and Risk Management System	5 4 3 2 1 5 4 3 2 1
▪ Business Process Management	
▪ Workflow Management System	5 4 3 2 1 5 4 3 2 1
6. The electronic and physical spaces where we store our knowledge kept up to date.	5 4 3 2 1
7. We have a formal policy that insures we share technology and ideas across unit	5 4 3 2 1
8. Training on new systems focuses on how these technologies can be used to improve the quality and efficiency.	5 4 3 2 1

9. Access the utility of IT tools in the following patterns.					
▪ Management of documents	5	4	3	2	1
▪ Using existing information	5	4	3	2	1
▪ Improving collaboration	5	4	3	2	1
▪ Providing better transparency	5	4	3	2	1
▪ Bringing together and consolidating information	5	4	3	2	1
10. In what manner the Technology Support would enhance the Capabilities of your Bank					
o Ease of Use					
o Access to data	5	4	3	2	1
o Security of Data	5	4	3	2	1
o Quality of Reporting	5	4	3	2	1
o Sophistication of data analysis	5	4	3	2	1
o Flexibility of Reporting	5	4	3	2	1
o Web-based	5	4	3	2	1
o Low Cost	5	4	3	2	1
	5	4	3	2	1

Section III score

Calculating your score

Number of Strongly Agree	* 5	=
Number of Agree	* 4	=
Number of Neither Agree nor disagree	* 3	=
Number of Disagree	* 2	=
Number of Strongly Disagree	* 1	=

Your Total Score

Total Point Score Possible 200

Your percent score
(Your point score divided by 200)

People - Human Issues (100)

Strongly Agree (5)	Agree (4)	Neither Agree nor disagree (3)	Disagree (2)	Strongly Disagree (1)

1. Our bank reward employee for sharing knowledge	5	4	3	2	1
2. We have accounting techniques to measure intellectual capital	5	4	3	2	1

intellectual capital					
3. Our bank provides training and development programs that emphasize knowledge management and sharing of other developmental programs	5	4	3	2	1
4. Employees engaged in cross training in other areas outside their current area	5	4	3	2	1
5. Training in the critical skills required in each unit is provided	5	4	3	2	1
6. Training opportunity are made available to all individuals	5	4	3	2	1
7. Appreciations and acknowledgements are freely given	5	4	3	2	1
8. Employees have the competencies needed in our bank to take us towards the ideal state	5	4	3	2	1
9. People are sufficiently motivated for sharing and using knowledge in the bank	5	4	3	2	1
10. The willingness to share knowledge among the employees is very high.	5	4	3	2	1
11. Everyone in our organization can explain the basics about or financials	5	4	3	2	1
12. Supervisors generally consult their workers whenever every problem crops up	5	4	3	2	1
13. Employees are encouraged for suggesting new ideas about the work.	5	4	3	2	1
14. Concepts of team spirit and cooperation are followed in the organization.	5	4	3	2	1
15. Banks actively recruits for qualified talent	5	4	3	2	1
16. The organizational values are communicated and are practiced in the organization.	5	4	3	2	1
17. Our bank has been awarded in the national/international market by quality concerns.	5	4	3	2	1
18. Outstanding performance is recognized.	5	4	3	2	1
19. Proper Suggestions are given to the employee when they commit any mistake	5	4	3	2	1
20. Career development activities are conducted with each individual	5	4	3	2	1

Section IV score

Calculating your score

Number of Strongly Agree	*	5	=
Number of Agree	*	4	=
Number of Neither Agree nor disagree	*	3	=
Number of Disagree	*	2	=
Number of Strongly Disagree	*	1	=

Your Total Score

Total Point Score Possible 100

Your percent score

(your point score divide by 100)

Business Process (100)

Strongly Agree (5)	Agree (4)	Neither Agree nor disagree (3)	Disagree (2)	Strongly Disagree (1)

1. Our Bank share information with the customers.	5	4	3	2	1
2. Our Bank using incentive for fostering knowledge sharing	5	4	3	2	1
3. Historical data is using for project planning and estimating.	5	4	3	2	1
4. We use standard templates for opening an account, internet banking, ATM, credit card etc.	5	4	3	2	1
5. Routine knowledge is well documented.	5	4	3	2	1
6. Our bank is adopting new ideas.	5	4	3	2	1
7. Measurement systems do not encourage individual and organizational creativity.	5	4	3	2	1
8. A defined process for knowledge sharing (contribution) and knowledge reuse (implementation).	5	4	3	2	1
9. New products and services are introduced quickly with the technology.	5	4	3	2	1
10. People have complete explanations when they make information requests.	5	4	3	2	1
11. We have a defined process for measuring customer satisfaction.	5	4	3	2	1
12. Groups and individuals routinely document and share information about their achievement.	5	4	3	2	1
13. People only request information when they really need it.	5	4	3	2	1
14. We have established ways for people to document and share information.	5	4	3	2	1
15. Office space is used as a symbol of status in our bank.	5	4	3	2	1
16. Information is shared across all levels of the organization.	5	4	3	2	1
17. Involving our customers in the process of creating and developing new products and services is a well-established practice in our bank	5	4	3	2	1
18. We have a process for scanning the external environment for new ideas, information etc.	5	4	3	2	1
19. There is a process to ensure that competitor information is kept up to date.	5	4	3	2	1
20. The available knowledge improves your effectiveness in performing your tasks.	5	4	3	2	1

Section V score

Calculating your score

Number of Strongly Agree * 5 =

Number of Agree * 4 =

Number of Neither Agree nor disagree	* 3	=
Number of Disagree	* 2	=
Number of Strongly Disagree	* 1	=

Your Total Score

Total Point Score Possible 100

Your percent score
(Your point score divide by 100)

Organization Structure (100)

Strongly Agree (5)	Agree (4)	Neither Agree nor disagree (3)	Disagree (2)	Strongly Disagree (1)

1. Our bank has a designation of knowledge management practices (e.g. Chief Knowledge Officer, Chief Learning Officer, Chief Information Officer, Knowledge Manager, and Knowledge Associate. Etc.)	5	4	3	2	1
2. Collective banking knowledge communicated and supported as an important and essential requirement of employee's work in the bank	5	4	3	2	1
3. The organizational structure of our bank is able to make internal knowledge transparent.	5	4	3	2	1
4. Our top management is pushing hardest to have some knowledge programme	5	4	3	2	1
5. Some special units in our bank are responsible for KM	5	4	3	2	1
6. Employees are eager to share ideas and information	5	4	3	2	1
7. Management personnel are regularly interested in how the business is doing	5	4	3	2	1
8. Different department and disciplines are interacting at some intervals	5	4	3	2	1
9. Our efforts in effective innovation and new-use recognized and rewarded	5	4	3	2	1
10. Our learning process often includes gathering feedback from customers.	5	4	3	2	1
11. It is very easy to talk to other project teams among the various units.	5	4	3	2	1
12. There is a complete freedom for the project teams.	5	4	3	2	1
13. People follow clear guidelines and instructions about work	5	4	3	2	1
14. My immediate supervisor keeps me informed about what is going on	5	4	3	2	1
15. Workers in my branch share information about what is going on	5	4	3	2	1
16. My coworkers openly discuss what they need of one another.	5	4	3	2	1
17. Top management keeps everyone in the organization informed about what is happening.	5	4	3	2	1

18. The sharing of information across banking units is open and easy.	5	4	3	2	1
19. Employees can get what they need from the banking units.	5	4	3	2	1
20. It is the goal of the banking for all employees to be as open in sharing information as possible.	5	4	3	2	1

Section VI score

Calculating your score

Number of Strongly Agree	*	5	=
Number of Agree	*	4	=
Number of Neither Agree nor disagree	*	3	=
Number of Disagree	*	2	=
Number of Strongly Disagree	*	1	=

Your Total Score

Total Point Score Possible 100

Your percent score

(Your point score divide by 100)

Compute your overall Knowledge Management Score

Section 1:
Section 2:
Section 3:
Section 4:
Section 5:
Section 6:

Your Total

Total Possible = 1000

Overall percent score
(Your total divided by 1000)

Index

A

Agriculture, 60, 64
Anova Test, 118, 120, 123
Australian Banking, 37

B

Bank
 Nationalization, 59
 of America, 38
 Training Programmes, 118
 Transparency, 72
Banking, 134
 and Technology, 86
 Industry, 73, 93
 Policy, 49
 Regulatory Act, 49, 50, 52
 Sector Reforms, 49, 66, 69
 Sector, 72, 86, 96
 System, 110
Basel
 Capital Accord, 80, 134
 Committee, 80
British Council, 37
Business
 Process Management, 30
 Strategy, 16
 Systems, 20

C

Canara Banks, 85
Capital Markets, 72
Central Baking, 74
Chinese Banking Corporation, 86
Citi Bank, 85, 102, 106, 124, 135, 138
Clearing Corporation of India, (CCI), 68, 74
Commercial Banking System, 56
Commercial Banks, 49-51, 53, 54-58, 60, 64, 66, 70, 73, 87, 130-133, 137
Committee on Technology Upgradation in Banking System, 71
Cooperative Banks, 83
Corporate Governance, 69
Credit and Risk Management, 120
Credit Information Bureau, 68, 133
Currency
 and Finance, 86
 Management, 74
Customer Relations
 Management, (CRM), 29, 125, 138
Customer Services, 77, 134

D

Data
 Envelopment Analysis (DEA), 89, 91-96, 98, 103

Management Methods, 30
Techniques, 99
Warehousing, 125, 138
Debt Recovery Tribunals, 68, 133
Decision
Makers, 51
Making Mechanism, 107
Making Units, (DMUs), 91, 92, 94-98
Making, 71, 140
Decreasing Returns to Scales (DRS), 96
Developing Countries, 27, 53
Development
Banking, 113
Economy, 54
Document Management Systems, 22

E

E-Business, 29
Economic
Development, 19
Resources, 17
Economy, 49, 60
Knowledge Based, 19
Residual, 57
Enforcement of Securities Interest Act, 133
Enterprise
Information Portal (EIP), 147
Resource Planning, (ERP), 125, 138
Europe, Japan and US, 33
European
Banking and Insurance Firms, 131
Banking, 35, 39
Centre for Knowledge Management, 35
Expert System, 30

F

Farming Community, 115
Financial
Institutions, 50, 76
Markets Transparency, 72
Markets, 19
Sector Reforms, 64, 133
Sector, 49
Services Sector (Australia), 37
Foreign
Banks, 57, 59, 83, 84, 102, 112, 123
Direct Investments (FDIs), 68
Sector Banks, 173, 175-177
Ranking, 174, 178

G

Global
Economy, 17
Markets, 49
Globalization, 80, 118
Globalized Capital Markets, 133

H

HDFC Bank, 114, 119, 124, 126, 135, 138
Health Sector, 39
HRD Policies, 119

I

ICICI, 119, 124, 125, 126, 135 138
ICICI, and HDFC, 85, 102, 104, 106, 114, 115
Imperial Bank of India, 58
Increasing Returns to Scales (IRS), 96

Indian
Banking, 59, 70, 75, 78
System, 142
Banks, 75
Commercial Banking
System, 39, 132
Commercial Banks, 39, 131, 132, 142
Financial Network, 67
Financial Sector, 64
Industrial
Companies, 26
Growth, 64
Sector, 60
Information
Management Systems, 30
Management, 28
Sharing, 29
System, 20
System Project, 28
System Role, 105
Technology, 16, 22, 27, 33, 34, 36, 38-41, 49, 60, 72, 74, 103, 110, 112, 120, 136, 142
Design, 21
Firms, 87
Impact of-, 72
Investment, 36
Projects, 80
Structure, 146
System, 38
Insurance Companies (UN), 36
Internet Banking, 105

J

J & K Bank, 85

K

Knowledge
Based Industries, 26, 27
Based Initiatives, 35
Based Organization, 39
Based Systems, 25
Based Topics, 35
Engineers, 25
Growth Stages, 144, 145
Management, (KM), 16-22, 23, 25-28, 30-32, 34, 35, 37, 38-40, 70, 86, 87, 103, 115, 117, 118, 119, 133, 134, 136, 139, 144, 146
Enabling Technologies, 30
Process, 23
Program, 31, 116
System Analysis, 130
System, 21, 22, 71, 131, 132
Technology, 22
Resources, 29
Sharing Culture, 130
Strategy, 34

L

Liberalization, 64
Lok Adalat, 68, 133

M

Management
Credit, 140
Development Program, 35
Forex, 140
Information System, 73
Process, 16
Relationship, 16
Risk, 71, 76, 140
System, 110, 134
Treasury, 143
Monetary Policy, 74

N

Narasimhan Committee on
Banking System, 58, 66

National Resources, 17
Natwest Markets, 37
Negotiated Delivery System (NDS), 69
Negotiating Dealing System, 133
Non-Banking Finance Companies, 69
Non-Performing Assets (NPAs), 73, 76, 78, 116, 134
Non-Scheduled Banks, 56, 57

O

Offshoring, 79
Off-Site Monitoring Surveillance (OSMS), 108
On Line Banking, 73
Organizational
    Culture, 27, 35
    Knowledge, 33
    Routines, 15

P

PERT (Program Evaluation and Review Technology), 130
Pharmaceutical Sector, 39
Private Sector
    Banks, 58, 59, 133, 168-171
    Ranking, 172
    Sector Commercial Banks, 56, 57
Project Management, 125
Promotion Policies, 118
Public
    Administration, 34, 39
    Sector Commercial Banks, 56
    Sector Banks, 58, 59, 64, 68, 70, 79, 84, 85, 102, 112, 133, 158, 162-167
    Ranking, 161
Public/Private Sectors, 83
Punjab National Bank, 85, 104, 106, 110, 125, 135

R

Reforms, 49
Regional Rural Banks, 56, 83, 132
Research and Marketing Intelligence Cell, 115
Retail Banking System (US), 36
Reward System, 35
Role of Information System, 132

S

Scheduled
    Banks, 56, 57
    Commercial Banks, (SCB), 58, 59, 83, 155, 156, 157, 159
    Cooperative Banks, 132
Securities Settlements System, 75
Securitization—Interest, 68
Shared Payment Network System, 67
Siam Commercial Bank, 86
Small Industries, 60, 64
Society, 64
Software System, 29
Standard Chartered Bank, 85, 102
State Bank
    Academy, 119
    Corporate Learning Centre, 119
    Group, 114
    of India, 59, 119, 126
SWOT (Strength, Weaknesses, Opportunities and Threats), 28

T

Technology, 17, 19, 30, 36, 49, 31, 69, 71, 72, 78, 134, 147
  Driven Distribution System, 115
  Environment, 17
  Infrastructure, 142
Total Quality Management, 130
Trade Association, 115
Training Program, 120
Transparency, 78
Treasury Management, 120

U

United Kingdom, 37
UTI Bank, 85, 105

V

Variable Returns to Scale (VRS), 96, 143
VSAT Technology, 67

W

World Development Report, 27, 75, 122